Social and Emotional Education in Primary School

Carmel Cefai · Valeria Cavioni

Social and Emotional Education in Primary School

Integrating Theory and Research into Practice

 Springer

Carmel Cefai
Dept. Psychology
University of Malta
Msida
Malta

Valeria Cavioni
Dept. Brain and Behavioral Sciences
Psychology Section
University of Pavia
Pavia
Italy

ISBN 978-1-4614-8751-7   ISBN 978-1-4614-8752-4 (eBook)
DOI 10.1007/978-1-4614-8752-4
Springer New York Heidelberg Dordrecht London

Library of Congress Control Number: 2013947927

Printed on acid-free paper.

Springer is part of Springer Science+Business Media (www.springer.com)

Foreword

This extraordinarily compact and valuable book integrates the best available theory, research, and practice internationally and services as an essential resource for practitioners, researchers, and policy makers. It is rare indeed that one book, in relatively few pages, can accomplish all of these goals. However, this book has done so.

The outset of the book establishes the need in children's lives for a new kind of education, Social-Emotional Education (SEE), that leads to academically, socially, emotionally literate young people:

> A relevant and meaningful education for the realities of the twenty-first century leads to the formation of academically, socially, and emotionally literate young people who have the skills, abilities, and emotional resilience necessary to navigate the uncertain but fast moving environmental and economic present and future. (p. 5)

Teachers know that the well-being and mental health of their students is an extraordinarily important determinant of their learning and behavior in school. Their reluctance to state this is because they do not want "one more thing" on their plate to have to address is. But this book is about a third way—not mental health experts in the schools, not referrals to the outside, but an complete integration of social, emotional, and character development into the rest of educational and pedagogical concerns. By attending to these matters systematically and systemically, woven into curriculum and instruction at the individual, classroom, and school level, student performance can be enhanced and the role of the teacher can become more fulfilling. Further, Prof. Cefai argues convincingly that the relevance of Heart for learning and performance has been rediscovered, not discovered, by recent cognitive neuroscience research. Indeed, concluding each chapter with ancient legends or fables from around the world that exemplify aspects of SEE is effective and serves to show the timelessness and universality of the SEE message. In *Talking Treasure, Stories to Help Build Emotional Intelligence and Resilience in Young Children* (www.researchpress.com, 2012), my colleagues and I took the same approach, using timeless stories as vehicles for parents and educators of young children to develop their emotional intelligence.

The SEE framework presented in Chap. 2 expresses the integration of a wide range of perspectives that support SEE and guide its full and proper implementation. And then, the remainder of the book is dedicated to operationalizing that guidance. Prof. Cefai's vision of SEE is multilevel, multicomponent, multiyear, and multipopulation:

> Both universal and targeted approaches have their place in a comprehensive whole school approach to SEE, and an integrated universal and targeted approach is more likely to be effective than one focusing on one form of intervention alone. ... A curriculum, classroom based approach to SEE needs to be accompanied and supported by a whole school approach with the whole school community in collaboration with parents and the local community supporting and reinforcing a climate conducive to SEE for all the school members. (p. 28)

The book provides an action-research/implementation and evaluation cycle to help educators get started with bringing SEE into their schools systematically. It wisely begins with creation of an infrastructure, an SEE leadership team, and an analysis of needs and potential implementation obstacles. This includes devoting more time to understanding the theory and pedagogy of SEE, rather than over-emphasizing the technical aspects of curriculum delivery. Also included is the concept of piloting, which allows opportunity for local learning, experimentation, and tailoring.

The curriculum framework adds to the seminal work of CASEL (Collaborative for Academic, Social, and Emotional Learning) elements from other aspects of the author's SEE framework. This leads to four foci, represented as "I am...," "I care...," "I can...," and "I will..." This simplified framework, reminiscent of that used by the Anchorage, Alaska, public schools (http://www.asdk12.org/depts/SEL/), but elaborated in important, new ways, provides clear guidance for educators about the dimensions most important to develop in students, though without the detailed developmental sequencing found in the Anchorage framework and other comprehensive, multiyear, empirically-based curricula. A very useful assessment tool matched to the framework, for both staff members and student self-ratings, is provided and can be of instant use to readers. Prof. Cefai also recommends and explains the use of a student SEE journal, a highly innovative technique that allows for assessment but also has clear pedagogical benefit.

Prof. Cefai also shares the methodology he and colleagues have used successfully in Maltese schools to build optimal learning environments and caring classroom communities. Of tremendous value is a self-guided assessment framework that allows teachers and pupils to monitor a wide range of indicators for creating caring classrooms and engage in a program of continuous, incremental improvement. The inclusion of a pupil version highlights the overarching theme in this book of the importance of student voice and their essential role in co-creating a positive learning environment. There is a parallel structure, with equally valuable tools, in Chap. 7 dealing with the entire school environment.

Among the innovative contributions of this book are the chapters devoted to intervention with students who are experiencing more difficulties than can be addressed by universal approaches. Prof. Cefai provides an accessible, staged approach for targeted, multilevel SEE interventions coordinated with the universal level for optimal synergy.

Finally, Prof. Cefai addresses two issues too rarely confronted: the emotional life and well-being of teachers, and engaging parents. For staff, focusing in particular on mindfulness, self-care, and mentoring-peer support techniques, the book provides another outstanding self-assessment tool for educators to monitor and improve the extent to which their schools are promotive of staff well-being. For parents, there are international examples of ways in which parents and other caregivers have been engaged and supported in greater involvement in their children's education, including a user-friendly self-assessment tool.

To summarize the message of this book, I cannot do better than quote from the concluding chapter:

> We now have enough evidence about how educational systems without a Heart can lead to pupils becoming alienated, disaffected and unprepared for life outside school…. Schools now have a very clear choice. Rather than 'educating for the past' (Gidley 2007), they need to be grounded in the current realities and challenges if they are to remain valid and relevant to the lives of children in the 21st century. We need both Head and Heart in education. (p. 181)

I have seen no better recent, international guide to carrying out this mission, which expresses a developmental right of all children worldwide, than this outstanding book.

Rutgers University,   Maurice J. Elias
New Jersey, USA

Acknowledgments

The author would like to thank Tracy Grech, Felicienne Mallia Borg, Bernice Mizzi, SueAnne Pizzuto, and Stanley Zammit for their contributions to an initial draft on which this book is partly based. Thanks to Dr. Valeria Cavioni, University of Pavia, Italy, for the social and emotional activities she designed for the book and which are included in the electronic supplemental materials accompanying this book. It is also important to acknowledge the invaluable comments and feedback provided by Prof. Paul Bartolo, University of Malta and Dr. Helen Askell-Williams, Flinders University, Southern Australia. Thanks also to Albert Debono who designed the main diagrams in this document and to Dr. Valeria Cavioni and Dr. Liberato Camilleri for their help with some of the figures in the book. The author would also like to thank Victoria Blakeney, the coordinator of the Social and Emotional Learning Curriculum at the Anchorage School District in Alaska, USA, for sharing the ASD Social and Emotional Learning standards, benchmarks, and checklists and agreeing to the adaptation of some of the material for the book.

Contents

Part II   Heart in the Classroom

Part III   Heart in the Whole-School Community

About the Authors

Carmel Cefai, Ph.D., CPsychol. is the Director of the European Centre for Resilience and Health, and He,ad of the Department of Psychology, at the University of Malta, Malta. He is founding Honoury co-Chair of the *European Network for Social and Emotional Competence (ENSEC)* and joint editor of the *International Journal of Emotional Education*. For a number of years he also worked as a school teacher and educational psychologist. He leads a number of international projects on social and emotional education, mental health and resilience in schools, and has numerous publications in the area, including the popular *Promoting Resilience in the Classroom: A Guide to Developing Pupils Emotional and Cognitive Skills (2008)*.

Valeria Cavioni, Ph.D. is an educational psychologist in Italy, and she's currently collaborating in research and teaching with the Department of Brain and Behavioral Sciences at the University of Pavia in Italy, and an assistant lecturer at the Università Telematica e-Campus in Milan. She is also involved in research projects on well-being with the European Centre for Resilience and Health at the University of Malta. Her field of research is social and emotional learning and emotional well-being in nursery and primary schools, and she is presently working on evidence-based programs in this area. She has published various scientific papers, book chapters and participated in numerous conferences on social and emotional development in childhood.

Chapter 1
Education That Matters in the Twenty-First Century

The rapid global, social, economic and technological changes taking place in the adult world today are exposing children to unprecedented pressures and challenges at a young vulnerable age. Increasing mobility, urbanisation and individualism weaken the social connectedness and support that the children used to enjoy with consequent decline in emotional security and sense of well-being. These trends are demonstrated in the growing number of children who live in a world marked by changing family structures and more fluid relationships, breakdown of neighbourhoods and extended families, weakening of community institutions, fear of violence, rampant competition, excessive consumerism, increasing social inequality and manipulation through the media (Layard and Dunn 2009; Elias 2009; Collishaw et al. 2004; Palmer 2006). This emotional deprivation (Palmer 2006) is aggravated by adults' preoccupation with the pursuit of their own individualism and materialism, what James (2007) calls 'affluenza', which erodes prosocial qualities such as empathy, kindness and care. It also widens the gap between adults and children in terms of the amount of time that children spend with adults as opposed to that spent with their peers (over 50 % of the total time spent), and contributes to the social, emotional and behavioural difficulties such as bullying, delinquency, anxiety and depression (Layard and Dunn 2009; Palmer 2006; Rutter and Smith 1995; WHO 2012).

About 20 % of school children experience mental health problems during the course of any given year and may need help from mental health services (WHO 2011b; Romano et al. 2001); this may go up to 50 % amongst children coming from socially disadvantaged areas such as urban regions (Adelman and Taylor 2010). According to the latest report by the Centre for Disease Control and Prevention (2013), the prevalence of mental health difficulties in children and young people has been increasing in the last twenty five years, with 13 to 20% of American children and teenagers suffering from mental health difficulties in a given year, the most prevalent being behaviour or conduct problems followed by anxiety and depression. KidsMatter, Australia (www.kidsmatter.edu.au), reports that every one in seven primary-school-age children has mental health difficulties, the most common being depression, anxiety, hyperactivity and aggression, while in a longitudinal study with early primary school children, Cefai and Camilleri (2011) found that 10 % of young children were at risk of developing mental health difficulties, either internalised or externalised.

C. Cefai, V. Cavioni, *Social and Emotional Education in Primary School*, DOI 10.1007/978-1-4614-8752-4_1, © Springer Science+Business Media New York 2014

This social and emotional landscape highlights the challenges children and young people are facing today. One must be careful not to take a simplistic and uncritical view of social change, such as embracing the 'crisis of childhood' without contextualising it within the wider social change, or attributing the current difficulties that children face simply to adults' psychological narcissism and excessive materialism (Myers 2012). However, the social systems in children's lives, such as family, school and community, do need to address the social and emotional challenges that children experience in meaningful and useful ways (Bronfrenbrenner 1989). A relevant and meaningful education for the realities of the twenty-first century leads to the formation of academically, socially and emotionally literate young people who have the skills, abilities and emotional resilience necessary to navigate the uncertain but fast-moving environmental and economic present and future (Zins et al. 2004; Fundacion Marcellino Botin, 2008; Cooper and Cefai 2009; Durlak et al. 2011). Children and young people will need to be creative in problem-solving and effective in decision-making, to build and maintain healthy and supportive relationships and to be able to work collaboratively with others. They need to mobilise their personal resources in times of difficulty, and sustain their psychological and social well-being. These are the qualities and competencies that must be fostered in children and young people if they are to become active and constructive citizens of the world (Benard 2004; Noddings 2012). As Linda Lantieri (2010) put it, 'our task as educators who are preparing young people to be citizens of the 21st century, is to make sure that not only is no child "left behind" but that no *part* of the child is left behind—that every aspect of being human is welcomed into our schools. Becoming a citizen ready for the 21st century requires a change in consciousness'. Global interdependence, maximising human growth, development and learning, and a commitment to collaboration, justice and peace need to replace the erstwhile emphasis on competition (Noddings 2012; Lantieri 2009a).

There are so many changes happening at this very moment—particularly in our advances in technology—that we can only guess what the future will be like and what competencies young people will need to be successful. My guess would be that SEL skills will be, without a doubt, the ones that remain on the list. (Lantieri 2009a)

Schools are ideal entry points to address these challengesas they provide access to children from an early age (Brown and Bowen 2008). An 'industrial era template' of educational practice (Dator 2000) focused on academic achievement and performance indicators, however, is clearly out of step with the contemporary world. The spirit of twentieth-century competition still pervades many schools and educational systems today (Noddings 2012) with children being bored and depressed by 'high-stakes bullet-pointed lists' and 'terrifying competition with one another' (Cigman 2012, p. 10). They continue to be punished for their circumstances and social and emotional difficulties (Spratt et al. 2010). As well put by Roffey (2010, p. 156), 'during the latter part of the 20th century, relational quality in education became a casualty of tightly defined and delivered curriculum targets, a competitive focus on academic outcomes and time-consuming testing'. Teachers may have to repress their tendency for emotional connectedness with children and bypass their understandings and insights of child development in the face of academic press and 'technical, rational models of practice focused on assessment and targets' (Watson et al. 2012, p. 199). They become driven by the 'science of deliverology' seeking to deliver results and reach set targets and performance indicators within a 'depersonalised education' (Pring 2012).

For instance, the Programme for International Student Assessment (PISA) standards are one of the key indicators used for measuring school effectiveness and student success these days. However, PISA is focused on academic achievement and assessment, and there is a danger that an overreliance on these standards may force educational systems and schools to put more value on academic achievement at the expense of other aspects of education, such as social and emotional education (SEE) (Rowlings 2012). They could turn out to be another league table, underlining the segregation of rich and poor into separate schools resulting from competition (Pring 2012). As Ravich (2010) put it, within such contexts, whatever cannot be measured does not count.

In contrast, we now have a sound evidence base supporting the relationship between SEE and academic learning, underlining the SEE foundation of academic achievement (e.g. Durlack et al. 2011). This needs to be underlined when citing the PISA standards (Rowlings 2012). In his review of over 800 research studies on what makes effective teaching and learning, Hattie (2008) underlined the importance of healthy and supportive classroom relationships as a key factor in teaching and learning challenges.

> Will the schools successful in generating conventional academic, and occasionally social, excellence through their predictability, cohesion, consistency and structure, be the schools to generate the new social outcomes of 'coping' and 'psychosocial resilience' that are needed for today's youths? We fear that the answer (is)… no. (Reynolds and Teddlie 2000, p. 342)

1.1 Heart in Education

The foundational role of emotions in learning and behaviour is not something new as some might be led to believe (see Dixon 2012), but the current interest in the area underlines the shift towards a broad-based, holistic conceptualisation of childhood development and education, a proactive approach to the promotion of growth, health and well-being (cf. Seligman 2011). Research and theory in child development and learning have drawn our attention to the need for educational practices informed by a developing understanding of the ways in which social, cognitive and emotional factors interact and contribute to the learning process. Bronfenbrenner's (1989) systemic development model underlines the importance

of the whole child and the need to take the various facets of the child's development in education. Developmental theorists such as Bowlby (1980) and Maslow
(1971) indicated that children could only achieve self-reliance, autonomy, self-
esteem and other higher needs once their basic physical and emotional needs are
adequately addressed. Effective social and cognitive functioning in children is
predicated on emotional competencies which involve the understanding and regulation of emotions as well as the ability to read and empathise with the emotional
states of others (Cefai and Cooper 2009).

> What has happened to the idea that education should help people to find
> out what they are good at, what they would like to do in life, and how they
> might live their lives as individuals, friends, parents and citizens? (Noddings
> 2012, p. 777)

One may argue that education is not and should not be about mental health and well-
being and that teachers are educators and not surrogate psychologists or mental
health workers (Craig 2009). This is a particularly salient point in contexts where
teachers face increasing pressure to ensure ever higher levels of pupil performance
and passes in examinations, and where their own, and their school's, effectiveness
are most often measured solely on the basis of pupils' academic outcomes. As already mentioned above, however, the current social and economic changes taking
place in families and communities, leaving many children without the erstwhile
protective networks of social support and connectedness, is making us rethink the
objectives of education and the role of schools as primary settings for health promotion. Social and emotional education, however, does not equate with mental health
difficulties or with turning schools from learning communities into therapeutic
centres (Ecclestone and Hayes 2009). The traditional deficit discourse may have
hijacked the idea of what mental health promotion in school is really about, namely
promoting well-being and maximising growth and potential for all.

The broad framework suggested in this book and espoused in more detail in the
next chapters, proposes a positive health and well-being perspective of child learning and development, depathologising mental health and positioning the classroom
teachers as effective and caring educators in both academic and social and emotional learning. This universal perspective is clearly different from interventions
simply targeting students experiencing social, emotional and behaviour difficulties
and mental health difficulties, though the latter are not excluded (see Vostanis et
al. 2013). Targeted interventions for pupils in difficulty, even if they are effective,
do not necessarily reduce the incidence of mental health difficulties in children
(Greenberg 2011). In contrast, besides promoting health and well-being, universal
interventions prevent the development of more serious difficulties later on, reduce
the impact of stigma associated with targeted interventions, and often lead to a
reduction in multiple problem areas in children, since many of the social, emotional
and behaviour problems experienced by children have overlapping risk factors and

comorbidity (Essex et al. 2006; Diekstra 2008a; Greenberg 2010; Bowers et al. 2012; Sklad et al. 2012).

> The schooling of children, has, for more than a century, been about accomplishment, the boulevard into the world of adult work…imagine if schools could, without compromising either, teach the skills of well-being and the skills of achievement. (Seligman et al. 2009, p. 293–294)

One of the concerns amongst some parents and educators is that SEE takes precious time from academic learning which may lead to lower academic achievement (Benninga et al. 2006). The evidence shows, however, that a focus on social and emotional processes in education does not weaken or detract from achievement. On the contrary, affective education is at the heart of teaching and learning, providing a foundation upon which effective learning and success can be built and socio-emotional competence developed. In classrooms where teachers keep all the goals of schooling in mind, students achieve more than in classrooms where exclusive focus is on achievement (Caprara et al. 2000; Willms 2003; Roffey 2010). A dual focus on academic and socio-emotional learning promotes academic achievement, engagement, positive behaviour and healthy relationships (Payton et al. 2008; Dix et al. 2012; Durlak et al. 2011) and acts as an antidote against both internalised and externalised problems (Waddell et al. 2007; Blank et al. 2009; Battistisch et al. 2004). It enables pupils to regulate their emotions, cope better with classroom demands and frustration, solve problems more effectively, relate better and work more collaboratively with others. Competencies like agency and initiative, self-efficacy, problem-solving, decision-making and collaboration also help to build a sense of entrepreneurship from an early age—one of the objectives of the European Union's educational vision for the twenty-first century.

   Children can learn and use SEE competencies effectively, given the right context and tools, particularly at a time when their personality is still developing and serious behaviour problems have not yet been manifested (Domitrovich et al. 2007; Weare and Nind 2011; Lanes and Menzies 2004). In contrast, children with poor social and emotional literacy skills are more at risk of experiencing learning difficulties and engaging in such behaviours as anti-social behaviour, substance abuse, violence and criminality, and to leave school without any certification or vocational skills, with consequently poor employability opportunities (Adi et al. 2007; Maes and Lievens 2003; Fergusson et al. 2005; Colman et al. 2009; Bradley et al. 2008; Miles and Stipek 2006; Mooij and Smeets 2009). Seen this way, such children and young people may end up as an economic burden on the country's resources, including health and social services. For instance the USA spends about US$ 247 billion a year on such services (Centre for Disease Control and Prevention, 2013). A comprehensive, whole-school approach to SEE, combining prevention with early, targeted interventions, thus, would also be cost effective in the long term (National Institute for Health and Clinical Excellence 2008; WHO 2013). As Dodge (2010)

put it, social and emotional competence is an 'important causal factor in life outcomes, from graduation to incarceration to employment'.

1.2   Outline of the Book

This book is about the social and emotional processes in education, the formation
of socially, emotionally and academically competent and resilient pupils prepared
for the tests put up by life in the twenty-first century. It suggests an integrated
psycho-educational framework of social and emotional well-being, one which is
based on health, growth and resilience. It proposes a multilevel, multitarget, multidimensional taught-and-caught approach to the promotion of well-being, health and
resilience in school. It is intended as a practical guide for classroom practitioners,
support staff, administration and other educationalists engaged in the promotion of
social and emotional education in primary schools. It may also serve as a resource
for educationalists engaged in policy-making, planning and curriculum development as well as a teacher education guide for both initial teacher education and
professional learning programmes.

The book is divided into three major parts. The next chapter proposes a SEE
framework for primary schools, suggesting how SEE may be developed as a
whole-school approach with interventions at classroom, school and community
levels, at universal and targeted intervention levels and with interventions for
pupils, school staff and parents. Universal interventions refer to programmes and
initiatives aimed at the whole classroom, school or community, while targeted
interventions are focused specifically on pupils who may be either at risk of or
manifesting difficulties in their social and emotional development. Chapter 3 describes an overarching whole-school framework to facilitate the implementation
of the SEE framework in various elements at the school. Part 2 describes how
social and emotional education may be organised at the classroom level at both
taught-and-caught level and at universal and targeted interventions. Chapter 4
presents a universal curriculum integrating social and emotional learning, positive education, resilience, mindfulness, inclusive education and a caring school
community's perspectives. It describes the curriculum content, goals and learning
outcomes and how it may be delivered, assessed and integrated in the other areas
of the curriculum. Chapter 5 describes how the classroom may be organised as a
caring community in the promotion of SEE. A school-based, staged and developmental framework to address the social and emotional needs of pupils in difficulty
is discussed in Chap. 6. Part 3 outlines the implementation of the SEE framework
at the whole-school level. Chapter 7 discusses how the whole school may mobilise its resources in implementing SEE at the whole-school level, recruiting the
active engagement of all staff and the collaboration of parents and the community in reinforcing and complementing the classroom practices. Chapter 8 underlines the need to address the health, well-being and resilience of the school staff,
while Chap. 9 focuses on how the school needs not only to engage the parents'

collaboration but also to enhance their parenting and own well-being. Chapter 10 concludes with a brief overview of the way forward for practitioners engaged in social and emotional education in schools.

Each chapter ends with a story, legend or folk tale from various regions of the world, illustrating one of the competencies presented in the SEE curriculum. The stories have been developed and modified by the main author to fit the scope and style of the book. They are also intended as illustrations of how classroom practitioners may use story telling as a medium for the promotion of SEE.

The book includes various excerpts from interviews with school staff carried out by the author in a number of schools in South Australia engaged in social and emotional learning and mental health initiatives.

The book also includes a set of SEE activities by Valeria Cavioni at two age levels (early years and primary school) in self-awareness, self-management, social awareness and social management, respectively, with various classroom and home activities in each area. *Timmy's Trip to Planet Earth: A Self and Social Adventure* is available at www.springer.com.

Part I
Heart in Education

'Educating the mind without educating the heart is no education at all.'

—Aristotle

Chapter 2
Social and Emotional Education: A Framework for Primary Schools

There have been various terms and definitions of social and emotional education (SEE), such as social and emotional learning (SEL), social and emotional literacy, social and emotional well-being and mental health amongst others. This chapter presents social and emotional education as a multidisciplinary, integrative construct drawing from six major perspectives in children's health and well-being, namely social and emotional learning, positive education, mindfulness, resilience, inclusive education and caring communities. It then reviews the literature on the effective processes underlying SEE in schools and presents a whole-school, multilevel and evidence-based framework for the promotion of social and emotional education in primary school.

2.1 Social and Emotional Education: An Integrated Well-Being and Resilience Perspective

'Social and emotional education' (Cefai and Cooper 2009) as used in this book, is defined as *the educational process by which an individual develops intrapersonal and interpersonal competence and resilience skills in social, emotional and academic domains through curricular, embedded, relational and contextual approaches.* The definition implies awareness, understanding and management of self and of others through social, emotional and cognitive processes. This includes understanding of self and of others, regulating emotions and enhancing positive ones, developing healthy and caring relationships, making good and responsible decisions, making use of one's own strengths and overcoming difficulties and adversity in social and academic tasks. The term 'education' places the emphasis on the conditions and processes, which contribute to the development of social and emotional competence and resilience, including both a curricular and cross-curricular-based approach, as well as an embedded classroom and whole-school climate perspective. SEE is concerned with the broad, multidimensional nature of learning and teaching, including the biological, emotional, cognitive and social aspects of learning and teaching (Cooper et al. 2011). It underlines a pedagogy for building social, emotional and

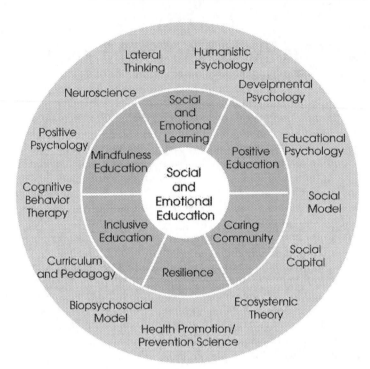

Fig. 2.1 The SEE framework

resilience skills as well as an 'intervention structure which supports the internalisation and generalisation of the skills over time and across contexts' according to the child's development and with the contribution of educators, parents, peers and other significant people (Elias and Moceri 2012, p. 427).

SEE draws upon such disparate fields as humanistic psychology, developmental psychology, educational psychology, teaching and learning perspectives, cognitive behaviour therapy, neuroscience, positive psychology, resilience, health promotion, prevention science, social capital, social model and the ecosystemic model of development (e.g. Weare 2010; Greenberg et al. 2003; Roffey 2010; Seligman et al. 2009; Benard 2004; Bernard 2006; Oliver 1996; Bronfenbrenner 1989). More specifically, it is based on the integration of six strands in the field of health and well-being in children, namely, social and emotional learning (Collaborative for Academic, Social, and Emotional Learning 2005; Mayer and Sallovey 1997), positive psychology and education (Seligman 2011; Seligman et al. 2009), mindfulness education (Kabat-Zinn 2004; Siegel 2007), resilience in education (Benard 2004; Masten 2001), inclusive education (Booth and Ainscow 1998; Oliver 1996) and caring community perspectives (Sergiovanni 1994; Battistich et al. 2004; Cefai 2008; see Fig. 2.1). These six perspectives are underpinned by the theory and practice of teaching and learning, with a focus on the twin processes of curriculum and pedagogy (see Chap. 4), and the use of social and emotional skills in the learning process such as persistence, goal setting, monitoring and academic regulation (Bernard 2012; Seligman et al. 2009; Noble and McGrath 2008).

2.1.1 The Six Perspectives Informing the SEE Framework

Social and Emotional Learning: 'The Heart of Education'

Over the past decades, social and emotional learning has been introduced in various schools at local, regional and national levels in various countries and regions in the world, with the help of initiatives such as the Collaborative for Academic, Social and Emotional Learning (CASEL) in the USA, KidsMatter and MindMatters in Australia, the European Network for Social and Emotional Competence (ENSEC) and the Social and Emotional Aspects of Learning (SEAL) in the UK. The CASEL identifies the key competencies required by children and young people in social and emotional learning, as '...the skills to recognize and manage their emotions, demonstrate caring and concern for others, establish positive relationships, make responsible decisions, and handle challenging situations effectively. These skills provide the foundation for academic achievement, maintenance of good health, resilience and civic engagement in a democratic society' (Collaborative for Academic, Social, and Emotional Learning 2005, p. 7). CASEL groups these skills into five major areas, namely self-awareness (ability to recognise emotions, describe interests and values and accurately assess strengths), self-management (ability to manage emotions and behaviour, manage stress, control impulses and persevere in overcoming obstacles), social awareness (ability to take the perspective of and empathise with others and recognise and appreciate similarities and differences), social management (ability to establish and maintain healthy and rewarding relationships based on co-operation) and responsible decision making. The CASEL framework incorporates the five domains of the SEAL programme in the UK (DfES 2005b), namely self-awareness, managing feelings and motivation (self) and social skills and empathy (others). The KidsMatter and MindMatters SEL components (www.kidsmatter.edu.au, www.mindmatters.edu.au) are also based on the five CASEL domains, namely self-awareness, self-management, social awareness, relationship skills and responsible decision-making. SEL programmes and their effectiveness in school are discussed in Sect. 2.2.

Positive Education: 'A Fresh Perspective in SEL' (Roffey 2010)

More recently, the positive psychology movement has been making deep inroads in the area of well-being and mental health promotion in schools (Seligman et al. 2009; Noble and McGrath 2008; Gilman et al. 2009) and has helped to develop and broaden the SEL perspective. The roots of positive education go back to the work of John Dewey, Maria Montessori and Elisabeth Hurlock amongst others, but the current emergence of the movement in education has been largely owing to the work of Martin Seligman who underlined the need for an evidence-based approach to health and well-being in education (Seligman 2011; Seligman et al. 2009). Positive psychology has shifted the erstwhile focus on deficit and mental health problems of traditional psychology towards wellness and health perspective. In education, it underlines the experience and expression of positive emotions and becoming aware and utilising individual strengths in achieving own and collective goals. It focuses on 'enabling' factors such as positive emotions, which facilitate adjustment, resilience, growth and well-being and prevent or reduce depression, anxiety and hopelessness (Seligman et al. 2009). Seligman (2011) underlines five key areas of well-being to be taught in school, namely, positive emotions, engagement through strengths/flow, meaning and sense of purpose, positive relationships and accomplishments (Seligman et al. 2009). Noble and McGrath's (2008) framework suggests 11 key foundations in positive education, namely:

1. Social and emotional competence, consisting of prosocial skills (respect, cooperation, acceptance of differences, compassion, honesty, inclusion and friendliness)

    • resilience skills (optimism, courage, coping, humour, and helpful thinking skills), social skills (sharing, cooperation, conflict resolution)
    • emotional literacy skills (eg managing negative feelings and amplifying positive ones, empathy)
    • personal achievement skills (identifying own strengths and limitations, persistence, goal setting)
    • meta cognitive skills
    • problem solving skills

2. Positive emotions: experiencing feelings of belonging, satisfaction and pride, safety, excitement and joy and optimism
3. Positive relationships, particularly classroom relationships
4. Engagement through strengths
5. A sense of meaning and purpose.

> The new century challenges psychology to shift more of its intellectual energy to the study of the positive aspects of human experience. A science of positive subjective experience, of positive individual traits and of positive institutions, promises to improve the quality of life. (Seligman and Csikszentmihalyi 2000, p. 5)

Mindfulness Education—'The Missing Piece to SEL' (Weare 2010)

Mindfulness education is an offshoot of positive psychology but it draws from other fields such as neuroscience, contemplative practices and SEL itself. Mindfulness is a state of self-awareness and attention, particularly related to the present reality (Kabat-Zinn 2004; Siegel 2007) that can induce plastic changes in the brain (Lutz et al. 2008). It has been linked to positive outcomes such as positive affect, optimism and self-actualisation as well as to reduced negative affect, anxiety and depression (Brown and Ryan 2003; Burke 2009). Mindfulness education is a universal classroom intervention, which seeks to promote social and emotional learning through mindful attention training, where pupils learn to become more mindful and aware of their present thoughts, emotions and behaviours. Pupils learn to focus on and live in the present by practicing such skills as breathing and sensation, mindful walking, sitting and movement. The consequent focused attention and enhanced awareness is then set to facilitate self-regulation and positive emotions such as happiness and optimism, engagement in learning process, as well empathy, perspective taking and prosocial behaviour. Rigorous research on the effectiveness of mindfulness education in schools, however, is still scarce and more evidence is required, particularly on the basis of randomised clinical trials, to substantiate the claims of this emerging field in education (Davidson et al 2012; Jennings et al. 2012). There are some indications, however, that it leads to decreased negative affect and increased calmness, emotional regulation and attention (Broderick and Metz 2009; Flook et al. 2010; Roeser and Peck 2009; Schonert-Reichl and Lawlor 2010; Huppert and Johnson 2010). In a recent quasi-experimental study involving 4th–7th-grade students, Schonert-Reichl and Lawlor (2010) found improved optimism, social competence and positive self-concept for mindfulness classes, particularly for the primary-school-age children, when compared to control groups. In a non randomised controlled study with 522 students aged 12–16 years in 12 secondary schools in the UK, Kuyken et al. (2013) found that the students who participated in the Mindfulness in Schools programme reported fewer symptoms of depression, lower stress levels and enhanced well-being when compared to controls. Another important issue in the use of the mindfulness education in schools in view of its origin is that it will be free of any religious connotations and presented as a secular and culturally sensitive and responsive tool (Davidson et al. 2012). Finally, mindfulness education with primary-school-age children needs to be developmentally appropriate for it to maximise the window of opportunity provided by the developing brain in emotional regulation and executive functioning (Jennings et al. 2012).

> Any use of contemplative practices in schools must necessarily be thoroughly secular, developmentally and culturally appropriate, and predicated on evidence-based practices. (Davidson et al. 2012, p. 153)

Resilience: 'Ordinary Magic' Within a Universal Perspective

The fourth perspective, which has contributed significantly to the mental health and well-being of children and young people, particularly those considered at risk, is that of resilience. Resilience has been defined as successful adaptation in the face of risk or adversity, but it is 'more about ordinary "magic" focusing on strengths rather than extraordinary processes' (Masten 2001, p. 228). It is a quality that can be nurtured and developed from a very young age and the systems impinging on the child's life, such as the school, have a crucial and determining role in directing the child's physical, social, emotional and cognitive development towards healthy trajectories even in the face of risk (Pianta and Walsh 1998; Dent and Cameron 2003; Masten 2007).

The literature identified two broad sets of factors that have been found to protect vulnerable children and facilitate their development into competent and autonomous young adults, namely individual qualities and characteristics and supportive social contexts in the child's life; children with high levels of these personal and social protective factors are more effective in coping with adversity than individuals with lower levels of protection (Benard 2004). The individual dispositional attributes, which have been found to contribute to successful outcomes in the face of adversity include problem-solving skills, flexibility, autonomy, sense of purpose, positive outlook of self and others, ability to recognise and express feelings constructively, being connected with, and seeking help from, others, sociability, humour, persistence, confidence, self-esteem and self-efficacy (Werner and Smith 1992; Masten et al. 1990; Rutter and the English and Romanian Adoptees Study Team 1998). These qualities may be an integral part of a universal, social and emotional education curriculum as they are essential not only for children at risk but also for normally developing children. Contextual protective factors at school include caring and supportive relationships between teachers and pupils and amongst pupils themselves, active pupil engagement in meaningful learning activities and positive belief and high academic expectations on the part of the teachers for all their pupils, particularly those at risk (Werner and Smith 1992; Masten et al. 1990; Rutter and the English and Romanian Adoptees Study Team 1998).

The resilience perspective coincides with and overlaps to a considerable degree with both SEL and positive psychology/mindfulness movements. It is concerned with developing competence and strengths as in SEL, but with a focus on children facing difficulties in their development. It is also closely related to positive psychology with its focus on strength, wellness and health, rather than deficits and remediation. Cefai (2007) has proposed a universal framework of resilience, which resonates with both the social and emotional learning and the positive psychology conceptualisation of wellness. It underlines the need to organise the curriculum and other aspects of the classroom and school contexts in a way that they address the developmental needs of all the pupils and to adopt processes that will promote social, emotional and academic development of all pupils in the classroom. These processes are grounded in the typical mechanisms involved in the development of social, emotional and academic competence. Self-awareness, strengths development, emotional literacy, social and prosocial skills, problem-solving skills, confidence, self-efficacy and persistence are key skills in the healthy development of both normally developing children and children at risk. This perspective also reflects on the current realities and challenges faced by our children today. Increasing economic, social and psychological stresses and developmental and situational challenges in children's lives today, underline the need for supportive contexts and systems for all children and a universal curriculum providing students with the skills to develop their strengths, overcome obstacles and be resourceful in problem solving (see Layard and Dunn 2009). Rather than just focusing on the impact of cumulative risks, a universal perspective of resilience underlines the value of cumulative protective and promotive factors in healthy development (Coleman and Hagell 2007).

Inclusive Education: 'A Nonpatholigising, Nonothering Stance' (Watson et al. 2012)

Inclusive education provides for the creation of a supportive community to which all can belong and are enabled to participate. It is a process of addressing and responding to the diverse needs of all learners through increasing participation in learning, cultures and communities and reducing exclusion and discrimination within and from education (Booth and Ainscow 1998; Oliver 1996). It is based on the right of all learners to a quality education that meets their needs, vulnerable and marginalised groups and individuals in particular, and develops the full potential of every individual. It underlines that every child has unique characteristics, interests, abilities and learning needs and education systems should be designed and educational programmes implemented to take into account such needs (UNESCO 2005; United Nations 2006). Acknowledging and modelling the rights of pupils through an inclusive pedagogy underline issues of justice and entitlement, and enhance pupils' well-being by strengthening their identity and empowering them to become self- and others' advocates in learning and social–emotional processes (Watson et al. 2010; UNICEF 2007).

The principles of inclusive education may be transmitted through the promotion of such values, attitudes and behaviours as appreciation and celebration of diversity and multiculturism, collaboration and equal participation, social justice and solidarity, human rights, equity and moral and social responsibility. Rather than serving as an instrument of exclusion and in turn, severing the link between learning and well-being and leading to disaffection and ill-being (Watson et al. 2012), the curriculum would thus become a 'hammer of justice and freedom' (Oliver 2004) for all pupils, the vulnerable and marginalised ones in particular. This stance is embedded in the social awareness dimension of the proposed curriculum framework, broadening the conceptualisation of one's well-being to that of others' as well, not only as an end in itself (social justice and human rights perspectives) but also as a creation of inclusive, caring, equitable and democratic communities having an added value to the well-being of all the individuals within those communities (e.g. Battistich et al. 1997; Cefai 2008).

Caring Classroom Community: A Safe, Empowering Base

The importance of community building as a basis for learning and well-being was already advocated a century ago by John Dewey, who wrote extensively on the relational and interpersonal aspect of education. In the 1930s, John Macmurray challenged the depersonalisation in education and argued for schools as inclusive and caring communities promoting communal or intersubjective knowledge (Fielding 2012). More recently, other researchers and educationalists have underlined the contribution of caring school communities to pupils' learning and social competence (e.g. Battistich et al. 1997; Noddings 1992, 2012; Sergiovanni 1994). Caring communities are defined by their caring relationships, active and influential participation and shared beliefs and goals. Community members care about each other, work together collaboratively and are actively engaged in the life of the community (Sergiovanni 1994). They share values and norms focused on pupils' well-being and learning and on prosocial values and behaviours. As Westheimer (1998, p. 142) put it, 'shared beliefs in…getting people together and acting in concert… in ensuring that marginalized voices are heard, are important not only for the fact that they are shared, but also that they reflect ideals of participation and egalitarian communities'. When pupils experience contexts focused on improving rather than proving competence, on sharing and supporting one other, they are more likely to feel connected to their group, become engaged in the classroom activities and consequently, improve their learning and behaviour (Battistich et al. 2004).

> The importance of community as the means and the end of human flourishing has been opportunistically co-opted and betrayed by the increasingly visible hand of neo-liberal market economics. (Fielding 2012, p. 687)

Caring classroom communities provide a dual pathway to social and emotional education. They provide an ethic of care through caring, supportive, prosocial and collaborative values, while they support pupils' social and emotional learning and resilience. Pupils with a sense of community are more likely to develop positive academic attitudes and behaviours. They participate in learning and other activities, engage in prosocial and collaborative behaviour and have a sense of competence and responsibility (Battistich et al. 1997, 2004; Cefai 2008). In an evaluation study in five elementary schools in the USA, Solomon et al. (2000) reported that the schools operating as caring communities showed gains, relative to the control schools, in pupils' motivation and engagement, personal and interpersonal concerns and skills and prosocial values and behaviours. Significant effects held for a broad variety of pupils, including those from low socioeconomic groups, urban areas and ethnic minorities. In a study with a number of primary schools, Cefai (2008) developed a framework of classrooms as caring and inclusive communities promoting social and emotional well-being and resilience. The communities were characterised by processes such as caring relationships; an ethic of support and solidarity; active and meaningful pupil engagement; collaboration; inclusion of all pupils in the learning and social processes; positive beliefs and high expectations and pupil autonomy and participation in decision making.

Although the caring community perspective puts particular emphasis on creating a classroom and school climate, which facilitates and promotes social and emotional well-being and learning (see Chap. 5), the curriculum itself can be a vehicle for creating and supporting such a context. 'Other' skills, such as prosocial behaviour, collaboration, inclusion, personal and social responsibility, healthy relationships and respecting and valuing the rights of others are key elements of SEE.

The curriculum framework and how it may be implemented in the primary schools are discussed in Chap. 4.

> If education is to be concerned with learning to be human, the challenge remains to reimagine socio-technical practices in education in ways that can be expressive of relations of friendship and mutuality, relations that are premised upon heterocentric contemplation of and care for others. (Facer 2012, p. 710)

2.2   Evidence Base: It Is Not Just Magic, Mystery and Imagination

Various reviews of studies have found consistent evidence on the positive impact of school-based SEE programmes on children of diverse backgrounds and cultures from kindergarten to secondary school in both academic achievement and social and emotional health (Greenberg et al. 2003; Zins et al. 2004; Hoagwood et al. 2007; Payton et al. 2008; Slee et al. 2009; Askell-Williams et al. 2010; Wilson and Lipsey 2007; Weare and Nind 2011; Durlak et al. 2011; Kimber 2011; Slee et al. 2012; Sklad et al. 2012). The largest average effect sizes appear to be in social and emotional learning, but the programmes also enhanced academic achievement and reduced internalised and externalised conditions, such as anxiety, depression, substance use and aggressive and antisocial behaviour (Durlak et al. 2011; Payton et al. 2008; Wilson and Lipsey 2007; Weare and Nind 2011; Sklad et al. 2012).

In their review of what works in social and emotional competence initiatives at school, Weare and Gray (2003) reported a wide range of academic, social and emotional benefits, such as improved positive behaviour, better learning and academic progress, improved social cohesion and inclusion and better mental health. In another review from the 52 reviews and meta-analyses of mental health in schools, Weare and Nind (2011) reported that overall, most of the interventions had positive effects, including positive mental health and well-being and social and emotional learning, externalising and internalising of problems and a positive attitude towards school and academic achievement. The authors identified various characteristics of the more effective interventions, such as teaching SEE skills, balancing universal with targeted interventions, starting early with young children and taking a multi-modal and whole-school approach. In another recent metanalytical review of 75 experimental or quasi-experimental studies on the effectiveness of universal school-based SEE programmes both in the USA and other parts of the world, including Europe, Sklad et al. (2012) reported the overall impact on all the seven outcomes measured, namely, enhanced social skills, positive self-image, academic achievement, mental health, prosocial behaviour, reduced antisocial behaviour and substance abuse. The largest immediate effects were for social and emotional learning, positive self-image and prosocial behaviour, followed by academic achievement and antisocial behaviour. At follow-up, the programmes still showed positive effects on all outcomes, but there was a substantial reduced effect for some of the outcomes.

In a metanalysis of more than 200 studies of universal, school-based SEL programmes from kindergarten to secondary school, Durlak et al. (2011) found clear evidence for the multiple benefits of SEL programmes. Students who participated in such programmes showed significant improvements in their social and emotional literacy, attitudes towards school, classroom behaviour, academic performance and social relationships as well as a decrease in conduct-related problems and emotional distress. These benefits persisted over time. Payton et al. (2008) provide results from three large-scale reviews of research on the impact of universal and indicated SEL programmes on primary and middle-school students in the USA. They reported a substantial increase in students' average academic test scores, in social and emotional literacy skills, an improvement in students' behaviour and a decrease in both externalised and internalised behaviour difficulties. And, in another review, Zins et al. (2004) report consistent evidence that SEL programmes in school lead to more prosocial and less antisocial behaviour, more positive attitudes and behaviours in learning, including motivation and engagement and higher academic achievement.

A recent evaluation of KidsMatter, a framework for the promotion of mental health in primary schools in Australia, reported a significant reduction in students' mental health difficulties with the greatest impact on students with social, emotional and behaviour difficulties. The evaluation also found improvement in student mental health such as optimism and coping skills as well as improved school work and academic achievement (Slee et al. 2009; Askell-Williams et al. 2010; Dix et al. 2012). Similar findings were found in an evaluation of KidsMatter in the early years, including closer relationships between staff and children, improved child temperament, and reduced mental health difficulties, with about 3% fewer children exhibiting mental health difficulties (Slee et al. 2012). Evaluation of the SEAL primary programme in the UK indicated overall positive impact on pupils' well-being and behaviour (Morrison Guttman et al. 2010; Humphrey et al. 2008; Hallam et al. 2006). The national evaluation of the primary SEAL curriculum by Hallam et al. (2006) found that the programme had a significant impact on pupils' well-being, confidence, social and communication skills, relationships, prosocial behaviour and positive attitudes towards school. A report by a group of researchers from the Institute of Education at the University of London in the UK (Morrison Gutman et al. 2010) underlined the value of the programme in primary schools, particularly for young children facing adverse circumstances in their developmental years, and the need to start such programmes as early in the child's school life as possible. Humphrey et al.'s (2008) evaluation of the primary SEAL small group work element reported a positive impact for some of the interventions. However, a number of issues about the effectiveness of the programme, particularly in secondary schools, have been raised, such as lack of consistent whole school approach and problems in implementation and monitoring owing to lack of staff training and school resources (Humphrey et al. 2008, 2010; Cooper and Jacobs 2011; Lendrum, Humphrey and Wigeslworth 2013).

In conclusion, our findings (based on 317 studies and involving 324,303 children) demonstrate that SEL programs implemented by school staff members improve children's behavior, attitudes toward school, and academic achievement. Given these broad positive impacts, we recommend that well-designed programs that simultaneously foster students' social, emotional, and academic growth be widely implemented in schools. (Durlak et al. 2011, p. 306; Payton et al. 2008, p. 6)

2.2.1   'Meta-Abilities' for Academic Learning

Neuroscience is providing hard evidence for the earlier 'softer' underpinnings of psychodynamic and humanistic theories linking emotions to academic learning. When a child feels afraid, anxious or angry, the lower areas of the brain controlling basic functions and fight and flight responses take over, neutralising the mediation of the cortex, which is responsible for higher-order thinking and processing. S/he will find it difficult to learn effectively if his or her basic needs for safety, security, belonging and self-esteem are not addressed adequately or has problems regulating emotions (Geake and Cooper 2003; Graziano et al. 2007; Greenberg et al. 2007). On the other hand, a sense of security and state of calmness facilitate learning, helping the child to remain focused on task, attend to instructions and put all his or her mental energy into solving problems and constructing knowledge (Greenberg and Rhoades 2008). Positive emotions such as pleasure and fun in learning, as well as intrinsic motivation where the activity is perceived as meaningful and relevant, also facilitate the operation of the working memory, including attention, information processing and recall (Greenberg et al. 2007; Greenberg 2010; Fredrickson and Branigan 2005). Emotionally literate children would be better able to regulate their emotions, cope better with classroom demands and frustration and solve problems more effectively. They will be able to relate better and work more collaboratively with others, which will not only help them to avoid entering into unnecessary conflicting situations, but also to synergise their learning potential through collaborative learning. They would also enjoy better relationships with the classroom teacher, which widens their opportunities for learning (Howse et al. 2003; Libbey 2004; Zins et al. 2004; Durlak et al. 2011). In this respect, they become 'meta-abilities' for academic learning as well (Goleman 1996).

> Brain science tells us that a child's brain goes through major growth that does not end until the mid-twenties. Neuroplasticity means that the sculpting of the brain's circuitry during this period of growth depends to a great degree on a child's daily experiences. Environmental influences on brain development are particularly powerful in shaping a child's social and emotional neural circuits. (Lantieri 2010)

In their meta-analysis of over 200 studies, Durlak et al. (2011) found that students who participated in universal social and emotional learning programmes, had a significant increase in their academic performance, scoring significantly higher on standardised achievement tests when compared to peers not participating in the programmes. The study clearly indicates that SEE does not hinder academic progress, and that any perceived 'extra work' on the part of the teacher with the introduction of SEE, is thus likely to be rewarded with enhanced learning and achievement. In a study in Australian schools, Dix et al. (2012) investigated the change in standardised academic performance across the 2-year implementation of an initiative to improve social and emotional learning in 96 Australian primary schools. They found a significant positive relationship between quality of implementation and academic performance, equivalent to 6 months of schooling. The study concluded that teachers' views also suggested an increase in academic performance as a result of SEL programming.

As Weare (2004) put it, it is crucial that those who seek to promote academic learning and achievement and those who seek SEE, realise that they are actually 'on the same side'. By underling the inextricable link between SEE and academic achievement, we are more likely to see SEE becoming an integral part of education (Elias and Moceri 2012).

> There's a huge push for well-being in our school, and that's what really underlines everything. I think children, if they are not happy, if they are not mentally right, they are not going to be in the right frame for learning. Our idea is to give them the strategies, help them and focus on their well-being to improve their learning. (Ms Grace, early years teacher)

Box 2.1   The benefits of social and emotional education (DfES 2005b, p. 7) © Crown

Where children have good social and emotional skills and are educated within an environment supportive to emotional health and well-being, they will be motivated and equipped to:

- Be effective and successful learners.
- Make and sustain friendships.
- Deal with and resolve conflict effectively and fairly.
- Solve problems with others or by themselves.
- Manage strong feelings such as frustration, anger and anxiety.
- Achieve calm and optimistic states that promote the achievement of goals.
- Recover from setbacks and persist in the face of difficulties.
- Work and play cooperatively.
- Compete fairly and win and lose with dignity and respect for competitors.
- Recognise and stand up for their rights and the rights of others.
- Understand and value the differences and commonalities between people, respect the right of others to have beliefs and values different from their own.

2.3   A School-Based, Whole School Approach to SEE

The WHO framework for health promotion in schools recommends a whole school approach to social and emotional education, which includes addressing social and emotional issues in the curriculum and in the organisation of teaching and learning, the development of a supportive school ethos and environment and partnerships with the wider school community (WHO 2007). Such an integrative approach leads to improved well-being and mental health and sense of belonging and connectedness (Battistich et al. 2004; Weare and Nind 2011; Adi et al. 2007; National Institute for Health and Clinical Excellence 2008; Weissberg et al. 2003; Bywater and Sharples 2012). SEE programmes need to be embedded within safe, caring and collaborative classroom and whole school communities where pupils have a sense of belonging and are actively engaged and empowered to practice SEE skills. Long-term effectiveness does not simply result from isolated programmes in schools, but from an integrated whole-school approach making use of interpersonal, instructional and contextual supports, sustained over time (Zins et al. 2004; DfES, 2007; Fundacion Marcellino Botin, 2008; KidsMatter 2012a).

In a systematic review of the effectiveness of promoting social and emotional well-being in primary school, Adi et al. (2007) reported that the most effective interventions were multicomponent programmes, which covered classroom curricula and school environment, together with programmes for parents. Children received a comprehensive curriculum in the development of social and emotional learning while the teachers were trained both in the new curriculum to be offered and in behaviour management. Similarly, the National Health Service Clinical Report on the well-being of primary school children in the UK (National Institute for Health and Clinical Excellence 2008) underlined the need for a supportive school environment with both universal and targeted interventions for pupils in difficulty. Such an approach also helps to avoid inappropriate referrals to intervention and support services, while identifying the needs of children who may need within-school support as early as possible.

SEE has greater impact when it is integrated into the primary school curriculum at taught-and-caught levels, with teachers teaching and reinforcing the curriculum in their interactions with the pupils (National Institute for Health and Clinical Excellence 2008; Greenberg 2010; Weare and Nind 2011; Cooper and Jacobs 2011; Greenberg et al. 2003; Durlak et al. 2011; Seligman 2009). Schools are more likely to be effective in promoting well-being, health and resilience if there is an emphasis on universal interventions for all children, supported by targeted interventions for children at risk or with additional needs (Adi et al. 2007; Diekstra 2008a, 2008b; Greenberg, 2010; Merrell & Gueldner, 2010; Cooper and Jacobs, 2011; Vostanis et al. 2013). Fragmented one-off, add-on SEE programmes are not likely to work in the long term (Ofsted 2007; Greenberg 2010; Durlack et al. 2011; Weare and Nind 2011). In a scoping survey of 599 primary and 137 secondary schools in England on mental health provision in schools, Vostanis et al. (2013) reported that most of the provisions were reactive, targeting students with mental health difficulties, were largely non evidence based and there was inadequate teacher education and support.

In their review of evaluations of the SEAL programme in the UK, Cooper and Jacobs (2011) attribute the lack of success of the programme owing to it not being embedded directly in the formal curriculum and the teaching staff not involved in its delivery and reinforcement. Hoagwood et al. (2007) reported that ecological and collaborative approaches, which included the classroom teachers amongst others, were the most effective in the promotion of both social and emotional learning and academic achievement. Sklad et al. (2012) found that the majority of the programmes in their review of studies were conducted by classroom teachers, and that teachers could deliver SEE programmes without compromising their effectiveness, concluding that the involvement of experts and specialists was not necessary for ensuring programme effectiveness. In their metanalysis of over 200 studies, Durlak et al. (2011) found that when classroom programmes were conducted by the school staff, they were found to be effective in both academic and social and emotional literacy, and that only when school staff conducted the programmes did the students' academic performance improve. On the basis of the review, they recommend that SEE programmes 'do not require outside personnel for their effective delivery' (p. 417) and are more effective when delivered by school than nonschool staff. Similarly, in another metanalysis, Weissberg (2008) reported that only when school staff delivered the programmes themselves did the students' academic performance improve significantly, not only because teachers are involved in the delivery of the mainstream curriculum and thus more likely to infuse the skills in their daily class-room practice but also as this is a reflection of an SEL-supportive whole-school culture.

One of the benefits of having classroom teachers delivering the SEE curriculum is that they are more likely to integrate and infuse the skills into the general class-room curriculum and daily activities. SEE has greater long-term impact when it is delivered in this way (Rones and Hoagwood 2000; Adi et al. 2007; Diekstra 2008). An evaluation of SEAL by(2007) in the UK, similarly reported that the greatest impact of the programme was when it was embedded in the curriculum, with the classroom teachers developing an understanding of students' social and emotional literacy skills, and consequently, using that understanding to develop healthier rela-tionships with the students in their teaching and classroom management and to ad-just their pedagogy according to the students' needs. Such an approach was found to be particularly useful in promoting prosocial behaviour amongst all students in the classroom as well as resilience amongst students considered at risk (Ofsted 2007).

Although classroom teachers are not expected to become surrogate psycholo-gists or mental health workers, they can still take responsibility for the social and emotional well-being of their pupils. It has been the traditional remit of primary classroom teachers to provide pastoral care and nurturance as caring educators to their young pupils (Spratt 2006; Noddings 1992; Nias 1999). This position reso-nates with the demedicalisation and depathologising of mental health and well-being in education, and the integration of academic learning and social and emo-tional learning (cf. Watson et al. 2010; Noddings 1992). The compartmentalisa-tion of education and well-being does not only lead to deskilling of teachers and short-changing of pupils, but also has been found to be fraught with difficulties in terms of implementation, service delivery, multidisciplinary collaboration and par-ticularly effectiveness (Spratt 2006; Noddings 1995; Greenberg et al. 2003). It also reinforces students' stigma of mental health, the largest barrier to accessing mental health services in school (Bowers et al. 2012). Specialists and professionals still have a key role to play in the promotion of well-being at school but more at targeted interventions. Even here, however, the more the interventions are school-based and carried out by school-based personnel or by professionals with close contact with the children and the school, the more likely they are to be effective (see Chap. 7). As Zins (2001, p. 445) puts it, 'now that we know more about SEL interventions, the shift must be done towards school-based personnel'.

I have argued over the past 20 years that the explicit teaching of social-emotional learning dispositions and behaviours is the missing link in schools' efforts to promoting school adjustment and achievement. (Bernard 2006)

Both universal and targeted approaches have their place in a comprehensive whole-school approach to SEE, and an integrated, universal and targeted approach is more likely to be effective than one focusing on one form of intervention alone

(Adi et al. 2007; Greenberg 2010; Weare and Nind 2011). Although universal interventions are highly beneficial for pupils experiencing social and emotional behaviour difficulties (Weare and Nind 2011; Cooper and Jacobs 2011), targeted interventions are necessary for pupils who are not responding to universal education or who need extra support in view of the risks or difficulties they are experiencing (Greenberg 2010; National Institute for Health and Clinical Excellence 2008; Payton et al. 2008; Weare and Nind 2011). The greater conceptual precision, intensity and focus of targeted interventions may be particularly effective in this regard (Greenberg 2010). Targeted interventions are also particularly essential in preschool and primary school years to reduce the development of more severe difficulties in secondary school, at which stage it is more difficult to change behaviour (Essex et al. 2006; Domitrivich et al. 2007; Merrell and Gueldner 2010). As well put by Lantieri (2009b, p. 15), 'If children learn to express emotions constructively and engage in caring and respectful relationships before and while they are in the lower elementary grades, they are more likely to avoid depression, violence, and other serious mental health problems as they grow older'.

A curriculum, classroom-based approach to SEE needs to be accompanied and supported by a whole-school approach with the whole school community in collaboration with parents and the local community supporting and reinforcing a climate conducive to SEE for all the school members (Adi et al. 2007; Weare and Nind 2011; Greenberg 2010). A positive school climate underlining caring and supportive relationships, inclusion, solidarity and prosocial behaviour, while supporting the well-being of all pupils, staff and parents, will help to support and reinforce the work being undertaken in the classrooms, thus providing a complementary, value-added approach (Adi et al. 2007; Weare and Nind 2011; Farrington and Ttofi 2009). The school ecology becomes a pervasive medium for the promotion of SEE throughout the school (Wells et al. 2003; Payton et al. 2008; Weare 2010). An evaluation of the KidsMatter framework in primary schools in Australia suggested that the framework was associated with a systematic pattern of positive changes to schools, teachers, parents and students, consistent with the international literature that a 'whole school' approach helps to enhance academic and social competencies through more positive interactions amongst all members of the school (Askell Williams et al. 2010).

The social and emotional well-being of the staff and parents themselves also needs to be addressed within a whole-school approach (Jennings and Greenberg 2009; Weare and Nind 2011; Roffey 2011; Sisak et al. 2013). For adults to be able to teach, role model and reinforce SEE, they would first need to be socially and emotionally literate themselves. This requires support structures, which provide information and education for staff and parents in developing and maintaining their own social and emotional learning, well-being and health. The focus is on the whole school community operating as an emotionally literate community, with each system connecting to, and supporting, the others (cf. Bronfenbrenner 1989). Primary school teachers would thus need to be provided with basic and ongoing training on how to teach and reinforce SEE in their classroom (Durlack et al. 2011; Lane et al.

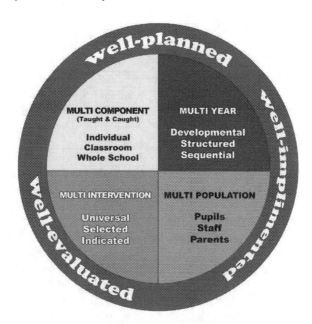

Fig. 2.2 A comprehensive, multidimensional SEE framework for primary schools

2006), support and guidance in the implementation of SEE (Jennings and Greenberg 2008). Parental collaboration and education in promoting and reinforcing the key skills being promoted at school are critical to the success of school-based programmes. In their evaluation of family SEAL, Downey and Williams (2010) found that both teachers and parents reported increases in the children's social and emotional learning as a result of the home programme implementation. Staff's and parents' well-being is discussed in more detail in Part 3.

2.4 A Roadmap for SEE in Primary School

SEE is a basic, fundamental educational goal directly related to learning, well-being and mental health of all pupils at school. It needs to be firm in theory and research, based on sound theories of child development, including approaches which have been found to be effective in bringing about long-term targeted outcomes. On the basis of the SEE curriculum framework described earlier and the evidence on the effective approaches for the promotion of SEE in primary schools, a multilayered, comprehensive, whole-school SEE framework is proposed for primary schools (Fig. 2.2). It consists of five elements: (i) multidimensional, (ii) multistage, (iii) multitarget, (iv) multiintervention and (v) well-planned, well-implemented and well-evaluated.

2.4.1 Multidimensional

SEE is organised as a comprehensive, universal approach at individual, classroom and whole-school levels. Explicit and regular teaching of SEE as a core competence by the classroom teacher is one of the key components of the framework. Direct teaching of evidence-based and developmentally and culturally appropriate SEE with application to real-life situations is required in the classroom. This necessitates a set curriculum and available resources to support consistency of delivery, one of the key criteria of programme effectiveness (Collaborative for Academic, Social, and Emotional Learning 2008; Durlak et al. 2011). One-off, pull-out, add-on programmes are unlikely to have any long-term effect on pupils' behaviour (see Chap. 4).

The teaching of SEE may follow the SAFE approach, that is, it is sequenced, active, focused and explicit. Research on the effectiveness of SEE programmes provides consistent evidence that effective programmes adopt sequenced step-by-step approach, make use of experiential and participative learning, focus on skills development and have explicit learning goals (Collaborative for Academic, Social, and Emotional Learning 2005; Durlak et al. 2010, 2011; see Chap. 4).

SEE is infused in the other academic subjects in the curriculum in a structured way. Opportunities are provided by the classroom teacher for the pupils to practice and apply the skills learned both in the classroom and outside, such as the playground and whole-school activities (cf. Elias 2003; Elias and Synder 2008; Greenberg 2010; see Chap. 4).

A positive classroom climate where pupils feel safe and cared for, and where they have the opportunity to practice the SEE skills being learned, is another component of SEE in school. Indicators for the classroom teacher and the pupils may help the teacher to evaluate the classroom community and make any changes necessary to make it more conducive to SEE (see Chap. 5).

A whole-school approach where the school community, together with parents and the local community, promotes SEE in all aspects of school life and where the skills addressed in the classroom are promoted and reinforced at the whole-school level in a structured and complementary way, helps to organise the school as a caring community for all its members (see Chap. 6). Such an approach helps to create supportive whole-school context and ethos through entire staff's collaboration, contribution and education, peer education and mentoring, parental involvement and education and community participation, leading to more effective SEE outcomes (Weare and Nind 2011; Greenberg 2010; Bond et al. 2007; Askell Williams et al. 2010).

2.4.2 Multistage

The structured and developmental teaching and promotion of SEE at individual, classroom and whole-school levels take place throughout the kindergarten and primary school years. Weissberg and Greenberg (1998) argue that social and emotional learning involves a similar process to that of other academic skills, with increasing complexity of behaviour and social contexts requiring particular skills at each developmental level. A developmental approach strengthens and builds on basic SEE skills from one year to the next, building on what pupils have already learned and equipping them with skills needed for different stages in their development. Four major areas of SEE relating to self-awareness, self-management, social awareness and social skills, form the basis of the curriculum from kindergarten to the final year of primary education, but with different learning objectives, standards, benchmarks and indicators for each stage in each of the four areas. A spiral curriculum, straddling the kindergarten and primary school years, revisits each of the four areas at developmentally appropriate levels, which are also adapted according to the individual needs of the pupils (Chap. 4). Early intervention is necessary to support children's social and emotional well-being and prevent serious difficulties from developing later on during school life (Shaw et al. 2006; Merrell and Gueldner 2010; Weare and Nind 2001).

SEE is evaluated at individual pupil level through a number of formative assessment strategies. A checklist of competencies for each stage and year is completed by the classroom teacher and the pupils themselves (the younger pupils will use other expressive strategies such as drawings and role plays). The focus of the checklists, however, is formative and developmental, providing the classroom teacher and the pupils with an indication of the strengths and needs of the pupils in the various areas of SEE. This is followed by a classroom discussion of the feedback during circle time. Pupils will also keep a weekly SEE learning journal, which is also discussed during circle time (Chap. 4).

2.4.3   Multitarget

Although SEE is primarily targeted at pupils, the training, education and well-being of both staff and parents are critical for its success. A whole-school approach includes education programmes in social and emotional literacy and well-being for both staff and parents (see Chaps. 7–9).

2.4.4   Multiintervention

SEE is implemented through a universal approach for all pupils, but it also includes targeted interventions for pupils facing difficulties in their social and emotional development at small group and individual levels. A staged, school-based approach puts the onus on the school, in partnership with professionals, parents, services and the community, to provide the necessary support for pupils experiencing difficulties in their social and emotional development. This prevents unnecessary referrals to mental health services and directs those services to the school as much as possible (Chap. 6).

2.4.5 Well-Planned, Well-Implemented and Well-Evaluated

A needs assessment of the school community to match interventions according to the needs of the school is another component of the framework. This includes identifying those practices and policies that the school has been doing well in SEE, and incorporating them into the initiative. Schools are provided with guidelines on how to choose available programmes, which might work best for them, underlining programmes, which have been found to be based on a sound theoretical and research basis, with evidence for their effectiveness (cf. Askell-Williams et al. 2010; Collaborative for Academic, Social, and Emotional Learning 2008; Chap. 4). All school staff involved receives specific training in delivering the SEE curriculum as well as mentoring and supervision by colleagues and specialised staff. The school makes provision for organisational supports and policies to safeguard the success and sustainability of the initiative, including supportive management, active participation in planning and implementation of the whole school community, provision of adequate resources and alignment with regional, district and school policies.

SEE is monitored, evaluated and improved regularly at individual, classroom and whole-school levels. Pre- and postinitiative pupil outcomes help to determine the effectiveness of the interventions in terms of pupils' social and emotional learning and academic learning. Data are collected from pupils, staff and parents, assessing pupils' behaviour through scales and checklists as well as pupils', staff's and parents' perceptions. Initiatives that are not adequately co-ordinated, monitored and evaluated are unlikely to work in the long term (Collaborative for Academic, Social, and Emotional Learning 2008; Greenberg 2010; see Chap. 3).

> Social and emotional well-being is establishing itself as a permanent fixture rather than a transitory blip on the radar screen of education…Schools are increasingly being held responsible for putting in place plans, programs and practices to promote positive student social and emotional health and to prevent problems of poor mental health. (Bernard et al. 2007, p. 2)

2.5 Conclusion

The evidence is clear and unequivocal. Our children need SEE as a preparation for a successful and fulfilling adult citizenship. To deny them this would be short-changing them by providing an inadequate formation for successful adulthood and denying them a fundamental right to a broad-based, meaningful and relevant education in tune with the demands of the twenty-first century. This book proposes an evidence-based framework on how this could be achieved at various levels. Reading through the book's chapters, however, some practitioners may feel overwhelmed by the multilevel, multitarget and multidimensional initiatives suggested in the book. The commitment, resources and time required to put the various elements of the framework into practice may appear daunting, and it may be easy for some to just write this off as a romantic, impractical academic exercise. Educational reforms in schools are replete with examples of failed initiatives, which did not take an account of the contexts, cultures and the day-to-day realities of schools and classrooms. Careful reading of this text, however, will show that this book, in fact, is an attempt to promote a bottom-up approach with the whole school participating in the planning and assessment of the needs of the school community, as well as in the implementation and evaluation of the proposed interventions. The book also suggests making use of and integrating the existing strengths, good practices and resources at the school. For instance, there may already be various initiatives taking place at a school to prevent and deal with bullying, to promote positive behaviour in the classroom, to facilitate collaboration and inclusion or to engage pupils actively in the learning process. The school will need to examine how these initiatives may be incorporated in any new SEE initiative. Moreover, the comprehensive and multilevel framework proposed in this book may need to be introduced in a phased approach in line with the school's resources and needs. Schools may feel overwhelmed with the complexity of the approach presented here, particularly if they are already suffering from reform fatigue. A staged approach and a focus on those areas considered to be most important to address the needs of the school are more likely to be sustainable in the long term in such instances. The framework presented in this book, thus, should not be taken as a prescriptive, one-size-fits-all recipe for schools across cultures and contexts. It is more of a road map, providing a framework for schools on their way towards the realisation of SEE, with the schools moving along that pathway according to their needs and realities.

The Oracle and the Gadfly

Delphi, Ancient Greece

440 BC

The inscription *'Know Thyself'* at the entrance of the temple welcomed the tired messenger from Athens. As Chaerephon made his way through the double door past the great Doric columns, he was embraced by the warmth and rustic smell of the pine fire tended by the white priestesses. He crossed the temple and walked down to the basement towards a round space below the temple floor. He was greeted by golden Apollo and kneeled to kiss the omphalos sacred stone, the navel of the world from where Zeus released the two eagles. Two priestesses in white led Chaerophon to the curtain hiding the adytum and asked him to make his request to the oracle inside. The laurel-purified and laurel-crowned Pythia on the tripod went into a trance as she inhaled the vapours emerging from the centre of the earth. The shaking, red-garmented messenger of the gods recited verses alien to Chaerephon. The two priestesses repeated to Chaerephon: 'The gods have not bestowed any greater wisdom than on the one who knows that he knows nothing. Go tell your master'.

Back in Athens the great master mused on the paradoxical message from the gods. How could he, the one who only knows that he knows nothing, be wise at all? His wisdom was limited to an awareness of his own ignorance. His only wisdom was to understand the path a lover of wisdom must take in his search for it. Confronted by this paradox, Socrates went round the streets of Athens, approaching the well-known wise men of the city in order to confirm his identity and refute the Oracle's verdict. After his lengthy elunchus with statesmen, poets, artisans and other prominent Athenians, he realised that although they thought they were highly knowledgeable and wise citizens, their wisdom was more conspicuous by its absence. Like Archimedes' eureka, it suddenly dawned on him that the Oracle was, in fact, correct. His fellow Athenians thought that they were wise when they were not. He knew that he was not wise, which thus made him wiser than the others. He was the only one who was aware of his own ignorance, of his own weaknesses and strengths. From that day, Socrates became the gadfly of the state, a social and moral critic pushing the Athenian citizens towards self-awareness and self-realisation. He questioned and attacked accepted traditional notions such as 'might makes right' and the unbridled pursuit of material wealth. Instead, he advocated self-development and the pursuit of goodness, friendship and true community.

Chapter 3
An Overarching Structure for the Implementation of Social and Emotional Education

The social and emotional education (SEE) framework presented in Chap. 2 is a comprehensive, taught and caught, universal and targeted approach at individual, classroom, whole school and community levels, and involving pupils, staff, parents/caregivers and the community. As such it needs an overarching structure which will facilitate its successful planning, implementation, monitoring and evaluation. This chapter provides a structure for schools wishing to embark on this process to ensure adequate training and resources, school community commitment, faithful implementation of the interventions, and regular monitoring and evaluation. It may serve as a guide to the school community in the planning, implementation and evaluation processes, while providing adequate space for schools to move along the path according to their needs and reality.

3.1 An Action Research Framework

Any change has to be introduced in a way that fits within the existing nature, culture and needs of the school community, with all school members examining their context to bring about change according to their own needs, strengths and resources, and building on good practice already taking place. It also needs to be owned by the school community, with the onus of responsibility for any SEE initiative falling on the school members themselves. There are three main cyclical steps in this action research oriented process, namely planning, implementing and monitoring and evaluation (Fig. 3.1)[1].

> (Social and emotional learning) is designed to help all schools become places where learning is valued, dreams are born, leaders are made, and the talents of students—the greatest resource shared by every community—are unleashed. (Elias 2003, p. 25)

[1] Some of the strategies in each of the three stages are based on the social and emotional learning (SEL) Implementation Cycle (CASEL 2006).

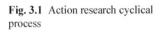

Fig. 3.1 Action research cyclical process

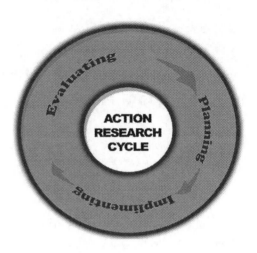

3.2 Stage 1 Planning

Leadership and Setting Up an SEE Team One of the tasks in starting the SEE process at the school is to establish a core team responsible for overseeing the planning, implementation, monitoring and evaluation stages of the initiative. It is crucial that all members of the team are committed to SEE and strongly believe in its value and usefulness for the school community. The team would be led by a member of the school community with the authority to move the process forward and with the resources to overcome potential obstacles. It would include members of staff, pupils, parents/caregivers and possibly the local community. It would link up with other support teams existing at the school, such as inclusion or behaviour support teams.

Needs Assessment and Plan of Action Before implementing any initiative, the team will carry an assessment of the SEE needs of the school community in order to develop a plan of action which will inform how the strategies suggested in this book may be adapted to suit the needs of the community, making use of its strengths and incorporating good practices already taking place. This task could be carried out in various phases, such as a staff development session for the whole school, followed by meetings with pupils, parents/caregivers and the local community. It may also include collecting data through surveys with staff, pupils and parents/caregivers. The final outcome would be a plan of action for a school-wide initiative at individual, classroom, whole school and family and community levels, at both universal and targeted interventions. It would be developed around the needs, strengths and culture of the school community, mobilising support and resources for its implementation. The action plan will have specific objectives and targets to be reached and a timeline for implementation and evaluation (CASEL 2006). It would have been understood, agreed upon and approved by all stakeholders involved, and would have discussed how the various stakeholders including staff, pupils, parents/caregivers and other partners, are going to contribute to the various strands of the initiative. One key ingredient for a successful SEE initiative at this stage is to include and make use of the existing strengths and resources of the school, such as linking it to other existing key initiatives (Elias 2003).

An important aspect of the initial task is to identify the potential implementation barriers that are likely to be faced by the school and how these may be overcome. Possible barriers may include limited or lack of human and physical resources, resistance, lack of commitment and disengagement by certain school members, lack of training of staff, lack of consistency in approach, academic pressure and devaluing of SEE, overwhelming pressures on classroom staff and problems in monitoring and in ensuring all school community members are following the implementation faithfully (CASEL 2006). In their review of the secondary social and emotional aspects of learning (SEAL) programme in the UK, Humphrey et al. (2010) identified the staff's 'will and skill' as a major barrier in many schools, particularly in the implementation process, in some instances leading to 'implementation failure'. Another barrier was physical, financial and human resource allocation and time constraints during the implementation. In their evaluation of the primary school programme (small group work), Humphrey et al. (2008) similarly reported that the key barriers to effectiveness included the attitudes of staff, misconceptions about the nature and purpose of primary SEAL small group work, and 'initiative overload'. Success was also impacted by the skills and experience of the facilitator and the availability of an appropriate physical space to conduct the sessions. Box 3.1 describes a number of strategies for engaging all stakeholders and dealing with resistance effectively.

Education of Staff and Provision of Resources The school staff may not have had adequate education in teaching and facilitating SEE in their classroom. Professional learning sessions on increasing understanding of well-being, resilience and mental health in children, and in using SEE in the classroom, is necessary for all classroom staff concerned. This will also include education in the use of the particular programme/package being used at the school. Members of staff, who have already received training in SEE, would be well placed to take a key role in school-based education in SEE. As already mentioned elsewhere, classroom staff will be provided with a resource pack for their respective year group with specified objectives, model lesson plans, necessary resources and assessment material (see Chap. 4).

Facilitating Parents/Caregivers and the Local Community Participation One of the key planning tasks will be to involve the parents/caregivers and the local community as key stakeholders and recruit their collaboration and support during the implementation. Various meetings with parents/caregivers and the local community, explaining the rationale and evidence for SEE, how they may contribute to the implementation, as well as how the school may contribute to the community's development, would help to lay down a framework of commitment and collaboration on the part of the parents/caregivers and the community to the initiative (see Chap. 9).

Box 3.1 Strategies for Involving all Stakeholders, from Diverse Perspectives, in the Initiative (Adapted from CASEL 2006)

1. *Set concrete goals.* Agreed-upon goals should form a shared agenda reached by consensus, thus creating a broad sense of ownership and strengthening communication among stakeholders. This step is critically important because if anything goes awry later in the change process, the stakeholders will be able to return to a shared agenda and refocus their intent and efforts.
2. *Show sensitivity.* Managing conflict means being aware of differences among individuals. Each stakeholder must genuinely feel he or she is an equal and valued party throughout the change process. All participants need respect, sensitivity and support as they work to redefine their roles and master new concepts.
3. *Model process skills.* Teaching through modelling the appropriate process skills and actions is fundamental to successful staff development initiatives. Staff developers may find, for example, that reflecting publicly and straightforwardly on their own doubts and resistance to change may help others. At the very least, honesty goes a long way towards building credibility. When staff developers model desirable behaviours, they give other stakeholders a chance to identify with someone going through the difficult process of change.
4. *Develop strategies for dealing with emotions.* All too often, educators concentrate on outcomes and neglect the emotional experiences—anxiety, fear, loss and grief—of change. Effective staff development programs should include ways to address those emotions. Focus on such questions as: How will our lives be different with the change? How do we feel about the changes? Is there anything that can or should be done to honour the past before we move on?
5. *Manage conflict.* Ideally, change is a negotiated process. Administrators and teacher union representatives should develop collaborative implementation plans to foster the positive development of all students.
6. *Communicate.* Openness in communication is a necessary component of collaborative problem solving. Communication that focuses on differences can move issues of concern out of the shadows. Another technique that increases communication is reflective questioning, i.e. when the questioner tries to help stakeholders explore their thinking, feelings, needs or attitudes. Such questions can include: Where are we in the change process? What has changed so far? Where are we headed?
7. *Monitor process dynamics.* The change process must be carefully monitored and appropriate adjustments made. Evaluation begins with the original assessment of the need and readiness to change and should be a key factor in a continuing reform effort.

3.3   Stage 2 Implementation

Piloting One of the decisions to be taken early in the process is how implementation is to be carried out. It is strongly recommended that before the actual, full blown initiative is launched; a smaller scale pilot project would be carried out to identify the initiative's strengths and weaknesses, including potential barriers which would still need to be overcome before it can work. For instance, the school may start by implementing a programme with only a 1 year group and following evaluation, make the necessary adaptations to the initial programme and decide whether it is ready to launch the programme for the whole school.

Commitment and Engagement of all Involved Once the initiative is launched, it is important not to let any individual or group slip through the net. The SEE team would need to ensure that all members of the school community, parents/caregivers and the local community are committed and actively engaged in the implementation process. It is also important to ensure that all strands of the SEE are in place as planned.

Constant Monitoring and Consistency Constant monitoring by the SEE team is necessary to ensure that the initiative is being implemented as planned. While an amount of adaptation may be necessary, faithfulness to the program will be paramount to its effectiveness and success. The team may distribute checklists where school members tick which part/s of the program are being implemented, carry out observations and meet and discuss with staff, pupils and parents/caregivers how the program is being implemented (see Chap. 4).

Troubleshooting and Support Monitoring will help to identify emerging problems which might threaten parts of, or the whole initiative, and enable action to resolve such problems as soon as they appear. Constant support including availability of physical and human resources and mentoring schemes, time to share practice and problems, and consultation, will need to be continuously provided to school members in the implementation phase. This is a stage where the expertise of specialist staff and the team will be particularly valuable to assist with the upskilling of regular classroom teachers.

Feedback and Celebration The school community will be kept regularly informed on how the implementation is going on at its various levels. Success will be shared and celebrated throughout the whole community.

3.4   Stage 3 Evaluation

The constant monitoring of the implementation will provide feedback on what is working, and help the school community to make necessary adaptations and improvements. All aspects of the initiative will be evaluated, including the taught curriculum in the classrooms, interventions for pupils in difficulty, the classroom climate, the whole-school ecology, the contribution of the parents/caregivers and local community, and initiatives to support staff's and parents' well-being, and how these different parts are working, and supporting and reinforcing one another. Crucial aspects for evaluation are the consistency and faithfulness to the initiative, such as whether all members of staff are actively committed and engaged and implementing the program as planned both in the classrooms and at the whole school level. The evaluation may be held at key stages of the implementation process, such as at the end of the school term, with feedback sought from all partners involved. The team may devise brief questionnaires for school staff, pupils and parents/caregivers, including items that address teachers' knowledge and competence in SEE, the school's provision of SEE learning opportunities and initiatives, and what worked and did not work in the various components of the initiatives (cf. Askell-Williams et al. 2010).

The evaluation will also provide information on the effectiveness of the initiative. The individual, classroom and whole-school checklists included in the subsequent chapters, will provide information on the standards and benchmarks of the pupils' social and emotional learning as well as on the functioning of the classrooms and the school community for pupils, staff and parents/caregivers. Other relevant available information related to the increase or decrease of positive or negative academic and social behaviours (e.g. improvements in learning, school attendance and behaviour, and reported decrease in violence, misbehaviour, exclusion and absenteeism) could also be indicators of the effectiveness of the programme. The Strengths and Difficulties Questionnaire (Goodman 1997) administered at pre- and post-intervention, would also provide data on the impact of the program on pupils' behaviour. The SEE team may also carry out a survey on such behaviours, seeking the feedback of staff, pupils and parents/caregivers on changes in pupils' social and academic behaviours. This exercise will help to identify both strengths as well as areas which will need further or more intensive interventions.

Evaluation is an ongoing cycle of action and reflection, with the school community itself seeking to refine and improve the initiative as it is actually unfolding in the field. Once the school community starts to see the benefits of the initiative, this will then lead it to decide on how to integrate and 'institutionalise' it into the daily life of the school community (Greenberg et al. 2003).

3.5 Conclusion

The following chapters will describe in more detail how the comprehensive SEE framework presented in this chapter may be put into practice at various levels as outlined in the framework. Part 2 lays out the roadmap for putting 'the heart in the classroom', describing how the SEE curriculum may be organised, implemented and evaluated as part of the daily classroom practice, and how it may be imbedded in both the academic curriculum and the classroom climate. It also presents a staged, school-based targeted intervention framework for pupils experiencing difficulties in their social and emotional learning and development. Part 3 then broadens the vision for a whole school approach to the promotion of SEE across the whole school, underlining the well-being and resilience not only of the pupils, but of the whole school community, including the staff and the parents/caregivers.

Bangarra, Gula and the Water Spring[2]

Tully Falls, Innisfail, Far North Queensland, Australia

As the dark orange sunset glow disappeared in the stifling hot air, the animals started to come out from their underground shelters for an urgent meeting amidst the shrivelled plants and burnt grass. The red kangaroo and the rufous-hare-wallaby, the brush-tailed possum and the ring-tailed possum, the sugar glider and the spotted-tail quoll, the mangrove goanna and the spiny-tailed goanna, the blue-tongued lizard and the perentie lizard, the broad-faced potoroo and the long-nosed potoroo, the short-beaked echidna and the burrowing bettong, the short-nosed bandicoot and the pig-footed bandicoot, Kookaburra the kingfisher and the bird of paradise, the gang gang cockatoo and the emu, the brown snake and the black bat, the crimson chat and the willie wagtail, all joined in a chorus of bellows, croaks, grunts, growls, hisses, howls, hums, squeals, squeaks, snorts, screeches, chatters, chirps, chuckles and chortles.

The angry red kangaroo accused Bangarra, the blue-tongued lizard, of having found water and kept it only for himself: 'Gudjilla has seen you drying yourself behind a rock. Where is the water, Bangarra? We cannot quench our thirst anymore chewing Gulbirra! We must share the water!' But Bangarra bared his blue tongue, and with a strong sweep of his tail, lurked away into the darkness. The animal assembly chose Gudjilla, the short-nosed bandicoot, to secretly follow Bangarra to his hideout. But Bangarra had shrewd sharp eyes and could see Gudjilla sneaking from behind a rock. Then they chose Jiggirrjiggirr, the willie wagtail, who flew from one giant eucaplyptus tree to another in hot pursuit. But Bangarra could easily spy Jiggiggjiggir's black and white feathers as he stretched his neck to spy on Bangarra. Midin, the ring-tailed possum, tried his luck as well, followed by Kookaburra, the spotted-tail quoll and the crimson chat, but Bangarra was too clever. The animals were at a loss what to do. Then Gula, the tiny short-nosed boodie, volunteered to have a try even if he did not drink so much water, and he was the smallest of them all. But the animals laughed at tiny Gula, he was too small to be of any use. He was even ridiculed by *Midin*, the proud ring-tailed possum, who told him to shut up and not waste the time of the assembly.

---

[2] Adapted from www.didjshop.com.

The hurt Gula believed he could find the water even if he was smaller than the others. When Bangarra thought someone was following, and looked to the left, Gula would jump to the right, and when Bangarra looked to the right, Gula would jump to the left. His small size and swift and agile movements, made it possible for him to hide from Bangarra's prying eyes. He pursued Bangarra to a spring hidden behind a big flat rock. He hurried back to the others and led them to the secret spring. The happy animals drank to their hearts' content and splashed the water in all directions, and Kookaburra swam and dug drains and gullies with his beak in front of the running water. This is how the mighty Tully Falls were created and the dry land became a waterland, with lush and dense rainforests. It became the wettest place in the whole continent to this day. Tiny Gula suddenly became a very important and valued member of the community. The red kangaroo declared that from that day on, all the animals were to call Gula 'the rat-kangaroo'. They also agreed that all animals, irrespective of their size and shape, had a right to have their say and to be listened to by all the others.

Part II
Heart in the Classroom

'All learning has an emotional base'.

—Plato

Chapter 4
Taught Social and Emotional Education: SEE in the Curriculum

High-quality classroom teaching of social and emotional education (SEE) as a core subject area in the primary school curriculum is one of the key elements of the SEE framework presented in Chap. 2. This chapter describes the SEE *content* areas to be taught, *how* SEE can be organised and taught and how the classroom teacher may *assess* the progress of the individual pupils in developing their social and emotional capabilities. The following sections describe the SEE content and goals for each area, the learning standards defining the learning needed to reach each stated goal, the staged benchmarks developed from each standard indicating the progress in pupils' learning of the skills in each standard, the method of instruction and the assessment of the skills taught (Fig. 4.1). This framework draws loosely from the one developed by the Anchorage School District Social and Emotional Learning in Alaska, USA, but it has been adapted according to the curriculum framework proposed in the book. There is also a section on how the curriculum may be embedded in the other areas of the curriculum, whereas the final section discusses the evaluation of the curriculum's effectiveness in pupils' SEE.

4.1 Curriculum Framework

Figure 4.2 presents a SEE curriculum content framework for early years and primary schools based on the six perspectives in well-being and resilience described in Chap. 2. It uses two main dimensions, which incorporate the various skills to be learned, namely self-social (others) dimension on one side and awareness-management on the other. The basic framework is loosely based on the ones by CASEL (2005)/ASD (2012) one, but it has been developed and extended to include other areas from positive education, mindfulness, resilience, inclusive education and caring community, which have not been included in the original SEL framework. It also draws on, and/or resonates with, the frameworks and approaches proposed by Roffey (2010), Nobles and McGrath (2008), Bernard (2012b) and lateral thinking (De Bono 1992). It is situated in the Western social and cultural contexts, reflecting values, attitudes, aspirations and behaviours developed and promoted in Western

C. Cefai, V. Cavioni, *Social and Emotional Education in Primary School*,
DOI 10.1007/978-1-4614-8752-4_4, © Springer Science+Business Media New York 2014

Fig. 4.1 The process of teaching and assessing social and emotional education (SEE) in the classroom. (Adapted from ASD 2012)

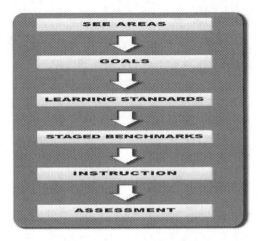

Fig. 4.2 The four key dimensions of the social and emotional education (SEE) curriculum framework. (Adapted from ASD 2012)

	SELF	SOCIAL
AWARENESS	I am..., Knowledgeable SELF CONFIDENCE	I care... Caring EMPATHY
MANAGEMENT	I can... Capable SELF CONTROL AND SELF MOTIVATION	I will... Responsible INFLUENCE

culture (Watson et al. 2012). Moreover, Western cultures themselves are becoming increasingly diverse and multicultural. In this respect, it is argued that the framework presented here may serve as a general one and the content areas may need to be adapted to the particular cultures and subcultures where it is being implemented.

The four areas developed from the two dimensions (self-awareness, self-management, social awareness and social management) incorporate the five social and emotional learning (SEL) areas proposed by CASEL (problem-solving skills has been incorporated in both self and social management) as well as other skills from the other five perspectives. Positive emotions, optimism, persistence, confidence and self-efficacy, autonomy/agency and sense of leadership are some of skills from both positive psychology and resilience literature (Seligman et al. 2009; Gilman et al. 2009; Benard 2004; Werner and Smith 1992; Nobles and McGrath 2008). The framework also includes success-oriented engagement, underlining the requisite skills students would need to maximise their learning potential, such as goal setting and achievement, planning, self-monitoring, academic regulation and persistence

(Bernard 2011a; Nobles and McGrath 2008; Seligman et al. 2009). Critical and creative thinking skills provide pupils with opportunities to learn about their learning process and develop their thinking and problem-solving skills and consequently take control of their own learning (Watkins 2010; De Bono 1992). This set of skills constitutes what NICE (2008) calls psychological well-being skills.

Emotional awareness and regulation is a key feature of the CASEL framework (CASEL 2005), but the present framework underlines awareness and regulation of one's thoughts also through positive self-talk (Bernard 2012b). Another important addition to the traditional SEL framework is spiritual development from positive psychology, mindfulness education and humanistic psychology. Sense of meaning and purpose (Roffey 2011; Nobles and McGrath 2008; Seligman et al. 2009) underlines the need to find meaning and purpose in one's life as a source of happiness, growth and self-actualisation (Seligman 2011; Maslow 1971). Related to this is the notion of mindfulness, the capacity to be aware of the present moment, accepting what comes without getting caught up in thoughts or emotional or physical reactions to the situation (Burrows 2011; Weare 2010; Kabat-Zinn 2004).

The social awareness and management areas within this framework underline the role of the individual in relation to the well-being of the social and physical environment. Besides having the skills to relate effectively, collaboratively and meaningfully with others, this framework underlines prosocial values and attitudes (Nobles and McGrath 2008), responsible decision making (Nobles and Mc Grath 2008; Roffey 2011), moral development (Cohen 2006; Noddings 2012; Elias and Synder 2008), inclusion, diversity and children's rights perspective (Oliver 1996; Booth and Ainscow 1998), belonging to, and participating in, classroom caring community (Sergiovanni 1994; Cefai 2008) and appreciation and care for the environment (Goleman et al. 2012). The addition of these components shifts the focus from the well-being and health of the individual to the well-being and health of the social environment as well, and to the responsibility of the individual not only to respect and care for himself/herself but also for others and the environment as well. This seeks to integrate the needs of the individual with those of the collective, underlining the benefits of contributing to caring communities not only for the individual but also the communities themselves. Although an excessive focus on the self in SEE may lead to unhealthy materialism and individualism (Crocker and Park 2004), taking into consideration and respecting the needs and rights of others, and underlining the values of solidarity, diversity and collaboration, help to create caring and supportive communities, which eventually benefit the individual himself/herself (Noddings 1992, 2012; Watson et al. 2012; Johnson and Johnson 2008). A sense of belonging, connectedness and community is a key factor to the well-being, health and resilience of the individual, serving both as a source of growth for normally developing children, but also as a protective factor for children in difficulty or at risk (Resnick et al. 1997; Pianta 1999; Battistich et al. 2004; Cefai 2008). Partaking in this 'shared humanity' (Roffey 2011) brings together the individual and collective needs in a synergetic maximisation of potential for both the individual and the community. It will help to offset the current growth of the dominance of individualism and the associated abdication of social responsibility in Western culture, which have become a major threat to the social and emotional well-being of children and young people (Cooper and Cefai 2009; Layard and Dunn 2009).

Similarly, appreciating and taking care of the physical environment does not only underline the role of respect and social responsibility towards the environment but also draws attention to the relationship between well-being and the environment and how a well-kept and protected environment contributes to the emotional and psychological well-being of the individual (Goleman et al. 2012; Reynolds et al. 2010; Cameron 2011).

> There is a need for a new structure in public school systems – An "Office of Social and Emotional Development". This office is focused on curriculum and policy and is NOT located with psychologists, counselors, social workers, and special educators, but in the central mission of schools – Curriculum. It involves both teacher training in quality teaching processes as well as specific curriculum. (Greenberg 2011)

4.2 Content

4.2.1 Self-Awareness

Pupils are able to recognise their emotions, describe their interests and values and accurately assess their strengths. They are able to reflect on their thoughts and learning process. They have a well-grounded sense of self-confidence, self-efficacy, agency and autonomy. They are hopeful about the future and have a sense of meaning and purpose. More specifically, this content area includes the following competencies:

- Recognition of emotions: identifying and labelling feelings.
- Knowledge and recognition of strengths: identification and cultivation of one's strengths and positive qualities, and using strengths to address limitations/weaknesses and maximise potential.
- Confidence and self-efficacy.
- Autonomy/agency, internal locus of control and sense of leadership.
- Self-advocacy and awareness of one's rights as an individual.
- Optimism about one's learning and life in general and hope for the future.
- Developing sense of meaning and purpose in life, self-actualisation.

4.2.2 Self-Management

Pupils are able to manage their thoughts, emotions and behaviour, manage stress, engage in positive talk, control impulses and persevere in overcoming obstacles.

They can set and monitor progress towards the achievement of personal and academic goals, persisting in the face of difficulties. They are able to engage in critical thinking on their learning and behaviour, to solve problems effectively and to make good and informed decisions. They express their positive and negative emotions appropriately in a wide range of situations and demonstrate mindful attention and focused awareness. They are actively engaged in social and academic tasks through their strengths. More specifically, this content area includes the following competencies:

- Self-regulation, emotional expression and dealing with negative emotions.
- Appreciating and enjoying one's positive emotions, such as happiness and excitement.
- Persistence and overcoming difficulties and setbacks.
- Goal setting and self-monitoring (establishing, planning and working towards achieving short- and long-term goals, including academic achievement).
- Making good decisions: analysing situations (accurately perceiving when a decision is needed and assessing factors that influence decisions).
- Problem solving (generating, implementing and evaluating positive and informed solutions to problems).
- Engaging in academic and social tasks through strengths.
- Critical, creative and lateral thinking skills: thinking critically about learning and thinking, learning about learning and developing better thinking skills.
- Positive thinking/self-talk—using rational and helpful thinking and positive self-talk to cope with negative events and feelings in one's life.
- Understanding and developing mindful attention and focusing awareness, sharpening awareness of self, others and environment through focused attention.

4.2.3   Social Awareness

Pupils are able to take the perspective of and empathise with others and recognise and appreciate individual and group similarities and differences, diversity and social inclusion. They have a sense of connectedness and belonging to community. They demonstrate prosocial values and behaviours are motivated to contribute to the well-being of their schools and communities and are able to seek out and appropriately use family, school and community resources in age-appropriate ways. They also appreciate and care for the physical environment. More specifically, this content area includes the following competencies:

- Engage in perspective taking (identifying and understanding thoughts and feelings of others).
- Empathise with others.
- Appreciate individual and group social differences and similarities, celebrating diversity and social inclusion, multiculturalism, solidarity and moral and social responsibility.
- Are aware of resources and support networks (family, school and community)

- Develop prosocial values and attitudes (honesty, respecting rights of others, feeling responsible for and supporting the well-being of others).
- Appreciate, respect and protect the physical environment.

4.2.4   Social Management

Pupils have good relationship skills, being able to establish and maintain healthy and rewarding relationships based on co-operation and collaboration. They resist inappropriate social pressure; constructively prevent, manage and resolve interpersonal conflict; and seek and provide help when needed. They demonstrate ethical behaviour and responsible decision making in the various contexts they operate, considering the needs and rights of others in their behaviour and decisions. More specifically, this content area includes the following competencies:

- Establish and maintain healthy and rewarding relationships with individuals and groups.
- Communicate effectively to express oneself and positive exchanges with others, using both verbal and non-verbal skills.
- Co-operate and collaborate with others.
- Deal with peer pressure (refusing to engage in unwanted, unsafe and unethical conduct).
- Resolve interpersonal conflict constructively (achieving mutually satisfactory resolutions to conflict by addressing the needs of all concerned).
- Seek and provide help and support.
- Engage in ethical and responsible behaviour and decision making (considering ethical standards, safety concerns, and respect for others, integrity and the likely consequences of various courses of action when making decisions).

4.3   Goals

1. Self-awareness
   I recognise who I am and how I am feeling relative to the world around me.
   Pupils will demonstrate a strong sense of self-awareness: The pupil becomes aware of who he/she is and his/her strengths and limitations; he/she recognises own emotions, describes own interests and values and accurately assesses own strengths. He/she has a well-grounded sense of self-confidence and self-efficacy, agency and autonomy and self-advocacy. He/she is optimistic about own success as a learner and hopeful for the future and has a sense of meaning and purpose.
2. Self-management
   I manage my behaviour in effective, positive, constructive ways.
   Pupils will be able to exercise self-management: The pupil becomes capable of regulating his/her emotions in effective and constructive ways, solve problems

effectively and make good decisions; he/she manages own thoughts, emotions and behaviour, experiences positive emotions, manages stress, engages in positive talk and perseveres in overcoming obstacles, setbacks and frustrations. He/she expresses own positive and negative emotions appropriately in a wide range of situations. He/she sets and monitors progress towards the achievement of personal and academic goals, persisting in the face of difficulty. He/she thinks and reflects on own thoughts and learning process and demonstrates mindful attention and focused awareness. He/she makes good and informed decisions, solves problems effectively and is actively engaged in social and academic tasks through own strengths.

3. Social awareness

   I demonstrate an awareness of the value of others in the greater communities.

   Pupils will show a strong sense of social awareness: The pupil understands and empathises with others; he/she takes the perspective of, and empathises with, others and recognises and appreciates individual and group similarities and differences, diversity and social inclusion. He/she has a sense of connectedness and belonging to the community. He/she demonstrates prosocial attitudes and behaviours, is motivated to contribute to the well-being of the school and local community and seeks out and appropriately uses family, school and community resources in age-appropriate ways. He/she also appreciates and cares for the physical environment.

4. Social management

   I interact in meaningful, productive ways with others.

   Pupils will demonstrate social management skills: The pupil will be responsible in relating constructively with others; he/she has good relationship skills, being able to establish and maintain healthy and rewarding relationships based on co-operation and collaboration. He/she resists inappropriate social pressure; constructively prevents, manages and resolves interpersonal conflict and seeks and provides help when needed. He/she demonstrates ethical behaviours and responsible decision making in various contexts, considering the needs and rights of others in their behaviour and decisions.

4.4 Learning Standards

The SEE goals are then translated into learning standards, that is, specific statements of knowledge, attitudes and/or skills clearly defining the learning needed to reach the stated goal. The standards are written in two formats: one for adults (teachers) and one for children (pupils), with a total of 30 standards for the four goals (see Table 4.1). The teacher version of the first learning standard for self-awareness is 'Pupils demonstrate awareness of their emotions', whereas the pupil version reads 'I am aware of what I am feeling'. These standards will inform the SEE learning benchmarks, curriculum, instruction and assessment as described later. Both the standards and the benchmarks include a combination of knowledge and skills, and

Table 4.1 Social and emotional education (SEE) learning standards. (Adapted from Anchorage School District Social and Emotional Learning 2012)

1. Self-Awareness (I am): Recognizing who I am and how I am feeling relative to the world around me.
1A. **Pupils demonstrate awareness of their emotions.**
(I am aware of what I am feeling.)
1B. **Pupils demonstrate self knowledgeof their personal traits.**
(I know what I do well,what areas I can work on, and in which areas I need help)
1C. **Pupils demonstrate a sense of meaning and purpose**
(I know what I want to do and achieve in lifeand how I can work towards it)
1D. **Pupils demonstrate a well grounded sense of agency and autonomy**
(I am aware of what I can do and what I need to do to achieve it)
1E. **Pupils demonstratea well grounded sense of self confidence and self efficacy**
(I am confident of myself and my abilities in learning and other activities)
1F. **Pupils demonstrate awareness of their rights and how to stand up for themselves**
(I am aware of my rights as an individual and how to stand up for them)
1G. **Pupils demonstrate awareness of their external supports.**
(I am aware of the supports Ihave around me.)
1H. **Pupils are optimisticabout themselves as learners and life in general**
(I am optimistic that I will learn and achieve and any problems can become opportunities)

2. Self-Management (I can): Managing my behaviour in effective, constructive ways.
2A. **Pupils demonstrate ability to manage their emotions constructively.**
(I can responsibly manage my emotions.)
2B. **Pupils demonstrate ability to appreciate and enjoy positive emotions**
(I can enjoy positive emotions such as happiness, satisfaction and excitement)
2C. **Pupils demonstrate effective decision-making skills.**
(I can make good decisions.)
2D. **Pupils demonstrategood and creative problem solving skills**
(I can solve the problems that I face)
2E. **Pupils demonstrate ability to set and achieve goals.**
(I can set and achieve goals that will help me to be successful)
2F. **Pupils demonstrate ability to persevereand recoverin the face of setbacks**
(I am able to keep going in the face of difficulties and setbacks)
2G. **Pupils demonstrate critical and creative thinking skills**
(Ican reflect on my thinking and learning)
2H. **Pupils demonstrate focused attention and awareness**
(I can focus my attention on my present thoughts, feelings and movement)
2I. **Pupils demonstrate ability to engage in positive self talk**
(I can use helpful thinking to cope with negative events and feelings)
2J. **Pupils engage actively in academic and social tasks through their strengths**
(I can engage inacademic and social tasks making use of my strengths)

3. Social Awareness (I care): Demonstrating an awareness of the value of others in the greater communities.
3A. **Pupils demonstrate awareness of other people's emotions and perspectives.**
(I am aware of others' feelings and viewpoints)
3B. **Pupils demonstrate consideration and care forothers and a desire to positively contribute to their community.**
(I care about others and do my part to make my community better)
3C. **Pupils demonstrate an awareness of cultural issues and a respect for human dignity and differences.**
(I care about and respect the individual differences of others)
3D. **Pupils can read social cues.**
(I am aware ofhow I perceive others and am being perceived by them)

Table 4.1 (continued)

3E. **Pupils demonstrate seeking out and appropriately using family, school, and community resources in age-appropriate ways.**   *(Iknow about and make adequate usefamily, school and community resources)*   *3F.* **Pupils demonstrate an awareness to appreciate and care for the physical environment**   *(I care about the physical environment)*

4. Social Management (I will): Interacting in meaningful, caring productive ways with others   **4A. Pupils use positive communication and social skills to interact effectively with others.**   *(Iwill interact well with others)*   **4B. Pupils develop constructive and caring relationships.**   *(I will work on having constructive and caring relationships)*   **4C. Pupils learn and work collaboratively**   *(I will collaborate with others in learning and social activities)*   **4D. Pupils demonstrate the ability to prevent, manage, and resolve interpersonal conflicts in constructive ways.**   *(I will deal with interpersonal conflicts constructively)*   ***4E. Pupils demonstrate ethical behaviours in their interactions with others***   *(I will act in an honest and responsible waywith others)*   **4F. Pupils demonstrateresponsible decision making in various contexts**   *(I will consider the needs and rights of otherswhen making decisions).*

are specific enough to identify the learning targets and to assess the achievement of those targets. On the other hand, they are not exhaustive, but more in line with the notion of a minimum curriculum, leaving room for teachers and schools to focus and adapt according to the needs of the pupils.

4.5   Staged Benchmarks

Learning benchmarks are progress indicators for pupils' learning of the skills in each standard, assessing their learning over time. The benchmarks are identified for the three main stages in kindergarten and primary schools, namely stage 1 (Kindergarten/nursery: 4–5 years), stage 2 (Early Primary: 6–8 years) and stage 3 (Late Primary: 9–11 years). They start at a very basic level in the first stage, increasing in complexity and becoming more advanced from one stage to the next. They are not designed to be exhaustive but to highlight important, representative features of each standard that instruction should emphasise at each stage. Although presented in four areas, the benchmarks are highly interrelated and teachers are strongly encouraged to integrate them across the various standards both within the respective goals and the other goals as well. SEE alignment is not only necessary with other academic subjects, but is also critical within itself as well, to ensure it is presented and taught in a coherent, integrated way.

Pupils are expected to reach mastery in each benchmark by the end of each of the three age stages. The benchmark is construed as an exit learning benchmark, that is, the progress the pupil is expected to achieve at the end of the respective stage. However, SEE is taught in a sequential, spiral approach, building upon skills in a developmentally appropriate way and providing opportunities for revisiting earlier skills. The benchmarks will also be adapted to match the developmental needs of the pupils. This will avoid SEE falling into a traditional paradigm of standardised norms and summative performance indicators, which has the potential to lead to segregation and failure for some of the pupils. Appendix, Table 4.5 at the end of this chapter presents a sample benchmark for stage 2, with indicators for each learning goal. The benchmarks for stage 1 will follow the same pattern, but at a more basic level, whereas those for stage 3 will be more elaborate and advanced.

> We, as the adults in children's lives, can't keep telling our children countless times to "calm down" or "pay attention" without providing them with some practical guidelines for how to do so. Teaching these practices to students can increase not only their social and emotional skills, but their resilience: the capacity to not only cope, but thrive in the face of adversity. (Lantieri 2009c, p. 10)

4.6   Instruction

Timetabling As the vehicle for developing core competencies, SEE needs a central place in the curriculum through regular, weekly structured sessions (CASEL 2008; Weare and Nind 2011; Greenberg 2010; Kids Matter 2011). It is suggested that classroom teachers would allocate one or two sessions per week of their regular timetable to SEE. These sessions may vary in time, from 15 min per session in the case of stage 1 to 30 min in stage 2 and 30–40 min in stage 3.

Instructional Design Research evidence has consistently shown that effective programmes make use of a sequenced step-by-step approach, employ active and participative learning strategies, focus on skills development and have explicit learning goals (cf. 'SAFE approach'; CASEL 2005; Durlak et al. 2010, 2011). Sessions will thus be interactive and experiential, make use of different learning styles and suited to sociocultural differences, learning difficulties and other individual needs. They focus on the development of pupils' attitudes and declarative (what), procedural (how) and conditional (when) knowledge, integrating attitudes, knowledge and skills in the development of SEE competencies. Pupils take an active part throughout the sessions, practicing learned skills through role play, group work and other activities and processing their experiences in teacher-facilitated group discussions. Coaching, discussion, modelling, feedback, processing and reflecting, peer mentoring and small group work are some of the strategies teachers may employ. Pupils are also provided with opportunities to practice the skills being learnt not only during the taught sessions but also during the other academic and social activities in the classroom, during play time as well as outside school, including home. The role of the classroom teacher is that of an empowering facilitator, providing opportunities for pupils to learn through hands-on, interactive, group-based activities, with the peer group being a key contextual element of the learning process.

SEE sessions also need to include extended activities and home-based/parents'/caregivers' activities. Extended activities are aimed at embedding the taught SEE topics in the other academic subjects, thus helping to reinforce the SEE attitudes, knowledge and skills being learned. SEE sessions also include home activities that involve the child working with his/her parents/caregivers to reinforce and encourage the skills learnt at schools to be practiced in other contexts. Parents/Caregivers thus become key stakeholders in implementing the SEL curriculum in a different social context. Research has found this home–school partnership to be critical for the skills learnt at school to be sustained in the long term and to be generalised to other contexts and real-life scenarios (CASEL 2005; Greenberg et al. 2003; Wear and Nind 2011; Cavioni 2013). The school needs to invest time, effort and resources to recruit parental co-operation and collaboration in the planning, development and implementation of SEE both at school and at home and deal with potential parental resistance related to such concerns as mental health stigma and fears of losing time on academic achievement (Downey and Williams 2010; Durlack et al. 2011; Weare and Nind 2011). Chapter 9 describes in more detail parents'/caregivers' collaboration, education and well-being in relation to SEE.

The SEE sessions would also need to be linked to whole-school activities during that week or month, including morning assemblies, pupil-led activities, newsletters, exhibitions, posters and display of pupils' work. In this way, pupils are being constantly reminded of the competencies being developed and provided with further opportunities to practice them in the school corridors and playground (see also Chap. 6). This level of intervention also works to develop a whole school, which promotes social and emotional learning, and it also feeds back into the classroom processes itself. For instance, whole-school support in terms of administrative support and quality of school environment is linked to the teachers' own implementation of SEE in the classroom (Jennings and Greenberg 2008; Ransford et al. 2009).

The sample activities developed by Valeria Cavioni in the online package *Timmy's Trip to Planet Earth: A Self and Social Adventure* provide various examples of classroom and home activities in the four SEE areas for early years (butterfly) and primary school years (seahorse; see Fig. 4.3). Figure 4.4 presents sample activities for each age group, namely a classroom activity for primary school children and a home activity for preschool children.

Staff Education Staff's own competence in teaching SEE as well as their own social and emotional competence impacts not only their teaching of SEE but also their attitudes, practice and relationships in the classroom. Lack of positive attitudes, knowledge and skills in SEE not only lead to uncommitted and disengaged staff who might regard SEE as being peripheral to education but also to fragmented

Fig. 4.3 Timmy's trip to planet earth: a self and social adventure. (www.springer.com)

and poor-quality teaching and programme implementation (Askell-Williams et al. 2012; Humphrey et al. 2008, 2010; Greenberg 2010; Lendrum, Humphrey and Wigeslworth 2013, 2011). For instance, poor implementation of SEE programmes in primary schools, particularly in self and social awareness and relationship management, compromises the effectiveness of the programme in terms of pupils' outcomes (Jennings and Greenberg 2008). On the other hand, teachers' understanding of, and commitment to apply SEE knowledge and skills in their daily classroom practice— as in relationship management and problem solving—are particularly crucial for programme effectiveness in terms of positive pupil outcomes (Conduct Problems Prevention Research Group 1999). Staff thus need to appreciate the importance of SEE as a core competence in the curriculum and in their classroom practice, and to have both the competence and the confidence in teaching and implementing SEE both in the classroom and at the whole-school level (Durlack et al. 2011). Louise Rowlings (2012) argues on the need to look beyond programmes and packages for effective SEL: 'we need to help classroom teachers develop their confidence and capacity in SEL, to understand the real drivers of change of social and emotional well-being in children'.

Furthermore, socially and emotionally competent teachers are more likely to be effective in their SEE teaching and programme implementation in the classroom (Solomon et al. 2000; Leithwood and Beatty 2008; Jennings and Greenberg 2008). Through explicit teaching, positive reinforcement, role modelling and confidence in themselves as socially and emotionally competent practitioners, the classroom teachers can create a strong classroom culture promoting the learning and practice of SEE as a daily classroom practice. As Sue Roffey (2011, p. 2) put it, 'teachers' own social and emotional competence and well-being is symbiotic with student well-being'.

Fig. 4.4 Sample social and emotional education (SEE) activities. (Valeria Cavioni)

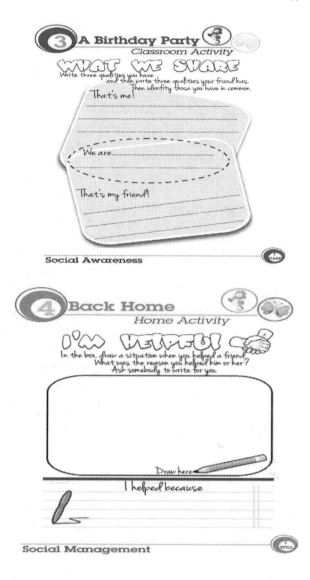

School teachers, however, frequently complain that whilst they believe in SEE and that they and the school do have a role in promoting children's well-being, often they are not provided with adequate education and resources in order for them to exercise such a role effectively (e.g. Reinke et al. 2011; Askell-Williams et al. 2005; Pace 2011; Vostanis et al. 2013). Any school initiative to promote SEE at classroom and whole-school levels would thus require in its planning and implementation, adequate teacher education and ongoing support, monitoring and mentoring (Elias 2003; Jennings and Greenberg 2008; Lane et al. 2006; Slee et al. 2012). It also requires that the staff's own well-being and health is considered as a key area for intervention. Tired and burnt out teachers, for instance, will lack the motivation and energy to effect high-quality implementation and will find it difficult to integrate SEE in their daily practice and relationships (Day and Qing 2009; Dworkin 2009). Staff's own health and well-being are discussed in more detail in Chap. 7.

Inclusive, Culturally Responsive, Developmental Approach Staff education also needs to address issues of reflective practice, which is essential for adapting the curriculum and pedagogy to the diversity of backgrounds and characteristics of pupils (Bartolo and Smyth 2009; Bartolo et al. 2007). Teachers need to be self-aware of their cultural baggage and open-minded to adopt affirmative approaches towards their pupils' diverse cultures. They also need to understand how the SEE curriculum can be diversified. One advantage of many existing SEE programmes is that they are based on experiential, hands-on, multimodal instructional strategies addressing the diverse needs of pupils. When content is experiential, it should enable individualisation as the content is brought up by the pupils themselves. Moreover, SEE programmes usually also include activities at various levels, which may be adapted according to the readiness and developmental levels of the pupils with different activities, resources, instructional designs, assessment modes and products for different pupils/groups of pupils. Adapting the material according to the cultural context of the school community will ensure that the pupils and their families will find the SEE curriculum meaningful and useful in their lives and thus more likely to engage with it. It would also facilitate the internalisation and generalisation of the skills to real-life contexts, helping to build their resilience skills to cope effectively with disadvantage and challenge (Merrell and Gueldner 2010; Whaley and Davis 2007). This is particularly relevant in SEE in view of the apparent relationship between social, cultural and economic disadvantage and mental health (Cole et al. 2005; Colman et al. 2009; Martinez et al. 2004). Introducing SEE initiatives without taking account of the contextual constraints and facilitating forces is likely to lead to difficulties in implementation and expected pupil outcomes (Askell-Williams et al. 2009). Elias (2010) suggests that programme adaptation to enhance coordination with existing programmes at the school need to be included in the planning phase. As one grade-3 primary school teacher in a South Australian primary school making use of an SEL package said, 'Programmes may not necessarily reflect the actual kids' reality outside and thus there is a need to adapt the programme according to our needs'.

A pertinent issue here is programme fidelity and dosage, and the challenge of finding a balance between retaining the programme integrity so as to maximise its effectiveness potential and adapting the material according to the individual needs and the social, cultural and linguistic contexts of the learners. Programme adaptation needs to be made in the light of the implementation guidelines of the particular programme being used so as to remain as faithful as possible to the key principles on which it is built and expected to produce outcomes. As per Weare (2010, p. 11), 'too much tailoring to local needs and circumstances can lead to dilution and confusion'. It will also lead to ineffective programmes in terms of pupil outcomes (Weare and Nind 2011; Cooper and Jacobs 2011; Greenberg 2010; Humphrey et al. 2010). The limited effectiveness of the social and emotional aspects of learning (SEAL) programme in both primary and secondary schools in the UK is attributed to lack of structure and consistency in programmes, such as teachers using only parts of the programme or using the programme only for a short period of time (Humphrey et al. 2008, 2010; Cooper and Jacobs 2011). Programme integrity in terms of high-quality implementation, fidelity and evaluation is a key indicator of programme effectiveness (Greenberg 2010) and usually programmes include manuals, guidelines and checklists to help the teacher in implementing it faithfully (Bywater and Sharples 2012). Pupils will thus be exposed to a broad-based curriculum rather than a restricted one, but with simplified and/or alternative activities and modes of instruction according to the developmental level, learning styles and the sociocultural context of the pupils. Use of language, examples, resources, activities and assessment will need to reflect the realities of the pupils concerned. In this way, the programme responds to the diversity of needs in the school without compromising its integrity. Adaptation could take place through a collaborative exercise involving the key stakeholders involved, including pupils, parents and other members of the community so as to identify the needs of the school community (Merrell and Gueldner 2010). As Durlak and DuPre (2008, p. 331) argue 'Expecting perfect or near-perfect implementation is unrealistic. Positive results have often been obtained with levels around 60 %; few studies have attained levels greater than 80 %' (p. 331).

> We see the development of pupils' social, emotional and behavioural skills as integral to good learning and teaching…This means teaching all pupils, from the beginning of education, to manage strong feelings, resolve conflict effectively and fairly, solve problems, work and play co-operatively, and be respectful, calm, optimistic and resilient. (DfES 2005a, p. 31)

Quality Circle Time Quality circle time (Mosley 1993) may be one of the mediums of instruction through which SEE is delivered and implemented in the classroom. Circle time is a child-friendly approach that facilitates the practice of SEE in an inclusive, caring and democratic climate. Through structured sessions within a safe and supportive setting, pupils can participate in developmentally appropriate tasks, games and discussions to help develop their social and emotional competencies (Mosley 2009). Circle time sessions follow a carefully structured five-step model, built around the skills of listening, speaking, looking, thinking and concentrating. Sessions are organised according to three key basic principles (ibid.):

- *Structure*: Sessions are a timetabled, weekly activity with a five-step plan. Each step has a specific structure and leads into the next step (see Box 4.1).
- *Solution-focused*: The atmosphere of safety is reinforced by the requirements of preventing put-downs and negative attitudes, teaching positive behaviours and attitudes and raising self-esteem.
- *Variety*: A wide range of teaching strategies are used, including group work, directed discussion, role play and processing.

During circle time, the teacher's role is facilitative and supportive, empowering pupils to express themselves and share their ideas, concerns and suggestions in a safe and positive atmosphere. Empathy, listening, providing feedback, recognition, encouragement and positive remarks are some of the key strategies the teacher needs to employ when leading a circle time session. Pupils take a more active role during these sessions than they usually do in more traditional lessons and the teacher provides space, opportunity and encouragement for the group to discuss personal and social issues. Circle time operates according to a number of rules, which ensure that a safe and supportive climate is maintained, such that only positive comments are made during the session; listening when somebody is speaking; having a right to pass if one wishes to and respecting confidentiality.

Box 4.1 The Five Steps of Quality Circle Time Meetings (Mosley 2009)

1. *Meeting up—playing a game*: Sessions begin with an enjoyable game to help the pupils relax and enjoy being in a group. Games often involve mixing the pupils up, providing opportunities for new friendships and collaboration and creating a supportive atmosphere.

2. *Warming up—breaking the silence*: Many pupils need to 'warm up' to speaking and this is achieved through a speaking and listening 'round', helping to reduce threat or embarrassment. The teacher introduces a sentence stem, such as 'My favourite animal is…' and passes a 'speaking object' to the pupil next to him/her who repeats the stem, adding their favourite animal. Any pupil who does not want to speak may say 'Pass' and pass the object on.

3. *Opening up—exploring issues*: This step is an opportunity for important issues to be discussed, such as exploring problems, concerns and hopes and developing a belief in one's ability to make responsible choices and decisions. Pupils practice specific skills, such as listening or speaking in turn and problem solving. They can be encouraged to ask the group for help. Members can suggest 'Would it help if…?' Step 3 utilises 'metaphor' through stories, role play, puppets and drama; this helps pupils to open up about their feelings without having the spotlight put on them.

4. *Cheering up—celebrating the positive*: To help pupils 'switch off' from issues of concern, pupils are provided with closing activities that ensure everyone leaves the meeting feeling calm and refreshed. This step celebrates the group's successes and strengths and gives pupils the opportunity to praise one another.

5. *Calming down—bridging*: Winding down in preparation for the next lesson may involve a calm game, a song or a guided visualisation.

4.7   Social and Emotional Education (SEE) Resource Pack

There are hundreds of SEE programmes, but the ones which have been found to be effective in promoting pupils' cognitive, social and emotional development in a sustained way are relatively few (Greenberg et al. 2003; Greenberg 2010). CASEL in the USA and KidsMatter in Australia provide a list of SEE programmes that are available in the market for schools. Both the *2013 Casel Guide* (CASEL 2012; see Box 4.2) and the *KidsMatter SEL Programmes Guide* (www.kidsmatter.com) are focused on programmes for early and primary schools and are intended to help make informed decisions on which programme/s are most suitable for their needs and contexts.

Schools may choose one or more programmes according to their needs and contexts. There are various factors that schools need to keep in mind when deciding which programme/s is the most suitable for their context. Firstly, the programme would need to fit to the needs of the school and resonate with its values, ethos, goals and priorities. A needs assessment exercise may be carried by the school to identify the SEE needs of the school community and which programme/s would be suitable in addressing those needs. This may result in choosing a generalist SEE programme, which covers the key SEE skills as well as a specific programme addressing particular needs. For instance, a school with a population facing high socio-economic challenges may opt for a resilience-enhancement programme to inoculate the pupils against the disadvantage they come across in their lives.

Secondly, programmes would need to have shown that they have been effective in promoting SEE amongst primary school pupils using rigorous evaluation criteria such as random controlled trials and longitudinal designs. Greenberg (2011) argues that we need to move from post-efficacy and effectiveness type of research evaluations to type 2 translation evaluation, which focuses on the adoption, maintenance and sustainability of scientifically based interventions at the practice level. There is a need for more research on the implementation process of effective interventions in real-life contexts; higher-quality implementation is likely to lead to more lasting change in children's social and emotional well-being (Ibid.). Ideally, the programme effectiveness evaluation is carried out by researchers not involved in the design and promotion of the package itself to exclude potential bias. The evaluation result would also need to match the school's intended outcome (MindMatters 2012).

Thirdly, SEE programmes need to be based on sound theoretical, educational and research basis with mechanisms for assessment and evaluation and appropriate learning strategies, skills and materials. They will be classroom-based and teacher-led, targeting the key SEE goals identified in the curriculum framework, structured and spiral, experiential and skills-based, multiyear from the Kindergarten/nursery through the primary school years and with extended cross-curricular activities and activities for parents (CASEL 2008; Askell-Williams et al. 2010; Weare and Nind 2011). This does not exclude, however, the use of parallel programmes targeting particular groups of pupils (see Chap. 7). Programmes would also include activities at the whole school level including the active involvement of parents/caregivers (cf. Durlak et al. 2011; Adi et al. 2007).

Schools also need to look at practical issues such as feasibility and sustainability of the programme, particularly in the long term (Merrell and Gueldner 2010). High-quality implementation and evaluation and programme sustainability, supporting the intervention over time by providing effective and adequate resources and services are key factors for programme effectiveness (Greenberg 2010). Issues such as readiness and capacity to bring about change, quality of material, supports available at the school and staff training need to be considered at both planning and implementation stages (Greenberg et al. 2005; Weare and Nind 2011). In their review of studies, Skad et al. (2012) reported that a majority of studies either indicated that the training manual was missing or did not mention its availability, arguing that this constituted a potential threat to implementation integrity. Schools also need to take account of contextual constraints and facilitating processes, seeking to remove the former and make use of the latter (Askell-Williams et al. 2009; Slee et al. 2012). As Durlack et al. (2011, p. 421) found in their meta analysis 'Capacity can be built through providing policy supports, professional development and technical assistance to promote educator knowledge and motivation for the best ways to identify, select, plan, implement, evaluate and sustain effective SEL interventions'.

Finally, as already indicated earlier on, schools will need to consider whether the programme/s are culturally responsive and can be easily adapted to diverse populations. Weare (2010) cautions against the blind adoption of programmes, which have been found to be effective in other countries with different cultural backgrounds. In their review of studies, Blank et al. (2009) conclude that even if programmes have been found to be effective, they would still require some adaption before being implemented in a different cultural context. Parents, for instance, may feel concerned that their children are being taught values, which differ from what they would like to inculcate in their own children (Arthur 2005). The staff themselves would need to feel confident about their competence in using the programme in their school and believe in its relevance and meaningfulness for their classroom (Askell-Williams et al. 2010). Teachers who have more positive views of teaching on emotions show better programme adherence and delivery (Jennings and Greenberg 2008). The school thus needs to choose a programme that the staff believes resonates with the realities and needs of their school and classrooms and which makes provision for adequate staff training in its use. The issue of ownership is very important here. As Graetz et al. (2008, p. 19) put it when referring to the Kids-Matter framework in Australian primary schools, 'although adequate resources are an important prerequisite of implementation, the capacity of schools to embed and "own" the initiative is likely to play a role in determining the longer-term success of KidsMatter in their school'.

...It needs to be recognized that for all their fundamental flaws and bold claims, actual practice within well-being programmes in schools has opened a door to understanding, listening to and working with children in new ways. (Watson et al. 2012, p. 217)

> **Box 4.2 Guide to Effective Social and Emotional Learning Programmes in Preschool and Primary Schools (Adapted from CASEL 2012)**
>
> The CASEL Guide identifies 23 universal and school-based programmes, which have been effective in promoting social and emotional learning in preschool and primary schools in the USA. They address five research-based social and emotional competencies, namely self-awareness, self-management, social awareness, relationship skills and responsible decision making. To be included in the Guide, programmes had to meet three main criteria, namely that they are:
>
> * Well-designed, classroom-based programmes that systematically promote students' social and emotional competence, provide opportunities for practice and offer multiyear programming.
> * Deliver high-quality training and other implementation supports, including initial training and ongoing support to ensure sound implementation.
> * Are evidence-based with at least one carefully conducted evaluation that documents positive impacts on student behaviour and/or academic performance.
>
> The Guide identifies three key principles that support the effective selection, implementation, impact and sustainability of SEL programmes, namely that school teams involve diverse stakeholders in programme selection, including parents, students and community members; the implementation of SEL programmes is made within the context of the school's overall priorities and needs and the consideration of local contextual factors including existing resources and challenges are addressed. The Guide then suggests a number of factors to be considered by the school when selecting the programme, such as whether the programme has been evaluated with similar student populations and whether the material is culturally and linguistically appropriate.

4.8   Assessment

Assessment is a necessary tool to gauge pupils' progress, identify strengths and needs and address the needs making use of the strengths. One may argue that assessment might be problematic for a subject like SEE. Not only could it become a reductionist and simplistic exercise in view of the complexity of human behaviour but also it could turn SEE into an examination-oriented and performance-driven subject (cf. Sultana 2008). A standardised, outcome-based assessment risks taking SEE into the trappings of academic press, seeking to fit 'quantitative proxies for qualitative understandings of broader (SEE) concepts' (Watson et al. 2012, p. 82), and exposing young children to labelling, pathologising and stigmatisation. Ecclestone (2012, p. 463) argues that the portrayal of well-being as a set of behaviours and the parallel push to measure them are 'rooted in a diminished view of an essential human vulnerability'.

There are important reasons, however, for including well-designed assessment in SEE, which will avoid the trappings of traditional academic assessment. Firstly, teachers and pupils will need to have feedback on the progress being made and the skills being learnt. This will provide valuable information on strengths to be celebrated and areas, which need further development. Secondly, assessment would be formative-developmental rather than summative-normative, providing feedback to both the teacher and the pupils on pupils' progress and targets for improvement for each learning standard. Rather than measuring a reduction in pupils' behaviour problems or enhancement in general social skills, the assessment would be focused and specific to the competencies being learnt. The benchmarks at each stage will help to guide the classroom teacher and the pupils to determine the progress and needs of each pupil according to his or her development, rather than making comparisons with any set of standardised norms. This will ensure that SEE will not become victim to the performance and achievement paradigm as in the case of the traditional academic areas. Thus, within a developmental approach, pupils are not identified as successes or failures according to standardised group norms in relation to their peers. Instead, the assessment will help to provide information of the level the pupil has reached in the respective benchmarks and then match the learning goals to the pupil's personal development accordingly. Assessment is also continuous with the teacher and pupils continuously monitoring and evaluating the competencies relevant to the SEE skills being learned in the classroom. A combination of individual and collaborative group assessment would also prevent assessment from becoming a competitive, individually driven activity, with pupils struggling to prove themselves at the expense of the others.

Another key principle of the assessment process is that the pupils will be encouraged to participate in the assessment themselves. This will help them to become more autonomous and self-reliant in their learning, gain more insight into their behaviour and into their strengths and weaknesses and thus become able to set learning goals for themselves. This approach resonates with the skills of agency, autonomy, self-efficacy, decision making and standing up for one's rights included in the curriculum framework proposed in this book. The fundamental differences between pupils' and teachers' views on various aspects of the learning experience (Spera and Wentzel 2003) underline the need to engage pupils in dialogue and give them a valid 'warranting voice' (Gergen 2001). What they have to say about their learning is not only valid and meaningful but also helps to provide a more adequate and useful evaluation. They are a source of knowledge and expertise, having unique and inside knowledge of what it is like to be a learner in a particular classroom (Cefai and Cooper 2010). They are also able to provide an accurate account of their own learning processes and how these could be enhanced by classroom teaching practices (Leitch and Mitchell 2007). Giving pupils the opportunity to express their views also helps them to gain an insight into their behaviour and its influence on their own and others' learning and relationships, thus empowering them to take more control and responsibility for their own behaviour (Kroeger et al. 2004).

At the moment I'm trying to create a little bit of a review system in my studio, whether it's for academic learning, whether it's for emotional things. I'm trying to have sort of individual interviews with my kids to have a talk about how we're going on in our learning, how we're feeling about certain things… we talk about what they enjoy doing, what they think might need to improve on, and what they do well in their learning, why they are good learners… I think these discussions help create a little bit of scaffolding in what they can do and how they feel about learning. I do this once every term with each kid. (Ms Mandy, Year 3 teacher)

4.8.1 Assessment Tools

There are various assessment tools that could be used to assess SEE, including assigning skills-related tasks, direct observation, behaviour rating scales, journals and self-reports. There are various pros and cons to any mode of assessment with issues of reliability, validity, practicality, feasibility and availability determining the most useful way of assessment. For instance, while objective measures like assigning skills-related tasks and direct observation of pupil behaviour could be highly reliable and valid measures, there are issues of availability and practicality, which may make it unrealistic to undertake such forms of assessments (Merrell and Gueldner 2010). The classroom teacher may use a simple, easy-to-complete checklist on the SEE competencies being learnt, completed on every pupil a number of times through the year. Behaviour and social skills rating scales are similarly useful instruments to assess pupils' social and emotional behaviour (see Denham et al. 2010). In many instances, however, they are quite generic and may not be necessarily related to the actual skills being learnt in the classroom. Many are also focused on difficulties rather than competencies. Moreover, more in line with the developmental and inclusive framework adopted in this book, standardised and normative rating measures may lead to labelling and some of the other limitations apparent in the traditional achievement assessment.

This book suggests a formative-developmental assessment of SEE making use of a combination of assessment modes, including a teacher-rating checklist based on direct observation, a pupil self-report, circle time discussion and a pupil journal, which includes practical tasks and illuminative techniques. Some of the programmes have readymade checklists to be completed by the teachers implementing the programme and the pupils themselves. Tables 4.2 and 4.3 provide a sample checklist along these lines, adapted from the Anchorage School District Social and Emotional Learning (Anchorage School District 2012) and adjusted according to the curriculum framework presented earlier. The checklists are to be completed by the classroom teacher and the pupils, respectively, for stage 2 (6–8 years) and they may be

Table 4.2 Sample of teachers' assessment checklist (stage 2). (Adapted from the SEL Standards & Benchmarks, ASD 2012)

Name of Pupil: _____ Date completed: _____	4- Advanced 3 – Proficient 2 – Making progress towards proficiency 1 – Making little progress 0 – No progress N/A – Not assessed at this time

Note: Pupils are progressing toward end-of-the-year learning standards in Social and Emotional Education. For the first reporting term, the pupil's **progress** toward those standards is assessed. Pupils who are making good progress are well on their way to achieving the goal of each standard by the end of the year.

SOCIAL AND EMOTIONAL EDUCATION		
1.SELF AWARENESS	1st	2nd
1A. Pupil demonstrates awareness of his/her emotions. *(I am able to identify and communicate how I am feeling)*		
1B. Pupil demonstrates self knowledge of his/her personal traits *(I am aware of what I like and dislike and of my strengths and challenges)*		
1C. Pupil demonstrates a sense of meaning and purpose *(I know what I want to do and achieve in life and how I can work toward it)*		
1D. Pupil demonstrates a well grounded sense of agency and autonomy *(I am aware of what I can do and what I need to do to achieve it)*		
1E. Pupil demonstrates a well grounded sense of self confidence and self efficacy *(I am confident of myself and my abilities in learning and other activities)*		
1F. Pupil demonstrates an awareness of their rights and how to stand up for themselves *(I am aware of my rights as an individual and how to stand up for them)*		
1G. Pupil demonstrates awareness of his/her external supports *(I am aware of where I can find help and support)*		
1H. Pupil is optimistic about self as learner and life in general *(I am optimistic that I will learn and achieve and that any problems will become opportunities)*		
2. SELF MANAGEMENT		
2A. Pupil demonstrates ability to manage emotions constructively *(I can appropriately handle my feelings)*		
2B. Pupil demonstrates ability to appreciate and enjoy positive emotions *(I can enjoy positive emotions such as happiness, satisfaction and excitement)*		
2C. Pupil uses effective decision-making skills. *(I can make appropriate decisions)*		
2D. Pupil demonstrates good and creative problem solving skills. *(I can solve the problems that I face).*		
2E. Pupil demonstrates ability to set and achieve goals. *(I can set and achieve goals that will make me more successful).*		
2F. Pupil demonstrates ability to persevere and recover in the face of setbacks. *(I am able to keep going in the face of difficulties and setbacks).*		
2G. Pupil demonstrates critical and creative thinking skills *(I can reflect on my thinking and learning).*		
2H. Pupil demonstrates focused attention and awareness. *(I can focus my attention on my present thoughts, feelings and movement).*		
2I. Pupil demonstrates ability to engage in positive self talk. *(I can use helpful thinking to cope with negative events and feelings).*		
2J. Pupil engages actively in social and academic tasks through own strengths. *(I can engage in academic and social tasks making use of my strengths).*		

Table 4.2 (continued)

3. SOCIAL AWARENESS		
3A. Pupil demonstrates awareness of other people's emotions and perspectives. *(I am aware of the feelings and opinions of others)*.		
3B. Pupil demonstrates consideration and care for others and a desire to positively contribute to the community. *(I care about others and do my part to make my school community better)*.		
3C. Pupil demonstrates awareness of cultural issues and a respect for human dignity and differences. *(I care about and respect the individual differences of others)*.		
3D. Pupil can read social cues. *(I am aware of how I perceive others and how they perceive me)*.		
3E. Pupil demonstrates seeking out and appropriately using family, school, and community resources in age-appropriate ways. *(I know about and make adequate use of family, school and community resources)*.		
3F. Pupil demonstrates an awareness to appreciate and care for the physical environment. *(I care about the physical environment)*.		
4.SOCIAL MANAGEMENT		
4A. Pupil uses positive communication and social skills to interact effectively with others. *(I will interact appropriately with others)*.		
4B. Pupil develops constructive and caring relationships. *(I will work on having positive and relationships)*.		
4C. Pupil learns and works collaboratively with peers *(I will collaborate with others in learning and social activities)*.		
4D. Pupil demonstrates ability to prevent and resolve interpersonal conflicts in constructive ways *(I will learn to handle conflicts in constructive ways)*.		
4E. Pupil demonstrates ethical behaviour in interactions with others *(I will act in an honest and responsible way with others)*.		
4F. Pupil demonstrates responsible decision making in various contexts *(When making decisions, I will consider the needs and rights of others)*.		

GENERAL COMMENTS:

Pupil strengths:

Pupil needs:

Targets for improvement:

adapted to the other two stages (3–5 years and 9–11 years). They are completed for each grade from the kindergarten/nursery to the last year of primary schools as well as at the exit of each of the three stages. The *grade-level* completion exercise serves as a continuous assessment tool for the teacher and pupils to evaluate progress and identify strengths and needs. The checklists will be completed by the class teacher and the pupils (with the help of the teacher, particularly in the early years)

Table 4.3 Sample of pupils' assessment checklist (stage 2). (Adapted from the SEL Standards & Benchmarks, ASD 2012)

	☹ I am weak in this ☹ I am not very good in this ☺ I am OK in this ☺ I am very good in this			
Name of Pupil: _____ Date completed: _____				
Social and Emotional Education				
Please tick the appropriate face for each statement:	☹	☹	☺	☺
I am able to identify and communicate how I am feeling				
I am aware of what I like and dislike and of my strengths and challenges				
I know what I want to do and achieve in life and how I can work towards it				
I am aware of what I can do and what I need to do to achieve it				
I am confident of myself and my abilities in learning and other activities				
I am aware of my rights as an individual and how to stand up for them				
I am aware of where I can find help and support				
I am optimistic that I will learn and achieve and that any probl ems will become opportunities				
I can appropriately handle my feelings				
I can enjoy positive emotions such as happiness, satisfaction and excitement				
I can make appropriate decisions				
I can solve the problems that I face				
I can set and achieve goals that will make me more successful.				
I am able to keep going in the face of difficulties and setbacks				
I can think reflect on my thinking and learning				
I can focus my attention on my present thoughts, feelings and movement				
I can use helpful thinking to cope with negative events and feelings				
I can engage in academic and social tasks making use of my strengths				

Table 4.3 (continued)

I am aware of the feelings and opinions of others				
I care about others and do my part to make my school community better				
I care about and respect the individual differences of others				
I am aware of how I perceive others and how they perceive me				
I know about and make adequate use of family, school and community resources				
I care about t he physical environment				
I will interact appropriately with others				
I will work on having positive and caring relationships				
I will collaborate with others in learning and social activities				
I will learn to handle conflicts in constru ctive ways				
I will act in an honest and responsible way with others				
When making decisions, I will consider the needs and rights of others				

What I learned most in the past 3 months:

 What I enjoyed most:

What I can do better/need to develop

What I would like to do do/see more

Other comments:

as a continuous assessment exercise, namely during the autumn, winter and spring terms, respectively, with targets for intervention being identified for the subsequent months. The checklists may also be completed at the end of each stage, here called exit-level assessment. The *exit-level* assessment gives a more definite profile of the pupils' strengths and weaknesses in relation to the learning standards expected to be achieved at that stage, and helps to identify areas that still need to be developed. It will also indicate any significant difficulties the pupil may be facing in SEE as early as possible and what intervention would be most appropriate to address those difficulties.

The teachers' checklist consists of the 30 learning standards divided into the four goals of self-awareness, self-management, social awareness and social management, respectively. Each learning standard will be scored on a 5-point scale ranging from 0 to 4, where 0 means that no progress at all has been registered on that standard, whereas 4 suggests that the pupil has reached an advanced stage. The staged benchmarks and indicators for each learning goal help the teacher to complete the checklist on the pupils' progress in that goal (see Appendix, Table 4.5). Each checklist has also space for qualitative comments at the end to provide formative information on the pupil's strengths and needs and potential targets for intervention. In order to cut down on report writing and paperwork, it is recommended that the teacher should be able to complete the checklists as a soft copy and that the checklists will be integrated into the mainstream school reports, reports to parents and teacher reports when referring pupils for assessment or additional support.

The pupils' assessment checklist may be completed in the same way, but instead of the 0–4 scoring key, a 4-point scale may be used as follows: 'I am weak in this, I am not very good in this, I am OK in this, I am very good in this'. It is suggested that with the younger classes, the checklist will be group-administered with the teacher reading, explaining and illustrating each learning standard followed by pupils ticking the correct response individually. The teacher may also devise more visual, practical activities to help them with this exercise of self-evaluation, such as use of drawings, role plays and circle time discussions (see Boxes 4.3 and 4.4). The checklist also has a space for qualitative comments to provide formative information on the pupils' strengths and needs, including what the pupils learned and enjoyed most, what they need to do better/develop and what they would like to see more of.

The use of information and communications technology (ICT) may help to make the checklist more child-friendly and interactive, with pupils also being given direct feedback for each item scored and once the whole checklist is completed, such as an automatic profile of strengths and needs, which may then be discussed with peers and the teacher. The total scores could be plotted as a graph to show the progress made by each pupil from one month or term to the other. The teacher may give general guidelines on the implications of the scores for each learning standard and total scores, while giving pupils the opportunity to share their findings with self-selected peers and with the teacher, should they wish to. A circle time session is also organised at the end of this exercise where the teacher and the pupils discuss together the results in a general collective way, such as discussing the classroom's SEE strengths and areas for improvement. Individual pupils and/or groups of pupils may also use circle time for particular issues related to their progress and may also use the whole group for learning support. At the initial phase, however, it is crucial that each pupil will have the opportunity to reflect on his or her progress in each of the competencies being assessed individually; this would avoid pupils copying the answers from each other.

Box 4.3 Pupil Well-Being Questionnaire (ReSURV 2012)

The Pupil Well-Being Questionnaire (PWQ) is an online, animated and interactive tool for primary school pupils developed recently by a team of educators in Edinburgh, UK. It is designed to help primary schools gain a deeper understanding of the emotional health and well-being of their pupils. It can be used to capture children's perspectives, attitudes and behaviours linked to social and emotional competencies, identify areas of strength and potential development for schools and track and measure the potential impact of whole-school approaches undertaken to support the development of social and emotional competencies. It uses 30 questions to capture attitudes and behaviours in relation to four key areas:

1. Self-respect and confidence.
2. Resilience and coping skills.
3. Empathy and relationships.
4. School ethos and culture.

The pupils' answers are then used to draw a profile of the class and/or the school in these four key areas of SEE.

4.8.2 Pupil Social and Emotional Education (SEE) Journal

Another useful mode of pupil self-evaluation is a pupil SEE journal, where pupils record their SEE experiences and learning on a regular weekly basis. It could be organised during the weekly Circle Time session where each pupil will be given the opportunity to reflect on his SEE learning. This could take a phenomenological perspective with pupils recording their thoughts and feelings about SEE for that particular week, making use of various modes of presentation, such as jotting down thoughts and feelings, writing a story, drawing something or adding a picture/poster/photograph of their completed work. The journal will record their SEE experiences in terms of what they like doing, what they are good at, what they have learnt, what they need to learn or develop more, where they need more help and what they would like to see more in SEE. The teacher may guide the pupils in this exercise through particular prompts, guiding questions, resources, specific tasks or illuminative techniques (e.g. completing statements such as 'one thing I have learnt this week…', making a drawing of themselves practicing some element of the skill learnt that week or completing a bubble dialogue), with more self-directed reflection and learning at a later stage (Weare 2004; see Box 4.4). The teacher may also assign specific tasks related to the learning goal, drawing from that learning goal's indicators. For example, in assessing the learning goal 'pupil demonstrates ability to manage emotions constructively', the pupils may make a list of reasons why characters in the story felt as they did, identify ways to calm themselves appropriately and write (and practice) different strategies for handling upsetting emotions. Once the pupils complete the individual activity, they can then discuss their learning experiences first in small groups and then with the whole group during circle time and also at home with their parents. Ms Kelly, an early-year teacher, describes how she makes use of a personal learning journey handbook for encouraging reflection on SEE learning in the early years:

> I keep a personal learning journey through preschool for each child, and within that we document everything the children are doing, with photos of pupils' work, their experiences, engagement, achievements, what they are going through and where they are at the end. It is also about well-being as the outcomes are about being engaged, being respectful… We find in our curriculum we don't have to write special targets for a lot of the children because the curriculum values what she brings with her and her engagement. The children then also have discussions with their parents on their journey, about what they have been doing, the skills learned, how they solved the problem, what they learned from it. And then at the end of the year we bind it as a book and give to the child to keep.

Box 4.4 Illuminative Assessment Techniques

Weare (2004) presents a number of illuminative techniques for school children developed with teachers and other educators across several European countries. These include children drawing and writing a story related to emotional literacy, completing sentences and filling bubble dialogues. The following examples illustrate how these three techniques may be used to asses SEE by primary school teachers.

1. Draw and write a story
   Draw a picture of a young boy/girl who is feeling anxious and draw around them what was making them feel anxious. Then write a short story about the drawing describing how the boy/girl is feeling and what made them anxious
2. Complete the sentence:
   When I am picked on by others, I feel…
   When I have a difficulty in completing a task, I can…
   One thing that makes me feel good about myself is…
   One thing I can do when I am angry…
   When I make a mistake, I say to myself,…

3. Fill the following bubbles

4.9 Embedding Social and Emotional Education (SEE) in the Other Areas of the Curriculum

One of the earlier debates in SEE has been whether SEE should be explicitly pro-grammed and taught to pupils or whether it should be embedded in the curriculum and 'caught' through the academic subjects instead. Research evidence suggests that rather than either/or dichotomy, the most effective way for the promotion of SEE in schools is through a dual taught and caught approach (Greenberg 2010; Weare and Nind 2011; Durlak et al. 2011). This involves explicit teaching of the area, supported by infusing the taught competencies into the academic and other areas of the curriculum as well as the creation of caring classroom and whole-school communities, where pupils will have the opportunity to observe and prac-tice the competencies they have been learning (Greeenberg 2010; Weare and Nind 2011). The curriculum framework presented here integrates the explicit teaching of SEE learning goals with the simultaneous infusion of the same goals into the academic curriculum and daily classroom practices. This will facilitate the trans-fer and generalisation of SEE to academic learning, setting a virtuous cycle where through the process of practice, modelling and positive reinforcement pupils will be able to integrate the SEE competencies into their daily behaviour repertoire. Besides reinforcing the SEE competencies being practiced, this process improves academic learning as well (Elias and Arnold 2006; Durlak et al. 2011). In this way, SEE becomes a central area of classroom practice and activities; as Ms Cathy a primary school teacher, said 'The SEL framework is at the back of my mind all the time in the classroom, across all subjects'. Ms Kyle, another teacher from the same school, remarks 'many of my kids are very shy sometimes so I help them to think ok during activities by saying "you can do it, be brave, be strong," and a lot of them will try, and it's the language they feed back to me saying "I was brave today because I did this!"'

Several SEE programmes include extended activities where the competence being learned explicitly is also being reinforced during other academic lessons in the classroom. Maurice Elias (2009) gives various illustrations how the infusion of SEE in the academic curriculum may take place. He describes, for instance, how the topic of 'Feelings' can feature in any area of the curriculum, such as identifying how passages reflect emotions (reading), using feelings vocabulary in journal entries, poetry and essay writing (written expression); drawing where people feel emotions (art); collecting and graphing 'feelings' data and tracking emotions during problem solving (mathematics); generating illustrations of feelings and downloading songs reflecting emotions (IT; Elias 2009). Figure 4.5 presents a more detailed illustration by Elias and Synder (2008) on how SEE can be infused into three key academic curriculum areas. Table 4.4 provides a sample template demonstrating how classroom teachers may infuse a learning standard into the various areas of the primary school curriculum. The school may set up a working committee to complete the templates for the 30 learning standards in each curriculum area for stages 1–3; the templates are then disseminated, discussed, refined and eventually adopted by the whole school.

4.10   Evaluation

The school may evaluate the adopted SEE programme for its usefulness and effectiveness by the end of the first year of implementation. The evaluation will examine teachers', parents' and pupils' views about the usefulness of the programme at the school. Purposely designed brief questionnaires will examine the teachers' knowledge and competence for teaching SEE and staff's, parents' and pupils' views on the impact on pupils' behaviour and learning, and on what worked, did not work or could be improved in the implementation of the programme. The evaluation also assesses the effectiveness of the programme in promoting social and emotional competence amongst the pupils. Measures of social and emotional competence and well-being, such as the Strengths and Difficulties Questionnaire (Goodman 1997), the Social Skills Improvement System (SSIR; www.pearsonassessments.com) and the Behaviour and Emotional Rating Scale (BERS-2; www.proedinc.com), completed at pre- and post-implementation, will provide data on the impact of the programme on pupils' behaviour and social and emotional competence. The evaluation may also help to examine the impact of the programme on pupils at risk for social, emotional and behaviour difficulties, establishing to what extent there was a decrease in such diffi-

Mathematics

- Use mathematics lessons as a way to examine problem-solving skills. Have pupils look at the stages they must go through to solve a problem.
- Ask pupils to articulate in detail how they solved a problem to foster self-awareness and insight.
- Use small group work as a way to build problem-solving and decision-making skills
- Reflect with pupils on the skills involved in problem-solving and occasionally ask them to consider how those skills can be used in life outside of class.
- Incorporate SEE into math problems by phrasing word problems in ways that reinforce emotional learning.

Language

- Use a "book talk" format to delve deeper into a story. Ask pupils to think about how characters feel about the situations they are in and what the character might want to happen. This can expand pupils' emotional vocabulary as well as promote inferential thinking. Questions to ask pupils might include:
- For each person or groups of people, what are some different decisions or solutions to the problem that might have helped them reach their goals?
- Do you agree or disagree with their solution to the problem?
- What would you have done in a similar situation? Why?
- What questions do you have based on what you read? What would you like to be able to ask one of the characters?
- Devote time and attention to discussing cultural differences, especially between Malta and the countries where English is spoken.
- Discuss cultural differences in Malta and the role English plays in our country.
- Address the natural frustration pupils may feel while learning a new language and use it as an opportunity to discuss the challenges that those from other cultures entering our culture, our town, our school must face.
- Discuss cultural stereotypes and where they come from
- Use skits and role-playing to build pupil's self-esteem and comfort with themselves in front of a group

Science

- Ask pupils to think about how the "scientific method" can provide helpful guidelines for other kinds of problem-solving outside of science.
- Assign pupils lab partners or groups for part of the year and ask them to establish group norms they want to have to guide their work together.
- Emphasize the importance of listening skills in gathering data, making observations, and following directions.
- Use hands-on experiences, such as science fairs and big projects, as an opportunity for pupils to learn to accept praise as well as constructive criticism.

Fig. 4.5 Infusing social and emotional education (SEE) into the academic areas of the curriculum. (Adapted from Elias and Snyder 2008)

Table 4.4 A sample template to be used for infusing SEE in the primary school content areas at stage 2

STAGE 2	SELF AWARENESS
Curriculum Area	**Learning Standard**
	Pupils demonstrate awareness of their emotions
Literacy	* Story telling, poetry, creative writing on a range of emotions and how they are experienced (eg. ask pupils to think about how characters feel about the situations they are in and what the character might want to happen)
Numeracy	* Ask pupils to articulate in detail how they solved a problem and how they felt to foster self awareness and insight * Phrase story sums in a way that reinforces social and emotional learning
Expressive Arts (Art, Crafts, Drama, Music)	* Use mime, role play, drawing and music to help pupils develop emotional vocabulary and emotional awareness, e.g. chart on how I am feeling today, posters and murals about 'me'
Health (PSHE, PE, Home economics)	* PE activities on how we feel when we lose, win * Feeling games such as running like angry lions, flying like happy birds * Relating different feelings to health, eg. feeling strong and energetic when happy, tired and sick when anxious
Science	* Discussions about physical body changes when experiencing different emotions such as mad, sad.
E-Learning	* Downloading emoticons from the internet to describe various feelings * Use of interactive games on different emotional states
Citizenship (Social Studies, Religious Education)	* Stories from historical/religious figures and how they felt in key episodes from their lives; how pupils would have felt if they were in such situations

culties and an increase in social and emotional competence, thus giving an indication of its effectiveness in promoting resilience. The programme evaluation may form part of a broader, whole-school SEE evaluation described in Chap. 3.

> The importance of a sound evidence base as a platform on which to build policy and provision is enormous. We therefore recommend that rigorous evaluation of the effectiveness of interventions be an integral part of any intervention strategy adopted. (Cooper and Jacobs 2011, p. 164)

The Skilled Archer and the Black Eagle

The Karakoram Range, Great Himalayas

As he reached the top of the mountain, the young man paused to enjoy the breath-taking scenery around him, the snow-covered mountain tops, the dense pine forests and the deep valleys stretching to infinity. He heard a snow leopard's haunting call echoing in the distance. The thin air, the blinding warm sunlight, the silence and stillness around him, the clouds around his feet, the sharp drops and sheer height made him dizzy and light-headed. The place felt outside time and space. He was a very skilled archer and in private he even defeated his master, but in public his hands trembled and his feet shook, and his shot was never near the mark. His master suggested it was time for a journey to the mountain to seek council.

Putting the cashmere wool goncha around him to protect against the biting wind, he made his way to the small cave where the hermit lived. The old bearded man dressed in shaggy yak hair, welcomed the archer into the small, dimly lit cave and offered him a cup of warm tea. The archer felt a warm tinge all over his body and a serenity and peace never experienced before. The eyes of the old man looked so kind, so understanding, so compassionate. His words were deep, insightful, wise. 'My son, Black Eagle is your name. You have her sharp eyes, her strong claws, her fast swooping dives, her precise hits. Tonight stay with me as we invoke her powers onto you. Sit down and slowly see yourself slowly transforming into the black eagle that you are with all her powers. See it dive down strongly and firmly. See and feel all her strength in your hands, in your mind, in your heart'.

As the old man retired, the archer imagined himself as the hermit had suggested, gradually starting to feel more and more confidence and power of the eagle within him. As the night grew young and his breath grew less frequent in the deep stillness of the dark mountains, he saw himself becoming stronger and lighter until he saw himself flying towards the brightly illuminated constellations above him. He flew from one star to another in a kaleidoscope of colours never seen before. His eyes were so sharp and keen, his hands so strong and firm. He saw himself diving at great speed, like a whistling arrow moving steadily and firmly to its target.

In the morning, the transformed archer looked for the old man but he was nowhere to be seen. He made his way down the mountain, now much lighter and swifter than when climbing up. As he wound down the ancient mountain path, he felt as if he was gliding down with splayed feathered wings holding him up. The next day the confident archer won his first archery trophy, it was followed by many more and the Black Eagle soon became the most renowned archer in the land.

4.11   Appendix

Table 4.5 Stage 2 (early primary) learning benchmarks (adapted from ASD SEL, 2012) learning benchmarks stage 1. (Adapted from the Anchorage School District)

Social and Emotional Education Standards and Benchmarks Key Stage 2 (Early Primary Years: 6-8 years)	
SELF-AWARENESS (I am...)	**Examples of Indicators**
1A. Pupils demonstrate awareness of own emotions.	* Recognise and label simple emotions * Recognise and label more complex emotions * Describe own emotions in various contexts * Explain what triggers own emotions
1B. Pupils demonstrate self knowledge of personal traits.	* Describe things they do well. * Identify their likes and dislikes * Describe an activity/task in which they can use their strengths * Describe an activity/task in which they may need help in order to be successful.
1C. Pupils demonstrate a sense of meaning and purpose	* Describe clearly what they would like to do and achieve * Identify those areas which are important for them and they would like to develop * Express belief that they can influence positively, and make a difference to,others * Express belief that they can use their strengths to contribute to the community * Express sense of belonging and co mmitment to the school community
1D. Pupils demonstrate a well grounded sense of agency and autonomy	* Express belief that they can take initiative in their academic tasks and social activities * Are able to get organised and take initiative during group work and other tasks * Voice their opinion regarding tasks and decisions * Are able to work on self directed work, pupil directed group work and enquiry based learning * Act in accordance with their own values rather than being led by others
1E. Pupils demonstrate a well grounded sense of self confidence and self efficacy	* Express belief that they will be successful in their academic work * Express belief that they will complete tasks successfully * Express belief that they will be successful in social tasks and activities * Are not afraid to take risks
1F. Pupils demonstrate an awareness of their rights and how to stand up for themselves	* Distinguish between rights and responsibilities * Describe the rights they have as learners and peers * Identify learning and social situations where they may have to stand up for their rights * Describe what they need to do to stand up for their rights

Table 4.5 (continued)

1F. Pupils demonstrate an awareness of their rights and how to stand up for themselves	* Distinguish between rights and responsibilities * Describe the rights they have as learners and peers * Identify learning and social situations where they may have to stand up for their rights * Describe what they need to do to stand up for their rights appropriately
1G. Pupils demonstrate awareness of their external supports.	* Identify an adult they trust * Explain situations in which they need to seek adult help (big problem/small problem). * Identify an adult and a peer whom they could turn for support * Understand how and where to get help in an emergency situation
1H. Pupils are optimistic about themselves as learners and life in general	* Express confidence and optimism in their ability to achieve and to solve problems * Describe positive strategies they will use to reach objectives and overcome difficulties * Express positive and hopeful thoughts in times of difficulty and challenge * Express belief that difficulties will become opportunities * Regard mistakes as learning experiences
SELF-MANAGEMENT (I can...)	**Indicators**
2A. Pupils demonstrate ability to manage their emotions constructively.	* Identify ways to calm themselves appropriately * Walk away or remove themselves from a triggering event * Keep control of their behavior no matter how they are feeling * Demonstrate constructive ways to deal with upsetting situations * Demonstrate coping skills in dealing with change and transitions
2B. Pupils demonstrate ability to appreciate and enjoy positive emotions	* Recognize positive emotions such as happiness, satisfaction, excitement * Appreciate the positive value of such emotions * Express and share such emotions * Use such emotions in their academic and social engagement
2C. Pupils use effective decision- making skills.	* Recognise they have choices in how to respond to situations * Identify and use choices to make effective decisions for self * Generate multiple and alternative solutions, considering pros/ cons and short/long term impact * Use lateral thinking strategies and other creative strategies in making choices * Participate in group decision-making processes

Table 4.5 (continued)

2D. Pupils demonstrate good and creative problem solving skills	* Describe the steps to be taken when faced with a problem * Identify effective strategies in problem solving * Identify creative and lateral thinking strategies in solving problems * Generate and implement positive and informed solutions to problems * Evaluate the evaluate the effectiveness of their solutions
2E. Pupils demonstrate ability to set and achieve goals.	* Define and set personal goals * Intentionally work toward a goal individually or as a part of a group * Identify and follow through the steps of a routine task or goal * Self monitor in goal achievement * Plan and manage time in goal achievement
2F. Pupils demonstrate ability to persevere and recover in the face of setbacks	* Have high expectations about own ability to succeed * Express confidence that they will accomplish tasks as planned * Keep working hard on tasks, even if boring or challenging * Can delay gratification/need satisfaction * Control frustration and anger when faced with difficulty or conflict
2G. Pupils demonstrate critical and creative thinking skills	* Describe their thoughts and feelings during problem solving and decision making * Describe their thoughts and feelings on the learning process * Use lateral thinking and creative strategies in learning and problem solving * Engage in critical thinking during learning activities
2H. Pupils demonstrate focused attention and awareness	* Focus attention on breathing, sensations, walking, sitting and mindful movements * Describe their present thoughts, sensations and emotions * Attend and concentrate to their present thoughts, sensations and emotions * Focus on tasks with ability to control intrusive thoughts
2J. Pupils demonstrate ability to engage in positive self talk	* State positive and helpful statements about themselves, their strengths and their work * Use positive statements to cope with negative events or work through and solve difficult tasks * Calm themselves down making use of positive statements * Express confidence that difficulties will become opportunities
2J. Pupils engage actively in academic and social tasks through their strengths	* Participate and contribute actively to the learning process * Identify and make use of strengths which are useful in learning tasks and products * Identify and make use of strengths which are useful in social activities and play * Make use of strengths to overcome limitations and solve problems

Table 4.5 (continued)

SOCIAL AWARENESS (I care...)	Indicators
3A. Pupils demonstrate awareness of other people's emotions and perspectives.	* Demonstrate ability to listen to, and consider, different perspectives * Demonstrate empathy toward others, i.e. relate own emotions and experiences to how others may be feeling * Allow others to express their thoughts and opinions without treating them judgmentally * Take steps to improve the situation when their actions have hurt others
3B. Pupils demonstrate consideration and care for others and a desire to positively contribute to their community.	* Share/take turns/help others in classroom settings * Express how they feel about hurting others * Recognise and stand up for the rights of others * Express sense of pride in being part of their group * Participate actively in classroom and school activities
3C. Pupils demonstrate an awareness of cultural issues and a respect for human dignity and differences.	* Describe and respect ways people are similar and different * Name human qualities that all people share * Include others in academic and social activities * Interact comfortably with all peers, including those manifesting any difference * Show respect to the rights of others to have beliefs and values different from their own.
3D. Pupils can read social cues.	* Identify and interpret accurately verbal and non verbal social cues * Demonstrate respect for personal space * Appropriately engage in play or work with others * Respond appropriately in a variety of situations (eg when to respond)
3E. Pupils demonstrate seeking out and appropriately using family, school, and community resources in age-appropriate ways.	* Mention at least two adult persons at school and at home whom they seek support in learning and socio-emotional difficulties * Mention at least one friend who helps with school work * Mention at least one friend whom they can play with * Describe the resources available to them when faced with learning difficulties * Describe the resources available to them when faced with social and emotional difficulties including bullying
3F. Pupils demonstrate an awareness to appreciate and care for the physical environment	* Describe the importance of taking care of the school, community and global environment * Describe how they can contribute to take care of their classroom, school, and community * Participate in keeping the classroom clean and well kept * Participate in keeping the yard, green areas and other parts of the school and community clean and well kept * Act responsibly when using public or other people's property.

Table 4.5 (continued)

SOCIAL MANAGEMENT (I will…)	Indicators
4A. Pupils use positive communication and social skills to interact effectively with others.	* Listen attentively and pay attention to others when they are speaking * Respond appropriately when spoken to * Demonstrate use of verbal etiquette (use please, thank you, excuse me) * Demonstrate awareness and use of other non verbal behaviours (eye contact, proximity, touch, gestures)
4B. Pupils develop caring and constructive relationships.	* Include others in academic and social activities * Support others in their work * Cooperate with others * Share the decision-making in social situations * List traits of good friends
4C. Pupils learn and work collaboratively	* Work willingly with any partner or group * Participate actively in collaborative work * Show teamwork during group work * Attend to, and consider, others' perspectives and opinions * Share and provide support to peers during work
4C. Pupils demonstrate an ability to prevent, manage, and resolve interpersonal conflicts in constructive ways.	* Demonstrate an ability to deal with conflicts as a natural part of social interactions * Distinguish between problems they can solve themselves and problems they need help with * Use a variety of appropriate strategies to solve conflicts * Distinguish between aggressive and assertive strategies * Resist inappropriate peer pressure constructively
4D. Pupils demonstrate ethical behaviour in their interactions with others	* Identify and state behaviours which are hurtful or disrespectful towards others * Consider the consequences of their actions on others * Show consideration and care for others in their behaviours * Engage in safe play without hurting or bullying others * Show such behaviours as honesty, trustworthiness, reliability and confidentiality in their interactions
4E. Pupils demonstrate responsible decision making in various contexts	* Consider the rights of others when making decisions * Consider the consequences of one's actions on others when making decisions * Take responsibility for their actions * **Make good choices respecting the needs and rights of others** * **Make good choices resisting inappropriate peer pressure**

Chapter 5
Caught Social and Emotional Education: A Caring Classroom Community

One of the most powerful contexts in the promotion of social and emotional education (SEE) is a positive classroom climate where pupils feel safe, secure and supported, where they observe SEE in action and where they have the opportunity to practice the SEE skills they have been learning. Learning and working in an emotionally literate classroom characterised by caring and supportive relationships and engagement in meaningful learning activities adapted to pupils' needs and making use of their strengths, provides the context for SEE to become embedded in the daily life of the classroom (Pianta and Stuhlman 2004; Osher et al. 2007; Payton et al. 2008; Libbey 2004; Battistich et al. 2004; Hamre and Pianta 2001). In such an environment, pupils are not only taught specific skills in SEE, but they have regular daily opportunities to 'catch' these competencies through observing them enacted by the classroom teacher/s and their peers, and through continuous opportunity to practice them in their daily classroom activities.

Watson et al. (2012, p. 223) argue that well-being is particularly about 'a relational ethics of care', with students engaged in meaningful dialogic encounters based on caring relationships, choices and rights, play and engaging learning experiences. In this way, social and emotional SEE becomes integrated in 'positive experiences of being, becoming and belonging'. This ethic of care and connectedness is particularly crucial in the kindergarten and primary school years when children are developing their social and emotional skills and where a caring teacher–pupil relationship provides a safe base for pupils' affective and cognitive development (Denham et al. 2012; Pianta and Stuhlman 2004). Young pupils experiencing difficulties in their social and emotional development stand particularly to gain from such a supportive relationship (Hamre and Pianta 2001; Pianta et al. 2002).

> In talks with teachers, I am often asked how they can 'do this'—establish a climate of care—'on top of all the other demands'. My answer is that establishing such a climate is not 'on top' of other things, it is *underneath* all we do as teachers. (Adapted from Noddings 2012, p. 777)

C. Cefai, V. Cavioni, *Social and Emotional Education in Primary School*, 81
DOI 10.1007/978-1-4614-8752-4_5, © Springer Science+Business Media New York 2014

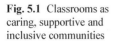
Fig. 5.1 Classrooms as caring, supportive and inclusive communities

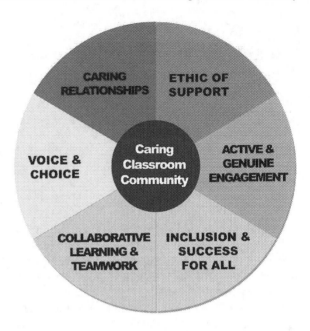

5.1   Caring Classroom Community

In a study in a number of Maltese primary schools working as optimal learning environments, Cefai (2008) developed a framework of caring classroom communities promoting SEE amongst young pupils. It construes SEE-promoting classrooms as caring, supportive and inclusive communities characterised by the following processes (see Fig. 5.1):

- Caring teacher–pupils relationships, where pupils feel safe, valued and trusted, built on connectedness, respect, understanding and support;
- Positive classroom management, where classroom management is built on behaviour for learning, making the right choices and mutual respect;
- An ethic of peer support with pupils caring for, supporting and mentoring one another;
- Collaborative learning with a focus on building learning experiences together;
- Active and genuine engagement, with pupils participating in experiential and meaningful classroom activities that make use of pupil-centred and activity-based instructional strategies connected to the pupils' own life experiences; the focus is on learning rather than just achievement;
- Inclusion and success for all, where all classroom members, irrespective of any difference in ability, background, interest or any other characteristic, have the opportunity to participate actively in the activities and to be successful in their learning;

- Voice and choice, where the pupils are consulted on classroom activities and behaviours, given choices and autonomy in their work and are aware of, and exercise, their rights as pupils;
- Positive beliefs and high expectations, where pupils feel valued as learners and individuals through recognition, positive beliefs and high expectations;
- Teacher–parent/caregiver collaboration, where the classroom teacher and the parents/caregivers work collaboratively to facilitate and support the pupils' learning;
- Staff teamwork, where the classroom teacher works collaboratively with other staff in the classroom, year teachers and other members of staff, and where staff support and mentor each other.

These processes help to create a sense of community that satisfies the basic psychological needs of young children, namely relatedness, competence, autonomy and fun. Needs satisfaction contributes to pupils' sense of being part of the classroom community and facilitates their internalisation of the academic and social values and norms in such communities, such as mutual understanding, respect and support, sharing, collaboration, solidarity and other prosocial behaviours. Pupils are also more likely to become actively engaged in the learning process, become confident in their competencies, experience a positive academic self-esteem and self-efficacy, persist in the face of difficulty, and deal more constructively with problem situations (Deci and Ryan 2000). As Dweck (1999) argues, pupils' beliefs about themselves, their abilities and learning are strongly influenced by the classroom processes and relationships.

An inclusive, caring community is the precondition of our human being and becoming. (Fielding 2012, p. 675)

As a school…we put a strong emphasis on valuing the knowledge and skills that children bring with them, so we are trying to focus on those aspects so that the children feel valued, that they have a place at school, they have a place in their learning, they have a place in others' learning, to build up their confidence and their inquiring mind…respect for others, respect for the environment. We try to show that school is not a place of punishment and strictness, but a place of learning and appreciating themselves, their environment and developing themselves and each other. Some of our children come with many problems from their homes and community, but what happens out there we have limited influence on that, so for that to be an issue is really a waste of time, and it does not help with the well-being of the child. We focus instead on their strengths, for them to be able to focus on what they can do and achieve… There are two little boys in the purple neighbourhood, they wanted sand, so they rang up and ordered it and it's there. So that type of confidence for early years' children, that's extremely significant and important to be able to value themselves and what they can achieve. They are in charge of their actions, the master and not the victim of their feelings. And there is the expectation that they will be able to be engaged in their learning, wherever they are coming from. It's their right, they have a right to be engaged in their learning and no one should be able to take that away. (Ms Grace, early years' teacher)

Box 5.1 Connecting with pupils (from Cefai 2008) Ms Erica, a Year 4 teacher, made it a point to spend half an hour Circle Time with her group every week, particularly during the first term. The first sessions were dedicated to getting to know each other, so that both she and the pupils could learn more about each other. Activities included:

- Sharing one thing about me with the others
- One thing I am good at
- If I were an animal
- One thing which can help me to learn better is…
- One thing about my family
- One thing I would like in the classroom

Later on, she used Circle Time to discuss issues related to the group's development as the scholastic year progressed and to discuss and resolve classroom issues such as episodes of bullying, helping each other with work or preparing for exams. Ms Erica found that this helped to create a positive climate in the classroom, with pupils being more open and trusting of each other and feeling more secure and happy. She also believed that it enhanced the teaching and learning process, as after the sessions the pupils became more motivated and engaged:

> I think that in the long term the use of Circle Time had a positive effect on the pupils' attitudes towards learning…and it helped me as well, I got to know the pupils more, what they like and do not like, their interests.

Box 5.2 Tribes Learning Communities (adapted from www.tribes.com) Tribes Learning Communities provide safe and caring classroom environments as the most effective way to improve behaviour and learning. In Tribes communities, pupils feel included and appreciated by peers and teachers, are respected for their different abilities, cultures, gender, interests and dreams, are actively involved in their own learning and have positive expectations from others that they will succeed. The classroom community functions around four main 'agreements', namely attentive listening, appreciation/no

put downs, mutual respect and the right to pass. Pupils learn a set of collaborative skills so they can work well together in long-term groups (tribes).
These include helping each other work on tasks, setting goals and solving problems, monitoring and assessing progress, and celebrating achievements. The
learning of academic material and self-responsible behaviour is facilitated
through teaching methods based on brain-compatible learning, multiple intel-
ligences, cooperative learning and social development research. The school
staff themselves also work in collaborative, supportive and collegial groups.

5.2 Indicators for Classroom Community

On the basis of the framework in Fig. 5.1, a number of classroom community indicators have been developed to assist classroom teachers to assess their classroom
climate at particular points during the school year. The list consists of ten general
indicators, with each general indicator opening into a number of specific indicators. The indicators are intended as a formative self-assessment guide for teachers
to identify strengths and targets for improvement in each area of classroom community. Table 5.1 presents the list of indicators of classroom community. It is construed as a helpful resource for classroom teachers as reflective practitioners, and
may be adapted to suit the needs of the particular classroom context assessed. The
indicators may be completed at the beginning of the scholastic year to identify the
strengths and needs of the classroom community, and plan targets for improvement in particular areas. The teacher may choose to focus on only one target for
improvement over a specific period of time or work on several targets over the
year (see Table 5.2). The teacher may also decide to have a more quantitative assessment of the classroom climate by scoring each specific indicator on a rating
scale, such as In Place (3), Partly in Place (2), Not in Place (1), and then drawing
descriptive graphs for the general indicators to illustrate the strengths and needs of
the classroom climate.

Table 5.3 presents a similar but simplified version of indicators to be completed
by the pupils. This will provide pupils with the opportunity to express their views
on the various facets of their classroom community and provide the teacher with
valuable pupil feedback on the strengths and needs of the group. The indicator list
is designed to be completed anonymously by the pupils to ensure more authentic
responses. In the case of younger pupils or pupils with learning difficulties, the
list may be completed as a group, with the teacher reading the indicators and the
pupils ticking the appropriate response individually. Alternative strategies may also
be used, such as drawing a picture, telling a story, filling balloons or completing
sentences (see Chap. 4). This information will provide the classroom teacher with
valuable and useful information on the pupils' own experience of the classroom
community (see Table 5.4). An easy way to analyse the information, would be for

Table 5.1 Indicators for a caring classroom—classroom teacher's version (general and specific indicators)

INDICATORS FOR A CARING CLASSROOM – TEACHER'S VERSION
General and specific indicators

A.	My relationship with my pupils is understanding, caring and supportive
A1	I try to make the pupils in my classroom feel safe and secure, such as by using humour and avoiding shouting with pupils
A2	I try to know my pupils well, such as finding time to talk with pupils and listen to their stories
A3	I provide opportunities for pupils to express their feelings and concerns both individually and in group discussions
A4	I consider and value the opinion, suggestions and perspective of the pupils in my classroom
A5	I provide adequate support to pupils experiencing difficulties in their learning
A6	I provide adequate support to pupils with social and emotional difficulties
A7	I demonstrate respect and concern towards my pupils, being attentive to their needs
A8	I recognize and celebrate the pupils' strengths, achievements and efforts, holding high but realistic expectations and providing constructive feedback
	Strengths: **Targets for Improvement:**

B.	My classroom management is fundamentally positive
B1	I provide the pupils in my classroom with clear and specific behaviour expectations
B2	My pupils are actively involved in the formulation of classroom rules and consequences
B3	I daily notice and reward positive behaviour
B4	I encourage pupils to take more responsibility for their behaviour
B5	I seek to teach pupils positive behaviour when correcting misbehavior.
B6	I demonstrate understanding and respect in handling conflict with my pupils, involving pupils in negotiating solutions
B7	I seek to be consistent and fair with the pupils in my classroom
B8	I consistently act as a good role model for expected behaviours
	Strengths: **Targets for Improvement:**

Table 5.1 (continued)

C.	My pupils support each other in my classroom
C1	The pupils in my classroom demonstrate care and concern for each other
C2	The pupils in my classroom support each other against bullying and harassment from others
C3	The pupils in my classroom find it easy to help and share things with each other
C4	The pupils in my classroom play with each other without frequent fighting and arguing
C5	The pupils in my classroom ask me or other members of staff for help when a peer is in difficulty
C6	The pupils in my classroom do not bully or harass other pupils
C7	The pupils in my classroom resolve conflict and disagreements constructively
C8	The pupils in my classroom include peers with physical and intellectual disability in their activities
	Strengths: **Targets for Improvement:**

D.	My pupils collaborate with each other in their learning
D1	Collaborative group work is a regular feature in my classroom
D2	The pupils in my classroom consult and discuss with each other during learning activities
D3	The pupils in my classroom have the skills to work with each other collaboratively
D4	Pair work, peer tutoring and mentoring is a regular feature in my classroom
D5	The pupils in my classroom do not compete with each other in their work
D6	The pupils in my classroom appreciate and recognise each other's strengths and achievements
D7	I regularly recognise and celebrate group effort and achievement
D8	I collaborate with the pupils and other adults in the classroom in lesson planning, delivery and assessment
	Strengths: **Targets for Improvement:**

E.	Learning activities are experiential, authentic and meaningful
E1	The pupils in my classroom are highly attentive during learning activities
E2	The pupils in my classroom often have fun during learning activities
E3	The pupils in my classroom consistently take an active part in the learning activities
E4	I make regular use of experiential and practical activities in my lessons
E5	I make regular use of multimedia resources in my lessons
E6	I consistently include pupils' interests and strengths in learning activities
E7	I consistently seek to make learning meaningful and relevant for my pupils
E8	I discourage competitive academic achievement in favour of learning and personal growth in my classroom
	Strengths: **Targets for Improvement:**

Table 5.1 (continued)

F.	All pupils are included in my classroom
F1	The curriculum offered in my classroom is diversified and accessible for all pupils
F2	The assessment offered in my class room is diversified, accessible and appropriate for all pupils
F3	My pedagogy, resources and activities match the diversity of pupils' backgrounds, needs and styles
F4	Together with the teaching assistant, I regularly develop individual programmes for pupils with learning difficulties
F5	Together with the teaching assistant, I seek to remove linguistic, cultural and social barriers to learning
F6	The physical layout of my classroom gives all pupils equal access to human and physical resources
F7	I make use of specific strategies to ensure that new pupils are supported
F8	In my classroom we celebrate and value pupils' family and socio-economic/cultural backgrounds
	Strengths: **Targets for Improvement:**

G.	My pupils have voice and choice in my classroom
G1	I include the pupils in my classroom in decisions related to setting learning goals and outcomes and classroom tasks
G2	I include my pupils in decisions related to evaluation of their work (eg. providing opportunities for self assessment)
G3	I include my pupils in decisions related to behaviour (eg. in classroom behaviour rules and consequences)
G4	I involve my pupils in solving classroom problems and conflicts
G5	I give my pupils roles of responsibility in the classroom (eg. organising mentoring and peer tutoring)
G6	I encourage and support pupils to become more autonomous in their learning (eg. organizing tasks where they do research by themselves)
G7	I respect my pupils' rights as learners in practice (eg. listening actively to their concerns)
G8	I teach my pupils on their rights as learners and how to stand up for them appropriately (eg. displaying their rights in the classroom)
	Strengths: **Targets for Improvement:**

H.	I hold positive beliefs and high expectations for all my pupils
H1	I hold high but realistic expectations for all my pupils (eg. consistently expecting all my pupils to learn and make progress)
H2	I encourage my pupils to believe in themselves and in their ability to learn and achieve (eg. consistently praising their effort and progress)
H3	I send messages of optimism and efficacy for all pupils through my practice (eg. frequently reminding them of their improvement)
H4	I help pupils to identify and make use of their strengths in learning
H5	I underline strengths as well as areas for improvement when giving feedback to my pupils
H6	I discourage comparison of my pupils' grades and achievements
H7	I acknowledge and recognise the work and achievement of all my pupils
H8	I encourage my pupils to acknowledge and celebrate each other's achievements (eg. organizing classroom celebrations and exhibitions)
	Strengths: **Targets for Improvement:**

Table 5.1 (continued)

I.	I work collaboratively with my pupils' parents/Caregivers
I1	The parents/Caregivers cooperate with and support my initiatives and recommendations
I2	The parents/Caregivers support their children with their homework, classroom and school activities
I3	The parents/Caregivers take an active interest in their children's education (eg. frequently contacting me about their children's progress)
I4	I encourage and make time for parents'/Caregivers' regular contact and discussions with me
I5	I keep parents/Caregivers updated and inform them regularly on classroom and school policies and activities
I6	I listen and address the parents'/Caregivers' concerns
I7	I ask the parents/Caregivers to give their feedback on classroom activities and homework, including their views on teaching and learning goals and activities
I8	I ask the parents/Caregivers to give their feedback on pupils' behaviour in the classroom, including their views on the behaviour policy
	Strengths:
	Targets for Improvement:
J.	**I work collaboratively with school staff**
J1	I and the other adults in the classroom plan and share practice together, such as schemes of work and learning plans
J2	I and the other adults in the classroom solve problems together (eg. supporting the learning of pupils with learning difficulties)
J3	I and my year colleagues plan the scheme of work and share resources together
J4	I and my year colleagues act as mentors and critical friends to each other
J5	I have a collegial relationship with colleagues at the school (eg. providing support to one another when in need)
J6	I participate actively in the social activities organised for the staff
J7	I am actively involved in curriculum planning and review and policy development (eg. being responsible for specific curriculum initiatives)
J8	I have frequent, positive communication with the administration and feel supported in exercising my role
	Strengths:
	Targets for Improvement:

Some of items in this and the other checklist in this chapter have been informed by other existing checklists, namely National Curriculum Council Focus Group for Inclusive Education (2002) and ASD (2012)

the teacher to do a visual inspection of each general indicator and list the strengths and targets for improvement before moving to the next general indicator. Another way is to present the data in the forms of bar charts for each general indicator. The five open-ended questions at the end will provide more qualitative information on what the pupils would like to see more in their classroom and what may help them to learn and develop their social and emotional competence (Table 5.5).

On the basis of the data collected from both the teacher and the pupil's checklists, the teacher will be able to draw a portrait of the classroom climate and identify those areas which need to be improved, while celebrating the strengths of the classroom community with all its members.

Table 5.2 Sample template improving classroom community (classroom teacher's indicators)

INDICATORS	Strengths	Targets for improvement
A. Teacher–pupils relationship		
B. Classroom management		
C. Pupil-pupil relationships		
D. Pupil collaboration		
E. Engagement		
F. Inclusion		
G. Voice and choice		
H. Beliefs and expectations		
I. Teacher-parent collaboration		
J. Staff teamwork		

Table 5.3 Indicators for a caring classroom—pupils' version (1 = rarely true; 2 = occasionally true; 3 = frequently true; 4 = true for most of the time)

INDICATORS FOR A CARING CLASSROOM–PUPILS' VERSION		
1= rarely true; 2= occasionally true; 3=frequently true; 4= true for most of the time		

A.	**Relationship with teacher**	
1.	My teacher cares for me	
2.	My teacher helps me when I have a problem	
3.	My teacher praises my work and effort	
4.	My teacher listens when I want to say something	
5.	My teacher understands how I feel	
B.	**Classroom management**	
1.	I feel safe in my classroom	
2.	I can say how I feel in my classroom	
3.	I know the classroom rules very well	
4.	My teacher listens to what I have to say when I misbehave	
5.	My teacher does not get angry at me when I make a mistake	
C.	**Relationship with peers**	
1.	I help other pupils when they have a problem	
2.	I play with my classmates without fighting or name calling	
3.	I am careful not to hurt the feelings of others in my classroom	
4.	I am friends with all pupils in my classroom	
5.	When I say something, the other pupils listen to me	
D.	**Collaboration with peers**	
1.	I do not compete with other pupils in my classroom	
2.	I share and discuss things with others when I am working	
3.	I learn a lot from the other pupils in my classroom	
4.	I work very well and learn a lot when we work in groups	
5.	When I have a problem, my peers help me to find a solution	
E.	**Engagement**	
1.	I like to be in this classroom	
2.	I learn a lot in my classroom	
3.	I participate actively in the learning activities	
4.	We do lots of fun things in my classroom	
5.	I greatly enjoy what we do in the classroom	
F.	**Inclusion**	
1.	All pupils can learn and do good work in our classroom	
2.	We are all equal in our classroom	
3.	I feel included and supported in my group	
4.	I have always someone to work and play with	
5.	My teacher always help me when I have any difficulties in my learning	

Table 5.3 (continued)

G.	Voice and choice	
1.	My teacher gives me choices in my work and activities	
2.	My teacher asks me what I would like to learn in class	
3.	My teacher encourages me to work and solve problems on my own	
4.	My teacher discusses classroom rules and behaviour with me	
5.	My teacher gives me responsibilities in the classroom	
H.	Positive beliefs and expectations	
1.	My teacher thinks I am a good pupil and that I can a learn a lot	
2.	My teacher is proud of me	
3.	My teacher frequently tells me I am improving in my work	
4.	My teacher knows what I am good at	
5.	My teacher shows my good work to others	
I.	Teacher-parent /caregiver relationship	
1.	My parents/caregivers communicate frequently with my teacher	
2.	My parents/caregivers and my teacher talk to each other about my work	
3.	My parents/caregivers know what I am doing at school	
4.	My parents/caregivers help me with homework and projects	
5.	My parents/caregivers are told when I do something good in class	
J.	Your comments	
	Write one or two things you like about your classroom	
	Write one or two things you would like to see in the classroom	
	Write one or two things which may help you to learn more	
	Write one or two things which may help you to behave better	

Some of items have been informed by, and adapted from, other existing questionnaires and checklists, namely National Curriculum Council Focus Group for Inclusive Education (2002) and ASD (2012)

Table 5.4 Sample template improving classroom community (pupils' indicators)

INDICATORS	Strengths	Targets for improvement
A. Teacher–pupils relationship		
B. Classroom management		
C. Pupil-pupil relationships		
D. Pupil collaboration		
E. Engagement		
F. Inclusion		
G. Voice and choice		
H. Beliefs and expectations		
I. Teacher-parent collaboration		

Table 5.5 Improving classroom community (pupils' suggestions)

What we like about our classroom:
What we would like to see in the classroom:
What may help us to learn more in the classroom:
What may help us to behave better in the classroom:

The Old Farmer's Treasure Chest

The Maghreb, North Africa

The old tired farmer knew that death was close by and he could already discern its long dark shadows looming on the dimly lit walls of the old farmhouse. The time had come for him to rest from his daily toil and join his ancestors. But one nagging thought would not let him rest. His four hard-working sons were constantly quarrelling and fighting with one another. He was worried that once he was gone, their differences and constant bickering would lead to the dismantlement of the prosperous farming enterprise he had built for them.

One day he summoned his four sons to his bed and asked them to each bring a strong stick with them. He put all the sticks together into one bundle and then asked each son respectively to try and break the bundle into pieces. The sticks were too hard to break for any of the men. The old man then opened the bundle again and gave the individual sticks to the sons, which they could break easily.

'My sons, a house divided amongst itself will fall. You will be each other's downfall. Your enemies will pick you one by one and break you like a stick. But united together you will be strong and stand like an unbreakable bundle, able to resist and overcome storms and tempests. You will be able to work this land and multiply its fruit. Now that my end is near, I would like to share with you a secret I have carried with me all these years. In my younger days as a pirate on the White Sea, I had once found a small but priceless box of precious stones, which I have hidden in our fields and which I would like to pass on to you. I would like you to work together to find this treasure and then share equally amongst yourself. My sons, to find this treasure you need physical strength and skilled quarrying, but you also need good planning and mapping, and determination and persistence. You have all of these together, but none of you have all these on your own'.

The four men soon forgot the bundle of sticks and the dead father's advice, and each tried to find the treasure on his own, arguing and fighting as usual. But the task looked too big for one man. They felt exhausted and disheartened, the land was too spread out, the excavations needed more time, strength and planning than they had imagined. Finally, they gave up and sat down to plan the treasure hunt together. They laid out a map of the all their lands, and the four of them together started to dig the extensive area section by section. Fired by the image of precious stones, they forgot their differences, and continued digging, day after day. The treasure, however, proved to be elusive, and after a month of digging they started to give up.

One day they came to an underground stream running through their fields. It was at that point they realised that this was their father's treasure, and that his real plan was that they would find the stream together and turn their fields into orchards of fruits and vegetables. They realised that they needed to pool all their energy and skills together to be able to bring the water to all their fields. As they sat down to plan the irrigation project together, they realised that the real treasure of their father was to bring them to work together and for each other.

Chapter 6
Targeted Interventions for Pupils Experiencing Difficulties

Social and emotional education (SEE) is a fundamental educational goal directly related to learning, behaviour and well-being for all learners. A comprehensive approach to SEE includes targeted interventions for pupils who are not responding to universal programming or facing difficulties in their social and emotional development (indicated interventions) or who need extra support in view of the risks they may be facing (selective interventions) (National Institute for Health and Clinical Excellence 2008; Greenberg 2010; Weare and Nind 2011) (Fig. 6.1). Within an integrated intervention approach, pupils would have access to both universal interventions and targeted interventions, tailored according to their needs. This may be particularly essential in pre-school and primary school years to reduce the development of more severe difficulties in secondary school, when it becomes more difficult to change more entrenched behaviours (Domitrovich et al. 2007; Weare and Nind 2011). Though percentages vary across countries, regions and contexts, there are some indications that about 20 % of children may need additional social and emotional support in some way or another during their school days; of these, 10 to 5 % may need more intensive support (Surgeon General's Report on Mental Health 2001; Ford et al. 2003; Cefai and Camilleri 2011; US Centre for Disease Control and Prevention 2013).

6.1 A Framework for Targeted Social and Emotional Education (SEE) Interventions

The framework for targeted interventions in SEE is based on three key elements, namely, that the interventions are developmentally appropriate and inclusive; that they are school-based and staged, and that they are child-centred and transdisciplinary (Fig. 6.2). In line with this book's SEE's portrayal of SEE as a developmental and inclusive process, pupils experiencing difficulties in the development of the requisite SEE competencies, will thus go through a school-based staged approach, with more intensive, individual and transdisciplinary interventions if difficulties become more apparent and significant. This will ensure that before a pupil is referred to outside agencies for additional or specialised support, the classroom teacher and the whole

C. Cefai, V. Cavioni, *Social and Emotional Education in Primary School*,
DOI 10.1007/978-1-4614-8752-4_6, © Springer Science+Business Media New York 2014

Fig. 6.1 A multi-level
intervention social and
emotional education (SEE)
intervention framework

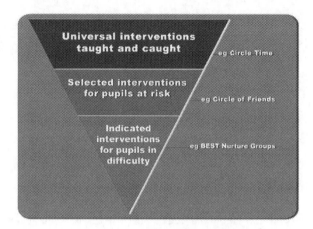

Fig. 6.2 Targeted intervention
framework for pupils experiencing
difficulties in social and emotional
education (SEE)

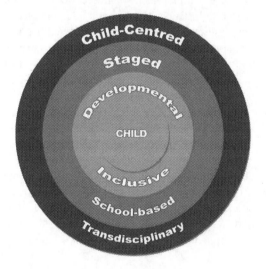

school would have already sought to address the needs of the pupil within their existing resources. It also makes it possible that a pupil may receive simultaneous universal and targeted interventions, thus benefitting from an additive and synergetic effect
on their social and emotional well-being and resilience (Merrit and Geuldner 2010).
A SEE team, including representatives of staff, pupils and parents, will coordinate
the targeted interventions in an efficient and effective way and integrate them with
the universal interventions and other whole school approaches in SEE. This implies
the active participation of the classroom teachers and the pupils as well. Engaging
pupils in the development and implementation of interventions would ensure child-
friendly and child centred interventions and avoid stigmatisation as well as resistance
and non adherence (Bowers et al. 2013). In their review of mental health promotion
in school, Franklin et al. (2012) reported that not only are teachers involved in the
delivery of mental health interventions as part of a mental health team, particularly in
selective and indicated interventions, but also they may serve as the sole provider of

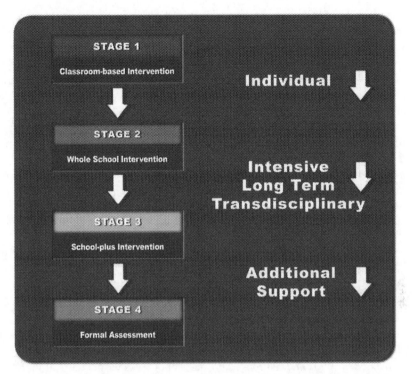

Fig. 6.3 A staged approach for targeted social and emotional education (SEE) interventions

such interventions, particularly universal ones. Interventions for aggressive behaviour and violence in schools, for instance, were more effective and sustainable when delivered by the teachers themselves (Wilson et al. 2003; Wilson and Lipsey 2007). In universal and selective interventions teachers and mental health professionals are likely to be found as partners in delivery of implementations, with more intensive intervention by the mental health professionals in indicated interventions.

Figure 6.3 describes the staged approach being proposed for targeted interventions for pupils exhibiting difficulties in acquiring the requisite social and emotional competencies. The approach, loosely based on the UK Code of Practice for Special Educational Needs (DfES 2001b), diverges in significant ways from typical medical models of intervention which tend to pathologise difficulties as individual problems residing within the child, requiring medical and psychological interventions by clinicians based in support services. It construes social, emotional and behaviour difficulties as part of a continuum ranging from high proficiency to significant difficulties in social and emotional learning. It puts the onus on the school and the classroom teacher to support the social and emotional needs of the pupils within the classroom and the school contexts and resources as much as possible, in collaboration with and supported by parents pupils, the school community and out of school support services. Teachers and schools thus cannot move directly to the stage where external support is utilised unless they would have tried to address the needs of the pupil at the classroom and school-based stages first.

Stage 1 follows the universal interventions already engaged in by the classroom teacher and the school, namely direct teaching of SEE, infusion of the skills learnt into the other areas of the curriculum, a caring and supportive classroom environment and a whole school approach to SEE. At this stage, the classroom teacher in collaboration with the pupils seeks to address the needs of any pupil experiencing difficulty in SEE, by adapting the curriculum, pedagogy, instruction and classroom management and organising additional support on a small group or one-to-one basis. Support may be provided by the teacher, the classroom learning support assistant, the classroom peers and/or parents/caregivers, and may include individual support, a teacher-led individual SEE program and mentoring program amongst others (Fig. 6.3).

In the second stage, the school supports an individual pupil or group of pupils within its own resources, making use of the support structures it has in place, such as whole school policies in SEE and behaviour, peer and staff mentoring, parental collaboration, LSAs, behaviour support teachers, PSHE teachers and other support staff amongst others. Initiatives at this stage may include the organization of a Circle of Support for a small group of pupils to support their learning of specific social and emotional competencies. Pupil mentoring by more emotionally competent peers, with the parents themselves being mentored by coaches linked to school, may form part of such interventions. These suggested strategies have been used effectively in the Fast Track Program in the USA to promote pro-social behaviour and reduce aggressive and disruptive behaviour amongst school children, particularly those considered at risk (Lavellee et al. 2005; Conduct Problems Prevention Research Group 2011).

At the *School Plus Interventions* stage, the school seeks further help for individual pupils/group of pupils, from outside sources such as educational support services, behaviour support teams, mental health services and child development assessment agencies. This may include requests for direct interventions by qualified practitioners with individual pupils, and support and education for teachers or parents. In the final stage, the school in collaboration with the pupil and the parents may refer the pupil for formal assessment (cf. Statement of Special Educational Needs) with a view for more intensive and frequent additional support and/or specialist provision. The framework has also a revolving door function, with the possibility of the process returning back to the previous stage(s) following an improvement in behaviour. For instance, following a school plus intervention, follow-up may require continued classroom teacher support at Stage 1.

The following section provides illustrations of interventions at each of the four stages. They are being presented as a general guide rather than a prescriptive, exhaustive list. Each school would adjust the type of interventions according to its needs, strengths and resources available. What is crucial, however, is that staff and schools would follow the staged approach when seeking to address the social and emotional needs of their pupils, having exhausted their resources at each stage before moving to the next one. In this way the pupils' needs would be addressed adequately and effectively as much as possible in their classroom, taking seriously the influences of environmental affordances and constraints on manifestations of pupils' behaviour. This emphasis on a "healthy settings" approach to pupil well-being and health, is consistent with World Health Organization recommendations for the promotion of mental health and well-being in children (WHO 2011b; WHO 2013).

6.2   Stage 1 Classroom-Based Interventions (From Universal to Selective Interventions)

At this stage, the classroom teacher seeks to provide his or her support to pupils who are finding it difficult to access the SEE curriculum. In line with the developmental-inclusive perspective of the framework proposed in this book, the classroom teacher assesses the needs of the pupil/group of pupils and adapts the curriculum and pedagogy to match their needs. Before seeking to implement any form of intervention, the teacher first ensures that the taught and caught SEE curriculum is being adequately implemented, with high quality classroom teaching, infusion of SEE in the curriculum, a positive classroom climate and a whole school ecology conducive to social and emotional learning. The teacher also examines the classroom climate by referring back to the checklists in Chap. 5, particularly if a number of pupils are showing signs of difficulties. Secondly the teacher conducts an assessment of needs of the pupil(s) concerned, identifying the gaps in learning and the pupils' strengths which might help to address those needs. The learning benchmarks and indicators and the assessment checklists in Chap. 4 provide guidance as to the nature of the gaps to be addressed, while a functional analysis of behaviour (see Box 6.3) helps the teacher in devising interventions based on the pupil's needs and strengths. Thirdly, interventions at this stage move from lightweight to heavyweight strategies, starting with low-level, non-invasive strategies with the least disruption to the classroom activities and without unnecessary involvement of third parties (Olsen and Cooper 2001). More heavyweight interventions such as individual programming and involvement of other parties follow the lightweight strategies. The teacher engages the pupil/s in the planning and development of these interventions.

The following are some examples of classroom-level interventions by the classroom teacher:

- individual attention by the classroom such as Bubble Time, where individual pupils ask the teacher for a one to one session to discuss personal issues;
- spending time to get to know more the individual pupil's needs and strengths, celebrating and making use of the latter to address the former (see example in Box 6.1);
- mentoring by the classroom teacher;
- examination of the classroom climate, particularly classroom relationships, classroom management, boundaries and expectations, and peer collaboration (see Chap. 5);
- curricular adaptation and differentiated teaching of SEE universal curriculum, including extra individual support by teacher and peers, additional and alternative activities and resources, and breaking down of skills into specific tasks;
- additional SEE sessions in identified areas, either individually or in a small group;
- more intensive infusion of identified SEE areas in the academic curriculum;
- consultation with parents/caregivers and how they may collaborate in addressing the pupils' needs;
- consultation and collaboration with colleagues and the classroom LSA;

- pupil support schemes such as buddy systems, peer tutoring, counselling and mediation schemes and mentoring schemes;
- sociometric test to help integrate pupils in the group, develop friendships and create more harmonious relationships (see Box 6.2);
- monitoring and recording of pupils' behaviour;
- functional assessment of behaviour to identify pupil's needs more systematically and how they could be addressed in the classroom, including designing and implementing an individual behaviour plan (see Boxes 6.3).

Box 6.1 Getting to know the pupils (from Cefai 2008)

THIS IS ME

Fill in this handout by completing the sentences about YOU

I am good in_____

I like_____

My hobbies are_____

I have an interest in _____

One subject I am good in is _____

One subject I am not so good in is _____

I have problems with_____

I need help in _____

I can help in _____

My friends are _____

Box 6.2 Sociometrics (from Cefai 2008)

The sociometric test is a simple but useful technique that may be used by the classroom teacher to promote more harmonious classroom relationships and identify and remedy any difficulties in such relationships. It is best used when pupils know each other quite well. The questions asked are determined by the information the teacher needs to collect. Samples of questions may include:

'Who is your best friend?'

'Which pupil would you like to work with in the classroom?'

'Which pupil would you like to play with during the break?'

In the beginning, it may be advisable to ask one or two questions and to restrict pupil choices to three preferences. Give pupils a piece of paper where they can write the names by the respective questions (you may also use pictures and photos instead of names in classes where pupils may have difficulty writing names). Tell the pupils that there are no right or wrong answers but that true and honest answers are important. Reassure pupils that their responses will be kept in confidence. Include absent pupils as well. Once you have collected all the responses, work out a matrix of all the pupils' preferences and then draw a sociogram which will give a graphic display of the classroom relationships, including the stars of the class, the cliques and pairs, and the isolated, neglected and rejected peers (see website address below for more details on how to do the matrix and the sociogram). Consider the changes you will need to carry out from the analysis of your data, such as helping rejected pupils by putting them in a small group of integrated pupils who did not reject them; organising class or arranging small groups so that the pupils can work more harmoniously; deciding on best seating arrangements for formal and informal work; and keeping pupils' views in mind when delegating responsibilities. More information on scoring and interpreting the responses of a sociometric test may be found at www.users.muohio.edu/shermalw/sociometryfiles/socio_introduction.htmlx

Box 6.3 A Classroom Teacher Framework for Analysis of Behaviour (adapted from Watkins and Wagner 2000)

1. What specific behaviour/s is causing concern?
2. In what situations does the behaviour occur? (events, time, with whom)
3. In what situations does the behaviour NOT occur?
4. What happens BEFORE the behaviour? (trigger, antecedent)
5. What happens AFTER the behaviour occurs? What seems to maintain the behaviour?

6. What skills/strengths does the pupil demonstrate?
7. What skills does the pupil NOT demonstrate? How may these be developed?
8. What views does the pupil have of the behaviour and him/self?
9. What appropriate behaviour could produce the same result?
10. What can be learned from previous efforts for the pupil about strategies that were ineffective, effective or only effective for a short time?

6.3   Stage 2: Whole School Interventions (From Selective to Indicated Interventions)

Whole school interventions seek to mobilise the school resources to address the more intensive and demanding needs of pupils experiencing social, emotional and behaviour difficulties. In a *Circle of Support* the pupils experiencing social, emotional and behaviour difficulties attend a program of further training in the particular skills required. The *Circle of Support* group consists of a small number of pupils experiencing difficulties and a similar number of pupils with good social and emotional competencies who will serve as mentors. The support group may be run by the school's behaviour support teacher and includes various activities in the areas targeted for the pupil(s) in question. Sessions take about 30–45 min per week for one school term, with the last phase bridging pupils back into the mainstream classroom accompanied by the *Circle of Support* facilitator. Targeted pupils are also paired with rotating peers in the classroom. At the same time the parents of the pupils experiencing difficulties are referred to (and supported to attend) sources of parenting education and support provided at the school and by other organizations (cf. Bierman and Erath 2006; National Institute for Health and Clinical Excellence 2008; Mosley 2009).

Mentoring is another key strategy that may be used as a whole school strategy to support pupils exhibiting social, emotional and behaviour difficulties. Peer-mentoring schemes may take various forms, but a cross age, well trained peer-mentoring group may take an active role in supporting pupils at this stage. Schemes may provide individual, group and specialist support such as counselling, conflict resolution or dealing with bullying (see also Box 7.1 on Peer Mentoring Schemes in Chap. 7). An adult–pupil mentoring scheme also provides the opportunity for pupils in difficulty to develop a close supportive relationship with an adult at the school. Finally the staff themselves may benefit from such schemes, such critical friends/peer mentors for the classroom teacher, particularly teachers in classrooms with pupils manifesting social, emotional and behaviour difficulties.

Another whole school strategy is early universal screening and identification of pupils exhibiting social, emotional and behaviour difficulties, accompanied by tracking, monitoring and recording of pupil's behaviour on a periodic and regular basis. Various screening measures, such as the Strengths and Difficulties Question-naire (Goodman 1997), the Behavioral and Emotional Screening System (Kam-phaus and Reynolds 2007), the Behavioural and Emotional Rating Scale (Epstein et al. 2012), and the Systematic Screening for Behavior Disorders (Walker and Sev-erson 1990) are available (see Box 6.4). Screening helps to identify the pupils who may be at risk of social, emotional and behaviour difficulties or already manifesting such difficulties, as early as possible. In a recent study with teachers of 4-year-old children attending regular classes, Greer et al. (2012) reported that most of the teachers found that emotional and behaviour screening provided them with valuable and useful information on the children, and that the screening results facilitated collaboration with parents and professionals and focused attention on the needs of particular children. The teachers also saw screening as an easy to do, worthwhile, 'non-stigmatising' tool for obtaining information about children's health and devel-opment which could help them to inform their practice. While early intervention is critical for the healthy social and emotional development of children (Weare and Nind 2011; Albers et al. 2007), care must be taken however, on the potential side effects of screening such as labelling and self-fulfilling prophecy. If it is going to be used, it needs to be used sparingly and cautiously and accompanied by other formative and strengths-based measures, and use of multiple informants (Dowdy and Kim 2012). Brief screening instruments will also be more feasible and practical to administer (Kamphaus 2012; Greer et al. 2012). Moreover, screening measures need to reflect the cultural, racial and linguistic diversity of the groups being as-sessed (Dever et al. 2012).

Other examples of whole school-level targeted interventions may include:

- use of additional specialist programmes to address the kind of difficulties en-countered (e.g. bullying prevention, coping with anxiety and depression, resil-ience building);
- use of the school's behaviour, bullying and socio-emotional education policies;
- introducing whole school positive behaviour schemes;
- curriculum planning, resourcing and adaptation;
- small group problem-focused sessions;
- more intensive school–home collaboration;
- use of the support staff at the school, including SEE coordinator, behaviour support teacher, Nurture Group staff, LSAs, complementary teacher, Personal, Social, and Home-Economics teacher as well as administrative staff;
- setting up a SEE support team at the school to provide guidance and support to individual pupils, groups of pupils, and staff. The team is also involved in inter-ventions at stages 3 and 4, such as referring a pupil for formal assessment and implementing the recommendations of the assessment process (see Box 6.5);
- introduction of breakfast/lunch clubs, and after school homework class;
- use of a relaxation room.

Box 6.4 The Strengths and Difficulties Questionnaire (Goodman 1997)

The *Strengths and Difficulties Questionnaire* (SDQ) is a brief, easy-to-use screening questionnaire used to identify children and young persons from 3 to 16 years who may be at risk for social, emotional and behaviour difficulties. It consists of four difficulty subscales, measuring emotional, hyperactivity, conduct and peer difficulties respectively. Emotional difficulties relate to anxiety and depression; hyperactivity to restlessness, over-activity and inattention; conduct to behaviour problems such as fighting, cheating and lying; and peer problems to bullying, loneliness and having problems in relating with peers. It includes a fifth subscale measuring pro-social behaviour, such as being considerate, helpful, caring and kind to others. The SDQ is completed by teachers and parents in primary school, and by teachers, parents and students (self-report) in secondary school. Used together with other assessment tools such as other behaviour checklists, observations, interviews and achievement tests, it may help to draw a profile of the pupil's strengths and difficulties and alert the classroom teacher to potential difficulties which may need to be addressed as early as possible. Caution is urged however, on the use of this test for diagnostic purposes, and educators' attention is drawn to the potential risks of labelling, emanating from the use of this test. The SDQ has been translated into more than 40 languages may be downloaded at www.sdqinfo.com

Box 6.5 A SEE Support Team at the School

A SEE support team at the school may consist of a multi-disciplinary team specialised in social and emotional education and in social, emotional and behaviour difficulties, but it will retain its identity as an educational service by specialised educationalists for schools. Besides SEE and behaviour support teachers, it may include pupils and parents specialized Learning Support Assistants, Personal, Social and Home-Economics teachers, Special Educational Needs Coordinators and other support staff at the school, and works closely with the school's psychologist, counsellor, social worker, youth worker and other professionals involved. The team provides education, guidance and support in socio-emotional education and behaviour support, working with individual pupils or group of pupils, classroom teachers, school staff and parents. Amongst other roles, it:

- provides direct work with pupils with social, emotional and behaviour difficulties at small group and individual levels;
- provides guidance, education and support to school staff and parents on best practices and policies for supporting pupils with their behaviour and social and emotional development, including the design and review of in-

dividual behaviour programs, behaviour management skills, peer-mentoring and parenting education;
- assists in the development, review and auditing of school policies designed to prevent and respond to behaviour problems and promote positive behaviour and social and emotional education, such as Circle Time and Circles of Support;
- trains, monitors and provides ongoing supervision and support for classroom teachers in the implementation of SEE as a core competence in the curriculum.

6.4 Stage 3: School Plus Interventions (Indicated Interventions)

Once the school's own resources have been exhausted and are outside expertise, support and intervention is indicated, the school then moves to the third stage of intervention. This constitutes a smaller group of pupils with evident and present difficulties which are interfering with their healthy development and posing difficulties in their learning, behaviour and relationships. It is suggested that the persons involved, including school administration, SEE coordinator, classroom teachers, LSAs parents, and pupil him/herself, form a behaviour support team to assess further, the presenting problem and decide on the intervention programme (see also Stage 2 and Box 6.6). The team may recruit the services of local or regional behaviour support teacher, early intervention support staff, Special Educational Needs Coordinator, counsellor, social worker, psychotherapist or educational psychologist as part of a transdisciplinary team depending on the nature of the difficulty. The school may also ask for the support of mental health services such as Children and Adolescents Mental Health Services, and Child Guidance Clinic, as well as Anti-Bullying Service, Child Safety Service, Family Therapy Services and similar services in the region. It is strongly recommended that a school-based professional, such as the SEE coordinator, coordinates the assessment, intervention and referral (where applicable) process. Clear referral pathways may be worked out at school, local or regional levels.

Interventions may include solution-focused approaches, cognitive behaviour interventions, play and drama therapy, counselling, psychotherapy, systemic family therapy, social skills training, social work intervention, occupational therapy, speech and language therapy, coaching and medical services amongst others. Interventions at this stage may also include:

- support for parents and parental education courses at both individual and group levels, at school or in the community;
- liaison with the local community for the provision of social and emotional learning programmes in the community, including day care centres;
- support and training to classroom teachers in behaviour management and individual behaviour programming by specialist consultants.

6.5   Stage 4: Formal Assessment for Additional Support/ Special Provision (Indicated Interventions)

A small percentage of pupils (3 to 5%) manifest social, emotional and behaviour difficulties which may be considered to be severe enough to warrant intensive, long-term intervention and/or additional support and specialist provision (Romano et al. 2001; Kaufman 2012). The school, in liaison with the local educational authority and related support services, may set up a formal SEE support team for the pupil to draw up a targeted programme for the pupil. The team is school based, transdisciplinary, follows the pupil regularly and includes the parents/caregivers and pupil him/herself, the classroom teacher and LSA, the school support staff involved in Stage 3, and professionals such as educational psychologists, counsellors, clinical psychologists, social workers, family therapists, psychotherapists, psychiatrists, occupational therapists, speech and language therapists and play therapists. It conducts a formal assessment of the pupil's needs and identifies the provisions required to address those needs. These may include amongst others:

- the services of a classroom learning support assistant;
- short term placement in a specialist provision with clear intervention targets, such as Nurture Groups or Assessment Research Centres;
- referral to regular and intensive specialist services as part of the programme of intervention.

Box 6.6 Hexthorpe Primary School: A Case Study of Targeted Interventions (DfES 2001a, pp. 49–50) © Crown

Hexthorpe Primary School, Doncaster, UK is located in a multi-ethnic, mainly working class area of high unemployment, and caters for over 400 pupils aged between 4 and 11. In the school, an increasing number of pupils with emotional and behavioural problems seemed to be struggling to cope with confusion in their personal lives. This manifests itself in low self-esteem, an inability to develop positive relationships with peers and feelings about being 'picked on' by those with whom they come into contact. The school developed an integrated whole school policy based on a multi-agency approach in order to respond more effectively to the needs of these pupils. A combination of Circle Time approaches, circle of friends, the setting up of play therapy/nurture groups and a programme aimed at the development of parenting skills helped to encourage an atmosphere of mutual trust and respect, leading to improved co-operative and supportive relationships between pupils, parents and staff.

The multi-agency group carried out a careful evaluation of the impact of the interventions. They found that although all interventions were only in place for a short period, the Circle of Friends and the Nurture Group, revealed the greatest impact. In relation to the Circle of Friends—for the two children selected for the intensive support (who were assessed as having low self-esteem and who were socially withdrawn) using sociograms and 'B/G esteem' measures, there was much subjective evidence and some quantifiable evidence to show that the Circle of Friends strategy was effective in promoting their inclusion. The strategy also had a positive impact for the other children involved in the groups. Staff in the school was committed to continuing the development of Circle of Friends approaches for other isolated children. The Nurture Group— set up to address the needs of Reception and Year 1 children demonstrating adjustment difficulties in the classroom, was by far the most successful of the project's interventions. Children were selected for involvement in the group by discussion with their class teachers; the primary criterion for selection was the child's difficulties in coping with the social demands of the classroom environment, e.g. mixing with peers, responding to adults, conforming to rules. In addition to this, the Box all diagnostic profile was used. Significant improvements were registered for two-thirds of the children involved in the Nurture Group, and it was felt possible that others would have benefited from a longer involvement—providing a clear indication of the value of this kind of intervention for young children who present emotional and behavioural difficulties in the classroom. All of the strategies employed by the school, except for Circle Time, involved the joint working of different professionals. The school reported of their experiences of this multi-agency working—'Where professionals shared an educational philosophy it was easy to develop complementary ways of working. Problems arose when educational and clinical professionals favoured the use of different methods. However, most difficulties were resolved and effective ways of working together were established'.

6.6 Conclusion

The framework proposed in this chapter is one which seeks to provide an integrated, comprehensive, and collaborative intervention, bringing together education, health and social policy, and providing integrated, transdisciplinary services in natural contexts as much as possible. This is in line with the stance taken in this book in depatholigising and destigmatising mental health and mental health difficulties and in broadening the educational agenda to a holistic, multifaceted one.

Oukonunaka and the Two Wolves

Keetoowah, Tuckasegee River, Great Smoky Mountains

The month of the wolf moon

The distant howling of the wolf sent shivers down the spine of young Oukonunaka as he entered the tipi. He sat down on the sage-covered floor, opposite the red-painted, cross-legged Attakullakulla. As the singing and drum beating subsided, Attakullakulla nodded his feathered head so that the young man could speak. "O great Attakullakulla, your wisdom and counsel I beseech for my troubled mind and tormented heart. It is as if I have two hearts, throwing arrows to each other. It is as if there are two wolves inside me, one grey and good, the other black and bad. The grey wolf wants me to live in harmony with the forest and the river, to be just, compassionate and forgiving, not to hurt others and desire and take what is not mine. But sometimes the black wolf gets too strong and his teeth sink deep into the grey wolf. He is wild, jealous, angry and resentful. His anger is easily aroused by others and he is wont to strike and hit back at the least provocation. He is jealous of what others have, and easily hurt by what they say. He fights all the time, his anger and bitterness at the deeds of others uncontrollable, clouding his reasoning and judgment. It is hard, o great Attakullakulla, to live with these two fighting wolves inside me. Heal my wounded heart, O Great Cherokee Leader."

As the singing and drum beating increased, the dreamy Attakullakulla started reciting a long repetitive invocation while examining the ancient black adolon between the thumb and index finger of his left hand, and another red bead between the forefinger and thumb of his right hand. The singers sat around the two men and increased their mantric recitations. As time passed, the red bead moved briskly in the old man's hand right, but the black one remained motionless. After a while, the old man opened his eyes and the singing, recitations and drum beating stopped. "There are many rings around your eyes Oukonunaka white owl, son of Wahy'a. You are being poisoned by these tempests inside you. This potion made from seven Haudenosaunee barks facing the sun, will purify your body from the poison and help you find peace from this struggle". "But which wolf will win and survive in my heart, O Great Attakullakulla?" "It is the one which you feed, Oukonunaka, son of Wahy'a."

Part III
Heart in the Whole-School Community

'The greatest wealth is health'.

—Virgil

Chapter 7
A Whole-School Approach to SEE: The School as a Caring Community

Schools are social systems functioning at various layers, with each layer carrying its own distinctive characteristic and having the potential to impact learning and behaviour (Bronfenbrenner 1989). The previous three chapters underlined the importance of classroom as the central context in which social and emotional education takes place. Processes occurring at the school layer, however, also impact pupils' learning and social and emotional well-being. SEE is more likely to be sustained and reinforced, and thus has an added value effect, when it is taught and caught both in the classroom and the whole-school layers. There is long-standing, consistent research on the significance of a positive whole-school climate underpinning the values and attitudes of the school community and consequently shaping the practices, behaviours and relationships of its members (Bryk and Driscoll 1988; Adi et al. 2007; Weare and Nind 2011; Battistich et al. 1997; Cooper and Jacobs 2011). When the whole school mobilises all its resources to promote the well-being and resilience of its members, it is more likely to be effective in promoting well-being and resilience in the classrooms, at the whole school and also beyond the boundaries of the school (Weare and Nind 2011; Greenberg 2010; Askell-Williams et al. 2010; DfES, 2007).

> Imagine a school where everyone in the learning community pays more attention in equipping the students with the skills they need to approach the 'tests of life' rather than having students' school experience to be composed of a 'life of tests'. (Lantieri 2009b, p. 12)

7.1 A Schoolwide Approach to SEE

This chapter proposes a framework of the school as a caring community for all its members, including the pupils, staff and parents/caregivers. When both pupils and staff have a sense of belonging to the school and their needs and welfare are adequately addressed, and when parents/caregivers are actively involved and supported, SEE is more likely to be effective and sustained. Figure 7.1 portrays schools

C. Cefai, V. Cavioni, *Social and Emotional Education in Primary School*,
DOI 10.1007/978-1-4614-8752-4_7, © Springer Science+Business Media New York 2014

Fig. 7.1 The school as a caring community

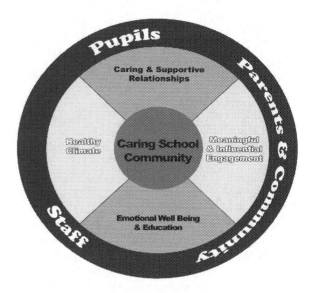

operating as caring communities promoting learning and social and emotional well-being of all their members, characterised by four major processes (cf. Bryk and Driskoll 1988; Solomon et al. 2000; Battistich et al. 1997; Cefai 2008; Weare and Nind 2011):

- Caring and supportive relationships, with pupils, staff and parents/caregivers feeling respected, valued, supported and having their needs addressed.
- Meaningful and influential engagement, with pupils, staff and parents/caregivers being actively involved in the life of the school and participating in the decision-making process.
- Adequate support to the emotional well-being and education of all members, including pupils, staff and parents/caregivers.
- Healthy school climate, including clear and shared goals and expectations, policy development and provision of support.

These four major characteristics are developed into a number of indicators, which will help the school to carry out an evaluation of how effective it is in providing social and emotional education and support to all its members at the whole-school level. On the basis of these indicators, the school may then decide to embark on a number of initiatives to reinforce and celebrate good practice and address areas that need further development. For instance, in the area of relationships, the school community may decide to strengthen and promote healthy and supportive relationships by introducing a pupil–teacher mentoring scheme, peer mentoring, cross-age tutoring and buddy systems, a bullying prevention programme, a weekly Happy Hour for staff, a mentoring scheme for new teachers, a Smart Play programme to encourage more positive interactions during playtime, more open and flexible learning environments to encourage connectedness and collaboration between and amongst pupils and staff in different classrooms, special whole-school assemblies to celebrate achievements and strengths, a Parent Hour where parents are free to come and discuss with staff in a relaxed and informal setting and a conflict resolution team, which helps to find constructive solutions to conflicts involving staff, pupils or parents.

Box 7.1 Peer mentoring schemes

MiniMentors, UK (www.minimentors.org.uk) is a mentoring programme for 5–11-year-old children in primary schools in the UK. It aims to promote friendship, inclusion, sense of belonging and taking care of one another amongst school children. Children learn the importance of looking after themselves and respecting each other, including others in their activities, and making friends with others. The MiniMentors (8 years and over) are trained in how to look after other children at the school, play with them, make them feel part of the school, listen to them when they want to share something and help them to solve problems. Usually, there are about 30 mentors in a school. MiniMentors consist of two programmes. The KS1 Programme for 5–7-year-old children seeks to teach children about the nature of good and bad friendships, bullying and online safety, making use of practical activities, creative play and traditional stories. The KS2 Programme is a more intensive programme, training mentors in friendship, bullying, peer pressure, cyberbullying, confidentiality and online safety. It uses various techniques and activities to help the young mentors to gain an insight into how they can be advocates for other children in friendship and in dealing with peer pressure, bullying and cyberbullying. CyberMentors is a sister programme providing online mentoring for secondary school students.

Youth Empowerment Process (*YEP; MindMatters 2012*) aims to promote peer mentoring. The process involves training of both staff and selected students in mental health promotion in schools, followed by an action team consisting of both students and staff to plan and implement the initiative. The students take a leading role in this process, supported by the staff and other professionals. The YEP framework consists of the following components:

- A school commitment to build an ongoing collaborative partnership between students and staff and amongst students themselves, based on trust and respect.
- Development of students' attitudes, knowledge and skills of mental health promotion so as to be able to make informed decisions about all aspects of well-being.
- Development of students' confidence in their ability to bring change in themselves and in others and to make a positive difference in the life of others.
- Creation of opportunities and responsibilities for action by students, including active participation based on sensitivity, openness and teamwork.

- Provision of active support, including being advocates for student voice, providing appropriate advice and support around issues of cultural or other conflict, ensuring a safe and supportive environment in which students are valued and are able to participate actively, and celebrating the strengths of students and the contribution they are making in promoting mental health and well-being.

Box 7.2 The school yard as an SEE laboratory (Ms Kathrine, behaviour support teacher)

The school yard provides a unique opportunity for social and emotional learning (SEL) at a whole-school level, for changing the culture of the school yard to a more prosocial and cooperative one. I do a lot of work with teachers on yard duty responsibility. I introduce Play Time in the yard as a teaching time. When you are on yard duty, you need to use that time as an opportunity for SEL, you do not just tell the kids, right go somewhere and play, but you go and interact and teach them SEL. The yard is another classroom, just outside, and probably it is richer ground for SEL learning because it is about real play—rather than just asking them what to do when you are playing, you help them actually do it. Teachers go round and reinforce good play behaviour, such as saying 'This is a really cooperative game here!' and 'That is a respectful way of using equipment!'. They also use behaviour incidents as opportunities for SEL. For instance, I worked on a case where the school was taking a rather punitive approach by removing a young child from the play area because he could not play. But in the classroom, if a child cannot read you do not say you do not get books because you cannot read, but we immerse them in books even further and become more creative in finding ways to get them how to read. So, in the yard, if they cannot play or make friends, they need help and support to do so. With a couple of schools, I am working on a programme called Smart Play, a designated space where a group of children are invited to smart play for a week, where a supervision teacher will teach a small group of children how to play cooperatively for a week, and then they go back to the whole play area. If a child runs out with the ball, instead of time out, the teacher gives the child the opportunity to observe another boy engaging in the appropriate behaviour for about 1 minute and let him go off to play.

7.2 Assessing the Whole-School Ecology

The following indicators are presented as a guide for school communities to engage in a self-evaluation and self-improvement process, one generated and directed by the school itself. The school SEE including members from each staff grade as well as representatives of pupils and parents/caregivers (see Chap. 3), distributes the indicators to staff, pupils and parents, followed by organised discussions amongst the various members. The discussion could be organised in various ways depending on the needs and interest of the school. The team may choose to discuss the results section by section and identify strengths and areas for improvement in each section; subgroups may draw a plan of action for a particular area, which is then discussed with the whole group. Every effort needs to be made to include and encourage the various members to participate actively in this process.

Following the identification of targets for intervention on the basis of feedback from staff, pupils and parents/caregivers, these are then prioritised, and a plan of action is developed to implement the chosen targets. The plan will detail what activities will be organised, the people who will be involved, the resources needed, the target date(s) for implementation and ways for monitoring and evaluating the action plan. In line with the collaborative approach suggested in the framework, the plan of action is drawn collectively by the staff in collaboration with the pupils and the parents/caregivers. The action plans, and the ways schools go about identifying and implementing it, are visible demonstrations to school communities of how to enact whole-school approaches to well-being and resilience. In other words, schools must 'walk the talk' of positive mental health. Collaborative planning, faithful implementation, continued monitoring and regular evaluation are critical to the success of any initiative. Action plans also need to be suited to the cultural needs and nature of the school community, building on the strengths of that community and the many good practices already taking place.

7.2.1 Staff Checklist

Table 7.1 shows the indicators checklist to be completed by school staff consisting of the four general indicators constituting the caring school community, with specific indicators for each of the four areas. The indicators are completed by all members of staff (or a representative sample of staff in the case of large schools) anonymously and returned to the SEE team. They may be completed and analysed visually for common patterns as in the case of the classroom community indicators in Chap. 5; in that case, the SEE team may input the data as in Table 7.2. If the team has the time and resources, a more detailed analysis for the quantitative data will be useful. The scores in each section of the indicators for each member of staff are totalled and then they are divided by the number of staff who responded to draw up an average score. These scores may then be presented in a table to give an indication of the strengths and needs of each area and of the school community as a whole (Table 7.3). Scores on the average or below the average indicate that the school needs

Table 7.1 Indicators for a caring school (staff version)

INDICATORS FOR A CARING SCHOOL – STAFF VERSION
1= Not in Place; 2= Partly in Place/Needs Improvement;3= In place.

	A. Caring and supportive relationships are the hallmarks of our school community	
A1	Our pupils get on very well with each other	
A2	Bullying is quite rare in our schools	
A3	I have close and collegial relationships with my colleagues	
A4	We work together closely as a team	
A5	I am understood and supported by the administration	
A6	I get on very well with our pupils	
A7	I show concern for the social and emotional needs of the pupils	
A8	I maintain regular communication with parents and seek to addresses their concerns	
	Examples of the above that are working well in our school	
	Targets for Improvement	
	B. School members are meaningfully and influentially engaged in the school community	
B1	Our pupils take an active part in the life of the school	
B2	Our pupils have a say in the design and review of our policies and procedures	
B3	I am actively involved in curriculum planning and policy development at the school	
B4	I participate actively and regularly in activities organized at the school	
B5	I plan, work and share practice and resources together with my colleagues	
B6	Parents are informed regularly on our school policies and activities	
B7	Parents have a real say in decisions on what happens in our school	
B8	The school works in close collaboration with the local community in various areas and initiatives	
	Examples of the above that are working well in our school	
	Targets for Improvement	

Table 7.1 (continued)

	C. The social and emotional needs of all school members are adequately addressed	
C1	SEE is organized regularly in our school, according to the needs of our pupils	
C2	I have adequate training, resources and time to deliver SEE effectively	
C3	The SEE team identifies pupils with SEE needs and provides information, and support to pupils, staff and parents/caregivers	
C4	SEE is implemented as planned and its impact is monitored and evaluated regularly	
C5	The available supports for pupils with SEE needs are relevant and appropriate to need	
C6	Our school recognises and actively addresses the staff's social and emotional needs	
C7	Our school has provisions and supports to safeguard the physical and psychological health and safety of our staff	
C8	Our school provides training and education for parents/caregivers including their children's SEE, both at school and in the community	
	Examples of the above that are working well in our school	
	Targets for Improvement	
	D. Our school's climate is conducive to SEE amongst all members	
D1	Our school is safe, warm and welcoming for all staff, pupils and parents/caregivers	
D2	Our school is well maintained and attractive for all members, including staff rooms, classrooms and play areas	
D3	Our school climate encourages mutual respect and understanding, open discussion of concerns and constructive problem solving	
D4	Our school policies and procedures reflect the rights and responsibilities of all partners concerned	
D5	Our school has in place updated policies and procedures with clear expectations on relationships, behaviour and pratices	
D6	Our school has in place procedures to prevent potential bullying of vulnerable groups or individuals	
D7	Our whole school behaviour policy encourages and reinforces positive relationships and behaviour amongst all members	
D8	Our school administration shows concern for the social and emotional well-being of the whole school community	
	Examples of the above that are working well in our school	
	Targets for Improvement	

Some of the items in this and the other two checklists in this chapter have been informed by other existing checklists, namely National Curriculum Council Focus Group for Inclusive Education (2002) and ASD (2012)

Table 7.2 Total frequency of numbers 1, 2 and 3 responses for each general indicator based on staff's responses

INDICATOR	Total number of 1s	Total number of 2s	Total number of 3s
A. Relationships amongst school members			
B. Members' engagement			
C. Members' social and emotional needs			
D. School's climate			

Table 7.3 Sample template: improving school community (staff indicators)

INDICATORS	Strengths	Targets for improvement
A. Relationships amongst school members		
B. Members' engagement		
C. Members' social and emotional needs		
D. School's climate		

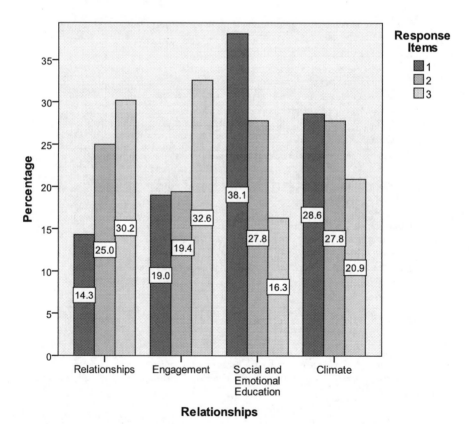

Fig. 7.2 Sample frequency chart of the four general indicators based on staff's responses

to work more in that particular area; scores above the average suggest that this area of school community could be either satisfactory or a relative strength. Once all the totals are in place, a bar chart for the four general indicators may also be plotted. Figure 7.2 presents an example of such a graph. The two open-ended questions at the end of each section may be analysed qualitatively, drawing up a portrait of the school's strengths and needs.

7.2.2 Pupil Checklist

The indicators checklist for pupils (Table 7.4) is completed anonymously by a representative sample of pupils at the school and returned to the team collecting the data. They may be completed and analysed visually for common patterns as in the case of the classroom community indicators in Chap. 4; in that case, the team will input the data as in Table 7.6. If the SEE team has the time and resources, a more detailed analysis of the quantitative data may be carried out. The response items 1–4 may be grouped in two, namely, needs improvement (response items 1 and 2: rarely or occasionally true) and satisfactory (response items 3 and 4: frequently or most of the time true). The team may go over section A (relationships) in all the checklists, counting first the total number of 1s and 2s and putting the total number (frequency of 1s and 2s) in the needs improvement box in Table 7.5. The process is then repeated for the total number of 3s and 4s, with the total number of both placed in the satisfactory box. This is repeated with the other three sections. The strengths and targets for intervention of each general indicator are then presented in a separate table (see Table 7.6). A bar chart for the four general indicators may also be plotted (Fig. 7.3). The qualitative data in section E are analysed for common recommendations emerging from the various respondents.

7.2.3 Parent/Caregivers Checklist

The indicators checklist for parents/caregivers (Table 7.7) is completed anonymously by a representative sample of the parents/caregivers and returned to the team collecting the data. These may be completed and analysed visually for common patterns (see Table 7.9). If the team has the time and resources, a more detailed analysis of the quantitative data is recommended. The response items 1–4 may be grouped in two, namely, needs improvement (response items 1 and 2: rarely or occasionally true), and satisfactory (response items 3 and 4: frequently or most of the time true). To score the responses, one may go over section A (relationships) in all lists, counting first the total number of 1s and 2s and putting the total number in the needs improvement box in Table 7.8. This is repeated for the total number of 3s and 4s, with the total placed in the satisfactory box. A similar exercise is then computed with the other three sections. Once all the totals are in place, a bar chart for the four general indicators may be plotted (Fig. 7.4). The strengths and targets

Table 7.4 Indicators for a caring school (pupils' version)

INDICATORS FOR A CARING SCHOOL – PUPILS' VERSION

1 = rarely true; 2 = occasionally true; 3 = frequently true; 4= true for most of the time.

A	Relationships	
A1	I help other pupils with work at school	
A2	I share things with other pupils at school	
A3	I work and play with others without fighting and arguing	
A4	I have one or more friends at school	
A5	Our teachers are kind and care for me	
A6	There are at least three adults at the school who care about me	
B	Engagement	
B1	I work hard and try to do well at school	
B2	I participate actively in school activities such as presentations and exhibitions	
B3	The teachers ask my opinion about how I can learn and behave better	
B4	I am given responsibilities at my school	
B5	My work is put up on display for all the school to see	
B6	My parents are told when I do something good at school	
C	Social and emotional skills	
C1	I learn how to listen and understand others at the school	
C2	I learn how to make friends	
C3	I learn how to express and manage my feelings	
C4	I learn how to solve problems	
C5	I learn how to make decisions	
C6	I learn how to identify and develop my strengths	
D	School Climate	
D1	Our school is nice, clean and spacious	
D2	I feel safe and secure at school	
D3	I am treated fairly at school	
D4	I was not bullied at school this year	
D5	I know whom to ask for help if I am bullied	
D6	I know and observe the school behaviour rules	
E	Recommendations	
E1	Write one to two things you like about your school	
E2	Write one to two things you would like to see in your school	

Table 7.5 Total frequency of numbers 1 and 2, and 3 and 4 responses for each general indicator based on pupils' responses

INDICATOR	Needs improvement (total number of 1s and 2s)	Satisfactory (total number of 3s and 4s)
A. Pupil relationships		
B. Pupil engagement		
C. Social and emotional education		
D. School climate		

Table 7.6 Sample template improving school community (pupil indicators)

INDICATORS	Strengths	Targets for improvement
A. Relationships amongst school members		
B. Members' engagement		
C. Members' social and emotional needs		
D. School's climate		

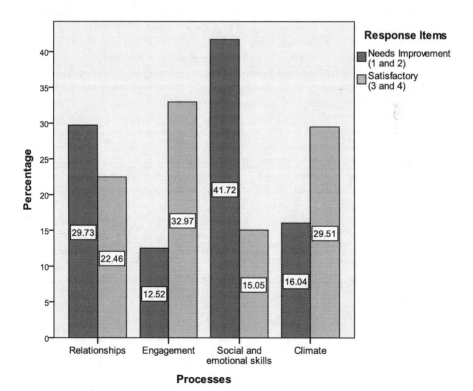

Fig. 7.3 Sample frequency chart of the four general indicators based on pupils' response

Table 7.7 Indicators for a caring school (parents'/caregivers' version)

INDICATORS FOR A CARING SCHOOL – PARENTS'/CAREGIVERS' VERSION
1 = rarely true; 2 = occasionally true; 3 = frequently true; 4= true for most of the time.

A	Relationships	
A1	I feel welcome at the school	
A2	I feel part of the school community	
A3	I am happy that my child/ren attend/s this school	
A4	I feel included and valued at the school	
A5	The staff listens to and takes action to address my concerns and issues	
A6	I have a good relationship with the class teacher and other members of staff	
A7	When there is a conflict with the school, I have the space to have my say	
A8	My opinion is listened to and valued at the school	
	Examples of the above that are working well at the school	
	Targets for Improvement	
B	**Engagement**	
B1	I can contact and discuss with staff when I feel the need	
B2	I am informed regularly on school policies and activities	
B3	I am informed when my child has been rewarded at school	
B4	I am asked to give my views on learning, behaviour and social and emotional education	
B5	I am asked to provide my help with learning, behaviour and social and emotional education	
B6	I am invited for school activities such as pupil presentations and exhibitions	
B7	I am given tasks to help my child/ren's social and emotional education	
B8	I support my child/ren with homework, classroom and school activities	
	Examples of the above that are working well at the school	
	Targets for Improvement	
C	**Education and well-being**	
C1	The school organises talks and courses on how I can help my child/ren learn	
C2	The school organises talks and courses on how I can help my child/ren behave and grow socially and emotionally	

Table 7.7 (continued)

C3	The school helps me to make contact with needed services and facilities in the community for my child/ren	
C4	The school organises talks and courses on how I can take promote my own health and well-being	
C5	The school helps me to make contact with needed services and facilities for my own health and well-being	
C6	I am encouraged by the school to organise activities for other parents at the school	
C7	The school provides opportunities where parents can meet and support each other	
C8	The school understands the difficulties I go through as a parent and provide needed support	
	Examples of the above that are working well at the school	
	Targets for Improvement	
D	**Climate**	
D1	The school where my child/ren attend/s is clean, spacious and child friendly	
D2	My child is safe and looked after at the school	
D3	I am satisfied with how the school deals with bullying and violence	
D4	My child is rewarded for good behaviour at the school	
D5	My child is taught how to communicate and make friends	
D6	My child is taught how to express his/her feelings appropriately	
D7	My child is taught how to identify his/her strengths and needs	
D8	My child is taught how to solve problems and make decisions	
	Examples of the above that are working well at the school	
	Targets for Improvement	
E	**Recommendations**	
	How may the school improve children's learning, behaviour and social and emotional education?	
	How may the school help you to participate and contribute more actively at the school?	

Table 7.8 Total frequency of numbers 1 and 2, and 3 and 4 responses for each general indicator based on parents' responses

INDICATOR	Needs improvement (total number of 1s and 2s)	Satisfactory (total number of 3s and 4s)
A. Relationships		
B. Engagement		
C. Education and wellbeing		
D. Climate		

Fig. 7.4 Sample frequency chart of the four general indicators based on parents' responses

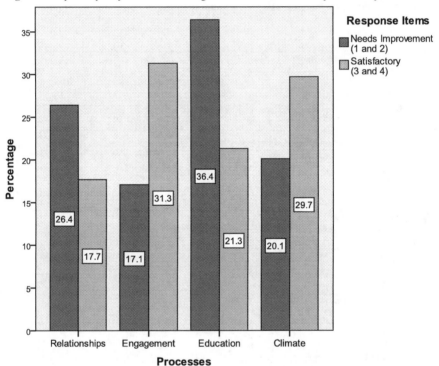

Table 7.9 Sample template improving school community (parent/caregiver indicators)

INDICATORS	Strengths	Targets for improvement
A. Relationships amongst school members		
B. Members' engagement		
C. Members' social and emotional needs		
D. School's climate		

for intervention of each general indicator are then presented in a separate table (Table 7.9). The qualitative data in section D are analysed for common recommendations emerging from the various respondents.

Box 7.3 An innovative whole-school approach to learning and well-being, integrating nature with leading technology

Blair Athol North Birth—Year 7 School in Adelaide, South Australia, was established in 2011 as an innovative school recognised by the Organisation for Economic and Community Development (OECD) as a model for school design for the twenty-first century. It is a category 1, multicultural and multilingual school with 42 different languages, 65% pupils having English as a second language and 60% of the pupils on the school card. One of the key objectives of the school is thus to foster resilience amongst the pupils, seeking to build the capacity of the children to believe in themselves and take control of their learning by focusing on their competences and assets.

The school provides a child-centred, multidisciplinary, high-technology and innovative learning environment inspired by its 3Bs: belonging, being and becoming. It adapted a set of capabilities and dispositions that it seeks to nurture amongst its pupils, encapsulated in its formula $7 \text{ Cs} \times 3 \text{ Rs} = \text{twenty-first century learning}$, namely critical thinking and problem solving, communication, collaboration, creativity and innovation, curiosity and inquiry, cultural understanding and care for self, others and the planet, and reflectiveness, resilience and risk taking. The school then developed six principles to enable it to foster these capabilities and dispositions amongst the pupils:

- *Intellectual quality/rigour*: Creating conditions for deep, active engagement in learning, making use of children's '100 languages' and integrating emotions and senses together with cognitive processes in learning.
- *Personalise and connect*: Viewing learners as capable and building on their interests, prior knowledge and understandings, following their passions and aspirations through inquiry, discovery and play and facilitating their choice, input, and self-direction.
- *Assessment and feedback*: Making learning visible for a range of audiences, involving pupils in joint construction and use of assessment modes, providing formative feedback and encouraging self-assessment and reflection as learners.
- *Twenty-first century multimodal digital tools*: Enabling learners to choose and use digital tools/social media anywhere and anytime, effectively, ethically and creatively; digital tools are used pervasively across the learning contexts, with some cohorts having 1:1 iPads.
- *Well-being and relationships*: Creating a culture of shared responsibility for feeling safe, respected and supported, through democratic and respectful relationships; nurturing and modelling positive values; addressing the physical, emotional and social well-being of the pupils; teamwork in

studios and neighbourhoods; actively valuing and respecting diversity; building and sustaining positive partnerships with families and community and caring for neighbourhood spaces.

- *Environment and spaces*: Making use of the learning environment as the third teacher, providing adaptable, connected and inviting spaces and fittings.

The open and flexible school design has brought down traditional barriers between classrooms to encourage connectedness, collaboration and enquiry amongst pupils and staff. The school buildings are called 'Neighbourhoods', classrooms 'Studios', classes 'Home Groups' and classroom teachers 'Learning Advisors'. The 'Learning Commons' are shared learning spaces that are joined to the studios. It is intended that the 'Piazza' serves as a central meeting area providing a strong sense of belonging and connectedness. As Ms Alice (grade 1 and 2 teacher) said, 'We are only one class...west and east are connected'. There is also a close connection with the outdoor areas such as the 'forest', 'wetland', and the play areas. Ms Nicole, an early-years teacher, remarked that 'you get to know everyone in the school and it really becomes a friendly place, it becomes a very positive working environment where everyone knows your name and says hello to you, it's really nice'. The layout similarly promotes teamwork amongst staff: 'We all know each other a little bit more in our neighbourhoods, our relationship keeps building on. We're becoming friends a little bit more and we can sit down and talk about what we want to change in our studios, it's a little bit of a "mountain top" where we can all share our ideas...it's very positive thing for our collaboration'.

The learning spaces are equipped with leading-edge technology, designed and furnished in a way to promote collaborative and inquiry-based learning and use of different learning styles and strategies, in line with the Reggio Emilia's approach of the '100 languages of children'. Pupils may wish to work together in a small group, individually, independently, teacher or peer guided and supported, making use of different learning spaces, multisensory strategies or digital tools. There are different work spaces available for all the pupils, with the 'camp fire' for whole group activity, 'watering hole' for collaborative group work, the 'cave' for individual work and reflection and the 'mountain top' for celebration. The atelier, the school studio and laboratory, is a place for experimentation with separate or combined visual languages, either in isolation or in combination with verbal ones. There are also mini-ateliers in the learning commons next to each studio used for extended activities, equipped with clay, wire, paint, pens, paper, beads, shells and a variety of recycled material. Real-life experiences are facilitated through the kitchen garden programme, TV studio and radio station, rock band, choir, and hip hop, percussion and ukelele groups, and ECO literacy (forest area and a wetland area). The school radio is run by the pupils, providing both live and prerecorded broadcasts. It provides pupils with an opportunity to present programmes with a variety of focus and interest areas, with a strong emphasis on literacy and music. The kitchen is fully equipped with a kitchen specialist and the garden is developed with fruit, vegetable and herb beds, and a chicken coup to provide eggs for cooking. Pupils are actively and collaboratively engaged in maintaining, growing and harvesting the garden and preparing dishes from the garden's produce.

This resonates with what Ms Helen said: 'pupils needs to be very active at school rather than sitting down for muscle development,...forcing children to sit down for long period of time, particularly young ones, is not only unnatural, but unhealthy... this is particularly true when even at homes and in neighbourhoods many children are not having adequate opportunity for play and physical exercise'. Ms Nicole added: 'these kind of activities help children to develop agency, empowers them to look after themselves, make decisions...many times they are not given these opportunities outside school... the administration team has given us permission to value well-being as much as academic learning for the whole school and to do things differently'. And Ms Grace, a grade 4 teacher, remarked: 'We make use of the knowledge they bring with them, in that way they feel valued and appreciated and develop their strengths...they are empowered to bring change themselves, helping them to deal with issues of powerlessness. We try to give them the power to feel masters not victims of their feelings and circumstances, that they can bring about change. There is the expectation that they will engage in their own learning, despite their background, that they have a right to. Today, we celebrated the hatching of the chickens at the school, it was a strong message for the kids, of the power to create rather than just change'.

The school premises include the Children's Centre, which is a place of engagement, learning and care for children and families from birth to 5 years. It offers a range of services and programmes for young children and their families, including the Learning Together Programme, which encourages parents to become more involved in their children's learning from birth, playgroups, a child care programme, preschool, pre-entry and early entry programmes, community development programmes, family services and parental education. One key feature of the Centre is the integration and multidisciplinary provision of health, social welfare and education services, facilitating easier access to families and the community, more effective and timely interventions, and less stigmatisation and pathologising of mental health services. Another feature is the significant role and contribution of the parents in the day to day life of the Centre. Parents do not only participate collaboratively with staff in some of the activities taking place at the school, but they also organise their own activities and educational programmes at the school. Ms. Kyle, an early-years teacher, describes how a problem was turned into an opportunity when a number of parents with refugee status were having difficulty accessing the services because of language difficulties. With the support of the school, the parents themselves organised a parent support group, which met regularly at the school and also offered English language classes for the parents. As Ms. Kyle said, 'our aim is to promote a rethinking of the role of parents in the school community, away from their traditional roles of fundraising and helping out, to parents becoming key partners with the school in their children's learning and well-being'.

Marjanna, the Marquis and the Falcon[1]

Medina, Malta

Medieval Times

The hesitant peasant knocked timidly on the door of the marquis' castle in Medina. As he observed the peregrine falcon on the marquis' coats of arms, his heart sank. The marquis was a hard, greedy old man, contemptuous of the peasants, and not known for his kindness or compassion. His anxiety increased as he was led into the rich sumptuous parlour, where the bent, crooked-nosed marquis was sitting, behind him a big stuffed peregrine falcon on a golden stand, rumoured to have been regaled to him by the great Emperor Charles V himself. 'My lord, as you know this year has been a very dry one. The crops and fruits shrivelled before harvesting time. The long illness of my wife has taken away the little money I had to find remedies for her health. My daughter cannot get married as I do not have enough for her dowry. Give me another year and I will be able to pay the rent, the last twelve days of the past year have predicted that the new year will be a wet and bountiful one. I have brought you some of what we have left, fresh cottage cheese and eggs, a jar of wild thyme honey, a jar of red wine, a jar of capers, a jar of sundried tomatoes, a jar of carob syrup,…'. 'Enough, you insolent fool' screamed the furious marquis, 'I will not tolerate this anymore. You will be evicted from my land and your farmhouse will be ransomed to make good for the money you owe me. Guards!' The panic-stricken peasant implored for compassion. 'Maybe there is another solution' the shrewd, slit-eyed marquis said slowly 'Give me the hand of your young daughter in marriage and your debts will be forgiven. She will be well cared for here, away from your poverty and misery'. The peasant recoiled in horror, the marquis looked older, meaner and uglier than usual, 'But my lord, she is so young…' 'Let Providence decide

---

[1] Inspired by De Bono (1973).

then…I will put two sealed small boxes in a money bag, one with a ring and the other empty, and your daughter will choose. If she chooses the ring, she will marry me and your debt will be forgiven; if she chooses the empty box, your debt will be forgiven. We will do this in the village square on Sunday morning in front of Dun Guzepp'.

The idea of Marjanna marrying the old wicked marquis threw Marjanna and her family into great sorrow. But the deeply religious family believed that Providence will not let Marjanna marry such a horrible old man. They walked barefoot to the holy shrine in the north of the island, and prayed fervently in front of the miraculous image for divine intervention. If Marjanna chooses the right box, they will build a small chapel in their fields.

Two days before the fateful day, somebody shrouded in a black faldetta knocked on their door during the late hours of the night. It was Katerina, one of the servants of the Marquis. She had seen the marquis wrapping two small square boxes in black linen, both had a ring in them. Marjanna and her family were at a loss what to do. They had just two days left to think hard and fast to come up with a plan to uncover the deceit of the marquis.

The whole village was gathered at the church square on Sunday morning. Marjanna's heart sank when she saw the old, conceited marquis, bent on a stick with a golden eagle on the knob. A hungry, wolfish look lurked on his deep-furrowed, wrinkled face. Marjanna put her hand in the money bag and drew one of the boxes. 'Open it' ordered the marquis. Marjanna put the box on the palm of her hand and slowly and hesitantly started to unwrap the box. Suddenly a red-footed falcon dived swiftly and silently from the church steeple above the square towards Marianna, snatched the box from Marjanna's open hand, flew high in the air and disappeared. Amidst the confusion, Marjanna said 'Let us look at the remaining box in the bag, we will know then which one I have chosen'. They knew that the marquis could not admit to his dishonesty without losing his honour in front of the whole village. In the meantime, unseen to all, the well-trained and faithful falcon stealthily made his way to his master, Marjanna's fiancé, hidden in the church steeple.

Chapter 8
From Neurasthenia to Eudaimonia: Teachers' Well-Being and Resilience

One hundred years ago, a survey amongst school teachers carried by V. J. Pavia (Government of Australia 1912) reported that classroom teachers were at risk of neurasthenia or 'brain fag' as a consequence of their profession. Strain was considered an inherent aspect of the profession, higher than in other professions, severe even to breaking point. Amongst the main causes identified in the survey, the authors mentioned poor salary, poor working conditions, overcrowded curriculum, inconsistent standards, large classes, long hours and blocked career paths. Many of the concerns raised about teachers' health 100 years ago, resonate with those faced by many teachers today. Working intensity, role overload, increased class size per teacher, unacceptable pupil behaviour and lack of support from management were the top five stressors amongst teachers in Europe (ETUCE 2007). Reviews of teacher stress in the UK, USA, Canada, Australia and New Zealand, similarly identified heavy workload, pupil misbehaviour, emotional demands, excessive reforms, performance appraisal and lack of time for personal and professional development, as some of the main concerns expressed by teachers today (Bricheno et al. 2009; Wilkonson et al. 2005; Williamson and Myhill 2008; Jamieson 2006; Johnson et al. 2005; Teacher Support Network 2009).

Teaching today is considered emotional labour (Hargreaves 1998; Bricheno et al. 2009) and a highly stressful career (Smith et al. 2000; Johnson et al. 2005) with increasing levels of burnout, turnover and attrition (Moon 2007; Ingersoll 2001). A survey amongst European teachers found that burnout, depression and emotional exhaustion are the most frequently encountered stress indicators and stress reactions for teachers, particularly in primary schools (ETUCE 2007). There is decreasing interest in young people entering the profession (Moon 2007), while as much as 50 % of newly qualified teachers may leave the profession within the first 5 years (Alliance for Excellent Education 2005; Ingersoll 2003). Teaching is turning more and more into a revolving door profession (Ingersoll 2001).

Bullough (2011)

C. Cefai, V. Cavioni, *Social and Emotional Education in Primary School*, 133
DOI 10.1007/978-1-4614-8752-4_8, © Springer Science+Business Media New York 2014

8.1 A Vulnerable Profession

Kelchtermans (2011) refers to a structural vulnerability inherent to the profession, with issues such as lack of control over working conditions, the limited extent to which teachers can show the impact they make on student learning and the lack of structure to facilitate decisions in their daily practice, posing threats to their identity as effective teachers. The intensive and extended interpersonal encounters involved in teaching and classroom management generate considerable emotional work, which may lead to job dissatisfaction, emotional exhaustion and eventually burnout (Day 2011; Day and Qing 2009; Kidger et al. 2010). Emotional stress, with consequent negative impact on sense of confidence and competence, is one of the main reasons teachers cite in leaving the profession (Montgomery and Rupp 2005; Gaziel 2004).

The social and emotional baggage pupils bring with them to school as a result of the changing social realities they are growing up with, adds pressure on teachers to provide more understanding and support to their pupils (Gillham 2005). An average 15 % of teacher time in the EU is spent on maintaining order in the classroom, hampering their efforts to perform at high level of effectiveness as classroom teachers (OECD 2009). Challenging behaviour in the classroom is one of the most stressful factors in the profession (Hargreaves 2000; McLaughlin 2008; ETUCE 2007; Bricheno et al. 2009; Barmby 2006; Spratt et al. 2010). Not only does it disrupt the teaching and learning process but also it is seen as a direct threat to the teacher's own competence and authority and to the school's attempts to achieve educational targets for academic excellence in market-led educational systems (Farrell and Humphrey 2009; DfE 2010). Indeed, when asked to consider the teaching of students with individual educational needs, classroom teachers often prefer teaching students with other forms of disability or difficulty, such as physical or intellectual disabilities, rather than students with challenging behaviour (Kalambouka et al. 2007; Tanti Rigos 2009).

The pressure on teachers to improve standards and performance is another key factor rendering teaching an unattractive and stressful career for many members of the profession. The neoliberal approach to teaching as a rational, performance-oriented profession with an accent on standards, assessment and accountability, reinforced by national and international high stakes testing, benchmarks and rankings, such as the League of Tables in the UK and the OECD's Program for International Student Assessment standards, puts continuous pressure on teachers to perform. As Hargreaves (1998) put it, teachers are expected to give more and more with less support. The academic press takes the heart out of teaching with less time for personal relationships, social support, collegiality, community development and curriculum flexibility and adaptation (cf. Jamieson 2006; Valli and Buese 2007; Oplatka 2009). At the same time, pupil underachievement is often blamed on teacher incompetence and ineffectiveness (Dworkin 2009; Jamieson 2006). Increased levels of accountability and reduced autonomy and professional responsibility are set to lead to lowered self-efficacy and self-esteem (Van Veen and Sleegers 2009) as well as sense of helplessness and burnout (Dworkin 2009).

The changes and challenges being faced by teachers are likely to have a negative impact both on their well-being as well as the quality of their performance. Stress and anxiety lead to lower morale (Ingersoll 2003), sense of vulnerability and uncertainty of professional identity (Kelchtermans et al. 2009; Kelchtermans 2011), poor self-efficacy (Van Veen and Sleegers 2009; Bullough 2011) and lack of commitment, sense of helplessness and burnout (Dworkin 2009). They may set off what Jennings and Greenberg (2008) call a 'burnout cascade' with teachers becoming demotivated, losing confidence in their competence and becoming emotionally exhausted. As Moore (2004, p. 10) put it, 'stories about the easy job of teaching are sheer fiction…good teaching is demanding and exhausting work, even in the best of work places'.

It is ironic that the increasing attention to pupils' well-being and resilience has not only been seldom accompanied by a complementary focus on teachers' own well-being, but also has seen a parallel increasing focus on performance and effectiveness, posing serious threats to their (teachers') well-being (Vallie and Buese 2007; Bullough 2009). Yet, evidence shows that teachers' emotional well-being is not only symbiotic with pupils' well-being (Roffey 2011; Kidger et al. 2010; Sisak et al. 2013), but also a necessary condition for their effectiveness (Day and Qing 2009). High-quality teaching is one of the most important factors in teacher effectiveness and student learning and achievement: raising teacher quality leads to substantial and significant increase in academic achievement (OECD 2005). High-quality teaching, however, is dependent on teachers' motivation, satisfaction, commitment and positive attitudes (Bullough 2011; Day and Qing 2009). These positive attitudes and emotions help to build the teachers' cognitive, social and emotional resources, which in turn contribute to their ability to cope with the demands and stresses of the profession and to their sense of well-being (Fredrikson 2004; Frenzel et al. 2009). This is particularly true of kindergarten and primary school teachers where relationships are closer and more personal (Hargreaves 2000; Hamre and Pianta 2001).

The following sections describe how school staff's well-being and health may be addressed through an interactionist approach to well-being, focusing on both the individual and the context.

> Teachers need to look for alternative resources and to the affective knowledge of themselves and their learners in order to subvert dominant traditions that are limiting to contemporary teaching and learning needs. (Zembylas and Schutz 2009, p. 376)

8.2   Promoting Teachers' Well-Being and Resilience: An Interactionist Approach

An interactionist, biopsychosocial perspective to well-being underlines the need to equip the staff with requisite social and emotional competencies while creating a caring context which promotes their health and well-being and provides support and protection against stress and burnout. An emotionally literate school context combined with personal, social and emotional resources serves to actively promote the staff's well-being and mental health, while reducing emotional labour and the risk of burnout and psychological difficulties. It builds the staff's personal resilience while promoting resilience-enhancing school communities (Jennings and Greenberg 2009; Response Ability 2009; NEF 2009; Cooper and Jacobs 2011).

> Creating schools as organisations which care for teachers as well as pupils is no longer an option, but a necessity in the contemporary contexts of teaching. (Day and Qing 2009, p. 28)

8.2.1   Teachers' Social and Emotional Competence as a Protective Factor for Well-Being and Resilience

School teachers need to be equipped to respond effectively to the cognitive and emotional challenges of working in difficult conditions, to strengthen the relationships with colleagues, students and parents, and sustain their own motivation, sense of efficacy and personal agency (Zembylas and Schutz 2009). While teachers with inadequate social and emotional competence experience difficulty in relationship and classroom management, social and emotionally competent teachers have not only a positive impact on the pupils' own social and emotional learning, but they are also able to understand, prevent and cope effectively with some of the many stressors inherent in the profession (Leithwood and Beatty 2008; Jennings and Greenberg 2009). In this respect, whilst lack of social and emotional competence constitutes a risk factor for teachers' well-being, its presence operates as a protective factor, leading to effective coping and resilience in the face of stress. Socially and emotionally competent teachers have high emotional awareness and understanding, being aware of their own strengths and weaknesses, and being able to regulate their emotions. They also have high social awareness and skills, being able to understand the perspectives and feelings of others, relate effectively, prosocially and collaboratively with others, and are able to engage in responsible decision-making (Jennings and Greenberg 2009). In their classroom practice, they are able to build healthy relationships, demonstrate more positive and effective classroom management and implement the social and emotional education (SEE) curriculum more effectively through role modelling. These practices contribute to the development of a healthy classroom climate which in turn feeds back into the teachers' own social and emotional competence and well-being (Bandura 1977; Jennings and Greenberg 2009). The positive emotions, supportive relationships, job satisfaction, and enhanced self-efficacy resulting from social and emotional competence in turn serve as antidote against the stresses teachers are set to face in their daily practice (Goddard et al. 2004).

Education in social and emotional competence may be organised in various ways at both initial teacher education and in-service professional learning, with experiential professional learning experience in emotional awareness and management and in social awareness and relationship building. It is particularly critical at initial education programmes so that prospective teachers would develop the requisite competencies earlier on in their career and would thus help to prevent burnout and attrition in the first years of teaching (Murray 2005).

Initial teacher education and in-service professional learning would also need to address the areas such as:

- *Child development and classroom management*: Knowledge of children's social and emotional development, learning and behaviour will increase teachers' insight into child behaviour and enable them to build healthy and caring relationships with children, create caring classroom climate, and deal effectively with challenging interpersonal contexts (Hargreaves 1998; Jennings and Greenberg 2009).
- *Teaching SEE*: Developing the competencies to teach SEE through experiential learning activities will enable classroom teachers to be more effective in supporting students' social and emotional needs and facilitate their social and emotional learning, which will in turn feed back into teachers' well-being through enhanced self-efficacy, sense of control, engagement and satisfaction (Goddard et al. 2004; Jennings and Greenberg 2009).

Box 8.1 Practical steps for implementing professional development on mental health and well-being (Mind Matters 2012)

- Have specific and regular professional development on mental health and well-being for staff.
- Focus professional development on key aspects like empathy, the facts about the lives of children, mental health research and practical ideas for the classroom.
- Use the occupational health and safety committee members as a possible focus.
- Ensure all staff has provision for quiet work areas.
- Have a staffroom where all the staff can gather.
- Build in regular appropriate social events.
- Include all staff in professional development on mental health and well-being.

- Survey staff on mental health and well-being regularly.
- Encourage opportunities for team teaching of social and emotional learning.
- Have interactive sessions, discussions and short social and emotional learning activities as starters or as part of the staff meetings.
- Allow time to talk through attitudes to the connections between academic outcomes, behaviour, education and social and emotional learning.
- Reintroduce and review staff-counselling arrangements.
- Provide updated information on student and staff mental health and well-being issues and research on the staff intranet.
- Review job role descriptions.
- Review the staff induction, exit strategies by asking staff recently arrived or needing to leave.

- *Mindfulness training*: Mindfulness is a useful tool to cultivate teachers' 'habits of mind' promoting their health, well-being and competence to develop supportive relationships with students and create classroom climate conducive to positive engagement and behaviour (Roeser et al. 2012). It has been linked to both emotional awareness and management and to social awareness and healthier relationships (Shapiro et al. 1998; Brown and Ryan 2003). Studies carried out with classroom teachers have found that mindfulness training enhances self-awareness, positive affect and compassion (Kemeny et al. 2012; Jennings et al. 2012; Lantieri et al. 2011), better relationships and equanimity in charged emotional environments such as the classroom (Burrows 2011a), and reduces stress symptoms, negative affect, depression and anxiety (Kemeny et al. 2012; Jennings et al. 2012; Thomas 2010; Winzelberg and Luskin 1999). Burrows (2011b) reported that awareness of thoughts, feelings and bodily reactions enabled a shift in teachers' attitude, facilitating self-regulation as well as openness, responsiveness and sensitivity. In a study with primary school teachers, Lantieri et al. (2011) reported that mindfulness training led to increased mindfulness and better relationships with colleagues, and to a better classroom climate which had a positive impact on students' engagement and emotional learning. In a review of mindfulness intervention studies with teachers in both primary and secondary schools, Jennings et al. (2012) reported significant positive benefits both for the teachers' classroom practice such as enhanced relationships with pupils and more effective classroom management, as well as improved sense of well-being and health. They concluded that mindfulness is a pathway towards the realisation of caring and effective teachers
- *Self-efficacy*: Enhancing teachers' self-efficacy is a key area for professional learning in view of its protective effect on teachers' sense of competence and effectiveness, and consequently their mental health and well-being. High self-efficacy has been found to protect stressed teachers from becoming burnt out and leave the profession (Schwarzer and Hallum 2008; Skaalvik and Skaalvik

2010), and is particularly crucial in the early years of teaching as teachers are establishing their professional identity in the classroom as well as in the profession (Day and Gu 2007). Furthermore, the staff's collective self-efficacy is instrumental in promoting a climate conducive to staff's health and well-being (Gibbs and Powell 2012). In a review of studies, Brown (2012) reported that the strength of the relationship between teachers' self-efficacy and burnout appeared to be stronger for one component of burnout, namely depersonalisation, which is the perceived sense of lack of control at work. The author suggests that a sense of classroom and school belonging and community would provide teachers protection from this component of burnout. This is discussed further in the next section.

Box 8.2 Mindfulness training with Australian teachers (from Burrows 2012)

One participant, 'Lea', an upper primary teacher whose focus for the mindfulness training project is 11-year-old 'Jade' who has been diagnosed with oppositional defiance disorder, became aware through her mindfulness practice of how her personal well-being was being effected by Jade's 'dominating loud voice' and demands, so much so that she began to feel 'emotionally lost' and that she 'could not go on any more'. One night she even dreamt there was an education inspector in her classroom. Then as she writes, something shifted:

That night I did the mindfulness practice with some focus on relaxing the tension out of my body. I woke the next day with a deep sense of hope. I decided to do the 15 min of no interaction mindfulness exercise you asked us to do, with him, just observing his behavior and not reacting. It was the longest 15 min ever. I noticed my urge to comment on his every action after 2 min. I noticed he kept looking at me for attention. I was relaxed and ignored him. After that I started standing back, watching my usual habitual thoughts instead of reacting to the content. That afternoon I began to interact with him differently and I noticed he seemed to cut back on yelling out in class.

The next day I woke without a headache, first time in 5 weeks. After the mindful walk I felt positive and inspired, ready for the day. I find I am becoming clearer in myself and when I am about to launch into my old pattern I step back and try a new tack. The space I give myself to respond helps calm my response somewhat and gives me a chance to consciously respond, not out of habit but giving a space for a new thought to come in. I am grateful for the changes in myself as they have helped Jade also change as I'm not 'nagging' him it gives him the opportunity to respond differently and improve.

Jade's behavior has improved out of sight. He has been able to change course. Jade ended the week with perfect behavior, he worked on a pine branch, sanding and filing it smooth during his break times. He was really proud of his work. He also wrote a beautiful poem on the environment. That night I dreamt that it was snowing and I felt peaceful.

I feel as though I have filtered out the extraneous negative and stressed thoughts and am left with the essential thoughts. Thanks.

8.2.2   A Caring Professional Community Supporting Staff's Well-Being

Teachers who work in collaborative, collegial and cohesive schools are more innovative in their work, more energetic and enthusiastic, and more open to personal and professional development; they are also more committed to addressing pupils' needs and supporting their learning (McLaughlin and Talbot 2006; Nieto 2003). Moreover, staff's own sense of belonging and community has a positive, added impact on pupils' learning and behaviour (Bryk et al. 1999; Battistich et al. 1997). When teachers' own interpersonal needs are addressed, they are more likely to pay more attention to, and feel more competent to address, the personal needs of their own pupils (Kidger et al. 2010; Sisak, 2013). Sergiovanni (1996) underlines the need to acknowledge the link between what happens to teachers and what happens to students: 'the idea of making classrooms into learning communities for students will remain more rhetoric than real unless schools also become learning communities for teachers' (p. 42). In caring school communities, staff enjoy caring and supportive relationships with colleagues, administration and parents, they are actively and meaningfully engaged in the life of the school, feel supported in their needs by the school administration and have an important say in what happens at the school, and share a collective common goal which they work collaboratively to achieve (Bryk et al. 1999; Battistich et al. 1997; Sergiovanni 1994; Cefai 2008). A supportive context does not only promote well-being and maximisation of potential, but also it mediates the negative impact of stress, helping to prevent burnout (Howard and Johnson 2004; Brown 2012).

The school administration plays a critical role in developing a sense of belonging and community amongst staff, establishing meaningful relationships, promoting a culture of trust and care, and providing opportunities for active, meaningful and influential staff engagement; conversely, restrictive and unsupportive administration leads to low teacher morale and confidence, absenteeism and burnout (Gaziel 2004; Dworkin 2009; Goddard et al. 2004; Brown 2012). Organisational school supports to promote staff well-being may include amongst others (MindMatters 2012; Response Ability 2009):

- Appropriate professional learning in the various aspects of student and staff well-being and social and emotional competence according to the particular needs of the school community;
- Supporting staff in the use of new procedures and technology;

- Providing structures for staff to work collaboratively and participate actively in school decisions while retaining their sense of autonomy, and to spend social time together;
- Ensuring equal opportunities;
- Providing opportunities for recognition and celebration of strengths and achievements;
- Providing psychological support to new staff and staff in difficulty such as buddy systems, critical friends and mentoring schemes, and counselling and other forms of psychological intervention.

Our leadership team is really supportive. They're very encouraging, they encourage us to do whatever we feel is the best way to go, and they help to facilitate that. We're working at the moment on creating spaces where our children can feel really safe to learn. Yesterday one of the leadership team came to our spaces to have a chat with my team on this project. It's really nice because I think in some sense they scaffold us in our own way, and they're very positive at doing it one step at a time. You know they hold our hand through it as well, and let us go when we're ready to go, and that's been a really positive experience for myself, as I'm still a fairly new teacher. (Ms Sally, primary school teacher)

We're made to feel that it's ok, if we need to take some time off for our family…. You know like sometimes with the pressures of family I need to do something for my kids…the school appreciates that our families are also important for us. Before, we were made to feel bad for being a mother and having to take time off in order to take care of a sick child. Here we don't, it's ok. When you get treated like that you give a 100% back. (Ms Amanda, primary school teacher)

Mentoring is an important pathway to caring relationships, collegiality and support, and has been found to act as a protective factor against attrition, particularly amongst early teachers (Kelley 2004; Smith and Ingersoll 2004; Marable and Raimondi 2007). In their review of the impact of mentoring and induction of newly qualified teachers, Ingersoll and Strong (2011) found that it has a positive impact on teachers' commitment and retention, teachers' classroom practices and student achievement. Mentoring may take different forms, addressing the various roles the teacher is engaged in, such as the transformative and reflective perspective (reconsidering and reconstructing knowledge of teaching), the situated apprentice perspective (underlining the sociocultural perspective on learning), and the critical constructivist perspective (helping the teachers construe a more emancipation-based professional identify; Blasé 2009). The humanistic perspective focuses on providing emotional support to help colleagues develop positive and productive professional identify, deal with the challenges and stresses of the profession, find solutions to problems and improve teacher confidence and self-efficacy (Bullough 2009). It has been found to be particularly effective in reducing teacher attrition, especially amongst new teachers (Blasé 2008). The mentoring processes involved in reducing attrition include having the mentors and mentees from a common subject/field in the same school, time and opportunity to work collaboratively with other teachers in the same field, well-prepared mentors, induction for new teachers and external support networks (Smith and Ingersoll 2004).

Box 8.3 The mentoring journal (Staff Matters 2005, p. 1)

Undertaking mentoring

- Mentoring works best if voluntary, for both the mentor and the mentee.
- Mentoring works best when there is a level of choice available to both mentor and mentee.
- Mentoring works best if all members of a group or staff undertake the exercise of mentoring in some form.
- Mentoring is best limited to a particular period of time or for a particular event.
- Mentoring needs resources—the main resource is time, but can also include a quiet space in which to talk, and tea or coffee and biscuits.
- Expectations of both parties need to be made clear very early in the process.
- Mentoring needs to have a two-way component, i.e. benefits for the mentor as well as the mentee. For the mentor this might be skills building and feedback on listening skills.
- Mentoring is not a substitute or another name for other staff development, e.g. a renewal program, supervision, line management or performance management.

The initial conversation

The initial conversation between people is important. Think about covering the following:

1. Your (both mentor and mentee) purpose for undertaking mentoring,
2. How to handle conflict or disagreement,
3. A meeting schedule,
4. A small standard agenda for each meeting,
5. Air time,
6. Resolution and action,
7. Recording,
8. Discussion topics,

9. Communication and cancellation procedures,
10. The skills and/or experience of the mentee,
11. The skills and/or experience of the mentor,
12. The resolution/celebration of the mentoring process,
13. The evaluation of the mentoring process.

8.3 Against the Odds: Promoting Resilience Amongst Teachers

Bruce Johnson and his colleagues at the University of South Australia have been working on identifying the factors that protect teachers from burnout, with a particular focus on factors which promote resilience in the face of teacher stress. Hardiness, namely an internal locus of control, agency and sense of commitment in the face of problems, lack of rumination on negative past events, distancing from, and objective analysis of, unpleasant experiences, and the presence of strong support from colleagues and administration are the key factors which have been found to help teachers to cope effectively with the demands and stresses in their work (Howard and Johnson 2004). Enhancing these personal and contextual factors will inoculate teachers from being burnt out and reduce the risk of teacher attrition. Johnson and his team (Johnson et al. 2010) have developed a resilience framework targeting early career teachers on the basis of feedback from such teachers and school leaders in a number of schools in South and Western Australia. The framework is designed as a heuristic tool to generate discussion amongst key stakeholders on how to support early career teacher resilience. It consists of five main themes with a number of key targets in each theme as follows:

- *Relationships*: the social and professional networks, human connections and belongingness experienced by early career teachers. Resilience is fostered when schools focus on their complex emotional needs by promoting relationships based on respect, trust, care and integrity as follows:

    - Promoting a sense of belonging, acceptance, and well-being
    - Fostering pedagogical and professional growth
    - Promoting collective ownership and responsibility

- *School culture*: the values, beliefs, norms, assumptions, behaviours and relationships that characterise the daily rituals of school life. Resilience is enhanced in schools that actively promote collaborative relationships, professional learning communities, educative forms of leadership and democratic decision-making:

    - Promoting a sense of belongingness and social connectedness
    - Developing educative, democratic and empowering ways of working
    - Providing formal and informal transition and induction processes
    - Developing a professional learning community

- *Teacher identity*: the development of one's awareness and understanding of self as a teacher. Resilience is more likely to take place when teachers successfully engage in processes of self-reflection and self-understanding, sustaining a coherent sense of personal identity while at the same time allowing for the emergence of a robust teacher identity:
  - Understanding the interplay between personal and professional identities
  - Engaging in self-reflection
  - Enabling the development of a strong sense of agency, efficacy and self-worth

- *Teachers' work*: the complex array of skills, practices, knowledge, relationships and ethical considerations that comprise the role of the teacher, acknowledging the ways in which teachers' work is being reshaped in the context of a broader set of economic, political and cultural conditions. Resilience is promoted when the focus is on understanding the complex, intense and unpredictable nature of teachers' work rather than on individual deficits and victim blaming:
  - Acknowledging the complex, intense and unpredictable nature of teachers' work
  - Developing teachers' curriculum and pedagogical knowledge and strategies
  - Providing support to create engaging learning environments
  - Ensuring access to appropriate ongoing support, resources and learning opportunities

- *Policies and practices*: the officially mandated statements, guidelines, values and prescriptions. Resilience is enhanced when systems' policies and practices show a strong commitment to the principles and values of social justice, teacher agency and voice, community engagement and respect for local knowledge and practice:
  - Providing relevant, rigorous and responsive preservice preparation for the profession
  - Creating innovative partnerships and initiatives that assist smooth transitions to the workforce
  - Implementing transparent, fair and responsive employment processes

---

Box 8.4 Risk and protective factors in teacher well-being and resilience (Response Ability 2009)

Personal factors:

Protective: job satisfaction, personal fulfilment from work, ongoing education and skills development, problem focused coping style, empathy and warmth

    Risk: social exclusion or isolation, lack of training/experience, inadequate coping strategies, feelings of helplessness, temperament

Organisational factors:

Protective: primary prevention in the workplace, support from other staff members, appropriate training and career development, support for new technologies, involvement of staff in decision-making, equal opportunities, culture of help seeking/disclosure, opportunity to demonstrate worth and talent

Risk: high workload, little support and low control, excessive admin duties, staff shortages, inadequate support and supervision, role conflict, lack of control over one's work, hierarchical communication, lack of recognition

Work factors:

Protective: additional supports, mentoring

Risk: demanding work, continuous and fragmented change, high-need students and clients

Most effective approach for staff mental health share responsibility for mental health between the individual and the organisation: supporting staff to build personal resilience while simultaneously creating a protective organisation that provides every opportunity for its members to operate at the peak of their capacity.

8.4   Promoting Teachers' Well-Being: Identifying Targets for Improvement

The staff well-being indicators in Table 8.1 are presented as a guide for the school staff to engage in a self-evaluation exercise to improve their health and well-being. The indicators are an extension and elaboration of those presented in the previous chapter and could be organised within the whole-school approach discussed in that chapter. Once completed by the school staff, the results are then used to identify the strengths and areas for improvement in each of the three areas, namely staff relationships, staff engagement and staff well-being. Subgroups may draw a plan of action for a particular area which is then discussed with the whole staff. Following the identification of targets for intervention, these are then prioritised and a plan of action is developed to implement the chosen targets. The plan will detail what activities will be held, the people who will be involved, the resources needed, the target date for implementation and ways for monitoring and evaluating the action plan. In keeping with the earlier recommended collaborative approach, it is recommended that plans of action are drawn collectively by the whole-school staff. Collaborative planning, faithful implementation, continued monitoring and regular evaluation are critical to the success of any initiative.

Table 8.1 Indicators for staff well-being

STAFF WELLBEING INDICATORS	
3= In place 2= Partly in Place/Needs Improvement 1= Not in Place	
Processes and indicators	
A. We have caring and supportive relationships	
A1	I am a proud member of the school community	
A.2	I feel valued in our school	
A.3	There is a strong sense of collegiality amongst our staff	
A4	Our staff understands, supports and cares for one other	
A5	I feel comfortable discussing work problems with my colleagues	
A6	Our staff solves problems together constructively	
A7	Our staff acts as mentors and critical friends for each other	
A8	I provide support to colleagues experiencing personal or professional difficulties	
A9	Our staff celebrates each others' achievements and events like birthdays	
A10	Our staff welcomes and values feedback from colleagues	
A11	Our staff value respects each other, irrespective of their roles	
A12	I have a very good relationship with the school's administration	
B13	New members of staff are welcomed, valued and supported at the school	
A14	I am understood and supported by the administration	
A15	Our administration is concerned and cares about the wellbeing of the staff	
C16	I feel understood and supported by the local educational authorities	
A17	I get on very well with our pupils at the school	
A18	I maintain frequent and regular communication with the parents/carers	
	Targets for Improvement	
B. We are meaningfully and influentially engaged in the school community	
B1	I am well informed about the school's policies	
B2	I am actively involved in various SEE activities across the school	
B3	I have autonomy to adapt the curriculum and assessment according to the needs of the pupils	
B4	I am given particular roles and responsibilities at the school	
B5	We have the space to discuss and resolve school issues together	
B6	I have the opportunity and support to develop my own strengths at the school	
B7	I participate actively in the activities organized at the school	
B8	I participate actively in staff meetings and school development sessions	
B9	I amactively involved in curriculum planning and policy development	
B10	Our staff is highly committed and sets high professional standards	
B11	I am provided with adequate support, resources and technology in my work	
B12	I plan, work and share practice and resources with my colleagues at the school	
B13	There are a number of teaching partnerships and mentoring schemes in our school	
C14	Our school has in place procedures to promote staff collaboration and constructive conflict resolution	
B15	All members of our staff are treated equally and their contribution is equally valued	
C16	I feel confident and competent in addressing the social and emotional needs of the pupils	
C17	Our school organises professional learning days for staff in teaching and promoting SEE	
C18	Our school organises professional learning days for staff in child development, mental health and behaviour management	
	Targets for Improvement:	

Table 8.1 (continued)

C. Our emotional well being and education are adequately addressed and supported		
C1	Our school organises professional learning sessions for staff in the development of its social and emotional competence	
C2	I have received education in developing my social and emotional competencies	
C3	Our school organises professional learning days for staff on its own health and wellbeing	
C4	Our school has a good understanding of the staff's social and emotional needs and addresses such needs proactively	
C5	Our school acknowledges and celebrates the staff's strengths and achievements	
C6	We have adequate designated areas where we can take a break	
C7	Our staff has ample opportunity to socialise and connect with each other	
C8	Our school gives importance to the staff's satisfaction and fulfilment in their job	
C9	I have ample opportunity to be creative and autonomous in my work	
C10	I have ample opportunity to apply for positions, roles and promotions	
C11	Our school is a safe and secure place to work in	
C12	Our school has adequate provisions to address staff bullying, harassment or discrimination by administration, colleagues, pupils or parents	
C13	Our school has provisions in place to safeguard the health and safety of our staff	
C14	I work in a physical environment which contributes to my physical and mental health	
C15	Our school has a policy to prevent and reduce staff stress and burnout	
C16	Our school has provisions to help staff cope with, and manage, stress and psychological difficulties	
C17	Our school provides extra support to staff working with vulnerable and/or challenging pupils	
C18	Our school has provisions for quick access to professional advice and assistance for our staff	
	Targets for Improvement:	

Some of items in this checklist have been informed by other existing checklists, namely National Curriculum Council Focus Group for Inclusive Education (2002) and ASD (2012)

The man with the lamp and the divine emperor

Corinth, Ancient Greece, 336 BC

The young king of Macedon headed an army of 3,000 cavalrymen south towards the Peloponnese to regain control of the rebel cities and states. City after city were added to the empire in the sweeping whirlwind from the north. At Corinth, Alexander asked to be taken to the old man living in a barrel near the Craneum in the market square. He wanted to meet the eccentric but wise Diogenes who had rejected the artificiality and vanity of his fellow human beings and their constant search for worldly pleasures and wealth. The one who called for a return to nature and simplicity, arguing that human beings had complicated every simple gift of the gods. At midday, he was frequently seen roaming the streets of the city with his burning lamp in search of the ever elusive human virtues such as honesty.

As the royal cavalry arrived at the market square, Alexander dismounted and walked to Diogenes who was enjoying the sunshine in the barrel. 'Noble doctor of the soul, your wise words have reached us up in Macedon. Let us know your wish and it shall be granted to you as a noble citizen of this city'. Diogenes thought for a little while and replied, 'Indeed I do have one, sire. If you move sideways, I can continue enjoying the sunshine'. Amidst the uproar of the crowd and the wrath of the generals, Alexander smiled and was heard saying 'But verily, if I were not Alexander, I would be Diogenes'.

That evening Alexander ordered a great banquet to celebrate his appointment as Hegemon of the city. His mind and heart were serene that night, free from the guilt of past misdeeds, the uncertainties of the future, and the burdens of his grand plan for the Levant and the Indus. As he sat down with his close and trusted friends that evening, he paused to enjoy the sound of the lyre music, the golden voices of the Delphi priestesses, the colours and elegant movements of the young dancers, the taste of the juicy, sun-kissed grapes. The music never sounded so melodious, the singing never so enchanting, the dancers never so mesmerising, the grapes never so delicious, the present never so serene, life never so worth celebrating! He never felt so close to his father Zeus. By Diogenes, long live the present!

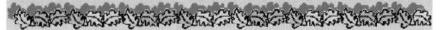

Chapter 9
Reaching Out: Parents'/Caregivers' Engagement, Education and Well-Being

A review of over 100 parent and family intervention studies underlines what we have long known, namely that parents/families and educators are both essential for children's academic and social outcomes in school (Carlson and Christenson 2005). Parents'/Caregivers' dynamic relationship with the school has long been recognized as a key factor in their children's education (e.g. Hattie 2009; El Nokali et al. 2010; Jeynes 2007; Fan and Chen 2001). There has been relatively less attention in educational research, however, to the impact of home–school collaboration on children's well-being and mental health, and to the parents' own social and emotional competence and well-being in relation to education. In its report on social and emotional well-being in primary schools, the *National Institute for Health and Clinical Excellence* (NICE 2008), suggests that one of the areas for further research is the identification of the most effective ways to involve parents/caregivers in primary school programmes to improve children's emotional and social well-being. This has gained particular significance with the introduction of social and emotional education (SEE) in schools in the past decades, and the realization that the home–school collaboration not only ensures parents' own collaboration in facilitating the school's goals for SEE, but also addresses parents' own education, well-being and resilience, which in turn impacts their children's social and emotional development (Weare and Nind 2011, Greenberg 2010; Humphrey et al. 2010; Downey and Williams 2010). Through such collaboration parents would develop positive attitudes towards SEE, dispelling fears about mental health stigmatization, and concerns about 'wasting' time on SEE at the expense of academic learning. They would also support the school's efforts in SEE by reinforcing and teaching the competencies being taught in school. They would also develop their own social and emotional skills in the process, and consequently their parenting skills.

9.1 Parents as Active and Equal Partners in Education

When parents/caregivers are engaged in a collaborative working relationship with schools in the implementation of social and emotional learning (SEL) initiatives, such interventions are more likely to be effective in promoting pupils' social and emotional

C. Cefai, V. Cavioni, *Social and Emotional Education in Primary School*,
DOI 10.1007/978-1-4614-8752-4_9, © Springer Science+Business Media New York 2014

learning. Various evaluations and reviews of SEE programmes in schools show that programmes which involve parents and the local community as key partners in the delivery of the programmes, are more likely to be effective in terms of pupils' academic, social and emotional learning (Downey and Williams 2010; Durlack et al 2011; Greenberg et al. 2003; Weare and Nind 2011; Catalano et al. 2004; Wells et al. 2003; Stormshak et al. 2005, 2000; Cooper and Jacobs 2011). Parental involvement and collaboration go beyond the more common but equally important exchanges about the learning and emotional needs and concerns of the child and/or family. Many SEE programmes include specific homework tasks for parents/caregivers to implement with their children, thus reinforcing the social and emotional competencies being learnt at school (e.g. Elias et al. 1997, Kusche and Greenberg 1994; Bernard 2012b; McGrath and Noble 2010; Cavioni 2013). Parents may also be invited at the school to participate more actively in the planning, implementation and evaluation of SEE programmes, or even help with teaching or mentoring pupils in these competencies in the classroom (e.g. Chapman 1999). Such an approach resonates with the more general framework on parents' involvement in education developed by Epstein et al. (2002) which identifies six types of parental involvement. These include parenting education; school–home communication about school programmes and pupils' progress; parental help and support for school programmes and pupil activities; providing information to parents/caregivers about how to help students with learning activities at home; including parents/caregivers in decision making at the school; and collaborating with the local community in making use of community resources and services for both the school and the families.

The school, in collaboration with the local community, may operate as an inclusive and parent-friendly centre for parental collaboration, education and well-being, providing accessible and culture-sensitive information and resources, support, links to community services and facilities, family learning assignments, parenting education programmes and personal development courses. This provides opportunities for parents/caregivers to make an authentic, meaningful and influential contribution to the SEE initiatives at the school, to contribute actively to the well-being of their children at home, to develop social and emotional competence both as parents/caregivers and individuals, to promote their own health, well-being and resilience, and to promote the well-being of their local community. Some of the school activities that promote parental collaboration, education and well-being may be included amongst others (MindMatters 2012; Centers for Disease Control and Prevention 2012):

- Consulting parents/caregivers about policies, events and initiatives
- Encouraging parental representation on school and community committees
- Inviting parents/caregivers to professional development with staff
- Organizing parent/caregiver focus groups on the role of the school
- Having regular parents/caregivers open days
- Including parents/caregivers in the design and evaluation of SEE initiatives at the school
- Providing a welcoming parent/caregiver resource centre at the school to serve as a basis for parents'/caregivers' engagement and education, and which includes parent/caregiver and community resources
- Sponsoring mentoring programmes and other SEE initiatives involving parents/caregivers

- Developing outreach parent/caregiver education facilities, such as mobile parent/caregiver centres in the community, use of community centres and facilities, and involvement of community groups
- Organizing meetings and seminars on child development, behaviour management, well-being and mental health for parents/caregivers
- Coordinating seminars and workshops on developing the parents'/caregivers' own social and emotional skills, parenting skills, and leadership and advocacy skills
- Holding family learning projects involving parents/caregivers and children working together on SEE projects
- Using a range of virtual and face-to-face communication strategies
- Hosting social and informal gatherings
- Holding school meetings in homes and the community
- Involving parents/caregivers in classroom activities and whole school activities, including teaching, mentoring and coaching.

9.2 Parental Education and Well-Being

Parental education is central to the success of universal interventions in the promotion of SEE in school, particularly at primary school level (Adi et al. 2007; Cooper and Jacobs 2011; Weare and Nind 2011; Wells et al. 2003; Cavioni 2013). Parental education has also been found to be one of the most effective strategies in supporting the education of children with social, emotional and behaviour difficulties (e.g. Borman et al. 2007; Ogden and Sorlie 2009; Cooper and Jacobs 2011; Shucksmith et al. 2007). Such interventions often include teaching parents key social and emotional literacy competencies which they can make use in their own interactions with their children. Weare (2004) cites various studies which have shown that children with social, emotional and behaviour difficulties receiving SEE stand to benefit when their parents receive parallel training in the area, not only because their (children's) social and emotional competence is reinforced at school and at home, but also as parents become more skilled in parenting.

> **Box 9.1 Home–school collaboration in the early years (Ms Ann, Early Years' Teacher)**
>
> We work very closely with the parents. When we start the year, we have a settling period where parents come in and stay at the school until the children feel safe and settled with us. We also have a handbook for parents where we give them information about our school, our curriculum, how they can communicate with us, how we can collaborate. I also organize a pocket system where I and the parents exchange messages through a pocket children bring daily with them. I am also in contact with some of the parents via email, but not all parents have emails. The administration also has a newsletter for parents and a section for parents on the school's website. I also organize home activities for parents

where they can help their children with some of the material we are doing here. I also keep a learning journey for each kid, documenting their learning engagement at school and which gives the child and parent the opportunity to discuss together the child's learning during that day. Sometimes we have morning tea for parents to come and discuss with us what we are doing at the school and how their kids are doing. We have a family support coordinator, offering parenting support and she liaises very closely with social services. Our school also has a community development support officer who works with the community, mostly with school community, sometimes with the border community. She does a lot of work with indigenous groups and minorities, such as running an aboriginal leadership team at the school, also bringing indigenous families to the centre/school, and organising BBQs and health checks for the family. The school was having a problem with the behaviour of a special needs child from an ethnic minority family, and the mum came to the school and said she needed help as the parenting skills course she was going to was not appropriate because the people organizing it did not understand the culture barrier for her. She was the only female in the household and did not know what to do. So the community development officer offered to organize a support group for women from similar ethnic-cultural minorities and got the community liaison office to come to the school to help them organise their own behaviour parenting support... now the group of families is getting bigger and it is run by the parents themselves, the community officer just provides space, information and resources.

In their review on parent education programmes that work, Cooper and Jacobs (2011) reported that empirically validated programmes contain common cognitive behaviour techniques, such as teaching parents/caregivers strategies to extinguish unwanted behaviour and reinforce desirable behaviour, and reflective and cognitive interventions such as reframing and behavioural contracting directly related to the behaviour. This resonates with another review by Carlson and Christenson (2005) who similarly found that parent education programmes that target specific behaviours to be learned are more likely to be effective. Cooper and Jacobs' (2011) review cite a meta-analytic review of studies by Kaminski et al. (2008) on successful parenting programmes for children aged up to 8 years. The review identified three key components of most effective parenting programmes, namely instruction in positive interactions with the child, encouragement of emotional communication and practising with their own child. Such programmes are also held at the parents'/caregivers' own community setting, such as schools, and are delivered by agencies that parents/caregivers trust and have faith in, such as having school staff as co-facilitators of components of the programme (Cooper and Jacobs 2011). Additional support systems addressing the particular needs of the community and the parents/caregivers, is another key factor of successful parental education. Parenting education programmes thus need to take into consideration the needs of the parents/caregivers themselves, including their socio-economic situation, cultural diversity and psychological well-being, besides parenting skills on their own (NICE 2008; Cooper and Jacobs 2011).

Cooper and Jacobs (2011) argue against taking a paternalistic, judgemental or even blaming approach in parental education and collaboration. In contrast to the deficit model, a well-being and resilience perspective regards parents/caregivers as active partners in a whole-school approach to well-being and health, contributing proactively to the efforts of the school in promoting SEE in the school community. As in the case of the staff themselves, the parents'/caregivers' own education and well-being as well as their social and emotional competence, are central to an effective whole-school approach to well-being. This puts the onus and responsibility on the school not only to recruit the collaboration and active participation of the parents and the community in its SEE programmes, but also to address the social and emotional needs of the parents/caregivers themselves in a collaborative, reciprocal partnership. It does away with such attitudes that schools are not responsible for parents'/caregivers' or families' well-being or that they should not 'interfere' in their affairs. Even in cases of parents/caregivers and families facing socio-economic, social and psychological difficulties, they need to be approached sympathetically and assumed to have an important contribution to make to the school's efforts in promoting SEE (Cooper and Jacobs 2011). When parents/caregivers believe that their contribution is welcome and that it will help to improve their children's well-being, they are more likely to take an active role in school activities (Green et al. 2007).

What is important here is that the approach taken by the school is respectful, inclusive and sensitive to the circumstances and needs of the parents/caregivers, families and the community (MindMatters 2012). It is sensitive to the diverse cultures in the community which the school is serving, particularly issues related to understandings and beliefs about mental health and well-being in the community. The school staff takes these issues into consideration when planning and undertaking SEE initiatives, and in its collaboration with the parents/caregivers and members of the community. In a review of the literature, Henderson and Mapp (2002) reported that schools that are successful in engaging parents/caregivers and families from diverse backgrounds have three key practices in common, namely they seek to build trusting collaborative relationships among teachers, families and community members; they recognize and address families' needs and class and cultural differences; and they share power and responsibility with parents/caregivers and families. Other strategies to develop sensitivity to families and community culture may include amongst others, involving cultural workers and community groups in school initiatives; celebrating and participating in cultural events; making school facilities available for use by community partners and organizations that will host activities for pupils and their parents/caregivers; promoting staff participating in cultural enrichment courses; and utilizing parent/caregiver and community expertise (MindMatters 2012; Centers for Disease Control and Prevention 2012).

CASEL together with the Mid-Atlantic Regional Laboratory for Student Success (2005b) provide online information on tools and resources for parents'/caregivers' education, including sections on SEL Parenting Articles, Tools, and Booklets; SEL Parenting Books; Child Development and Healthy well-being Books; and Online Social and Emotional Development Resources. Similarly, KidsMatter (2012b) has an online section on Family Matters providing information sheets and other resources for parents'/caregivers' education.

Box 9.2   The role of the school in promoting parents'/caregivers' collaboration, education and well-being (KidsMatter 2012a)

Kids Matter Primary (2012a) is a national framework for the promotion of mental health in Australian primary schools. The framework consists of four components, namely positive school community, social and emotional learning for students, working with parents and caregivers, and helping children with mental health difficulties. The family/caregivers component consists of three major school initiatives in working with parents/caregivers:

1. Collaborative working relationships with parents/caregivers. The school planning, policies and practices support collaborative working relationships with parents/caregivers: this includes proactive strategies to engage the parents in collaborative efforts to promote children's mental health, well-being and learning.
2. Support for parenting. School staff communicates effectively with parents/caregivers about their children in areas related to child development, learning and mental health and well-being, and identifies and facilities access for parents/caregivers to resources and services that support parenting.
3. Parent/Caregiver support networks. The school provides opportunities for parent/caregivers to connect with each other and develop support networks, and identifies and promotes community groups as sources of support for parents/caregivers.

9.3   Promoting Parents'/Caregivers' Engagement, Education and Well-Being: Identifying Targets for Improvement

The following indicators are presented as a guide for parents/caregivers to engage in a self-evaluation exercise in examining their engagement at the school as well as their school's efforts to enhance their education and well-being as parents/caregivers. The indicators are an extension and elaboration of those presented in Chap. 7 and could be organized within the whole-school approach discussed in that chapter. Once completed by the parents/caregivers, the results may then be used to identify strengths and areas for improvement in each of the three areas, namely parents'/caregivers' relationships, parents'/caregivers' engagement, and parents'/caregivers' well-being. It is highly recommended that this exercise be undertaken by the parents/caregivers themselves with the support of the school as necessary. Following the identification of targets for intervention, these are then prioritised and discussed with the school staff so that a plan of action is developed collaboratively. The plan will detail what activities will be held, the people who will be involved, the resources needed, the target dates for implementation and ways for monitoring and evaluating the action plan. Parents–staff collaborative planning, faithful implementation, continued monitoring and regular evaluation are critical to the success of any initiative (Table 9.1).

Table 9.1 Indicators for parents'/caregivers' engagement, education and well-being

PARENTS'/CAREGIVERS' ENGAGEMENT, EDUCATION AND WELL-BEING INDICATORS

4 = true for most of the time
3 = frequently true
2 = occasionally true
1 = rarely true

	Section A: Relationships	
1	I feel welcome at the school	
2	I feel part of the school community	
3	I am happy that my child/ren attend/s this school	
4	I feel included and valued at the school	
5	This school is open for everybody whatever background or difference	
6	I work very well with the school staff	
7	I have frequent contact with the class teacher and other members of staff	
8	I attend school meetings and activities regularly	
9	I take an interest in what happens at the school and communicate frequently	
10	The staff listens and takes action to address my concerns	
	Targets for improvement:	

	Section B: Participation and involvement	
1	I am encouraged to contact and discuss with the school staff when I feel the need	
2	I am kept informed on what takes place at the school	
3	My opinions are listened to and valued at the school	
4	I am informed regularly on school policies and activities	
5	I am asked to give my views on learning and behaviour at the school	
6	I am asked to give my views on social and emotional education at the school	
7	I am asked to provide my help with learning and behaviour support at the school	
8	I am invited for activities such as special assemblies, pupil presentations and exhibitions	
9	I am given tasks to help my child/ren's social and emotional development skills	
10	When there is a conflict, I am given the opportunity to express my views	
	Targets for improvement:	

	Section C: Education and wellbeing	
1	The school organises talks and courses on how I can help my child/ren learn	
2	The school organises talks and courses on how I can help my child/ren develop their social and emotional skills	
3	The school organises talks and courses on how I can develop and improve my parenting skills	
4	The school helps me to make contact with needed child support services and facilities in the community	
5	The school provides information and organises talks and courses on how I can take care of my own health and wellbeing	
6	As parents we are encouraged to organise our own activities both at school and in the community	
7	The school understands the difficulties I go through as a parent and provides needed support	
8	As parents we are provided with the opportunity and school space to connect with each other and develop support networks	
9	The school is sensitive to the cultural diversity amongst families in our community	
10	As a parent I am encouraged and supported to take an active role in the local community	
	Targets for improvement:	

Table 9.1 (continued)

Section D	
How may the school help you to participate and contribute more actively at the school?	
How may the school help to develop and improve your skills as a parent?	
How may be school help to promote your own social and emotional well-being?	

Some of items in this checklist have been informed by other existing checklists, namely National Curriculum Council Focus Group for Inclusive Education (2002), and ASD (2012).

Nasredin and the donkey

Caravanserai's Courtyard

The Ancient Silk Road, 1290

It was a late summer afternoon and the weather-beaten travellers were seeking refuge from the stifling heat under the shade of a big palm tree in the middle of the caravanserai's courtyard. Nasredin was serving them hot tea with fresh mint from his huge black teapot. The wide loose djellabaya and white turbans were helping to keep the heat, sand and flies away. The reeking smell of the tired camels surrounded the courtyard like a heavy hanging cloud. Nasredin's old donkey was engaged in a repeated ritual of tail shaking and leg stamping to get relief from the persisting flies. Nasredin was recounting the story of the donkey belonging to a Bedouin family in an oasis nearby. Ali and his son Mustapha were on their way to join the big celebrations in town on the occasion of the coronation of the new sultan. From afar they could see the colourful banners and flags flying on the town towers and minarets and people flocking towards the old town gate. It was a hot day, and the father and son decided to give their donkey some respite, and walked along with the donkey. A group of men under a palm tree laughed and jeered at them, asking how could they be so stupid not to ride the donkey in that heat. They decided to ride the donkey again to the applause and approval of the men. As they arrived at the main road leading to the gate, a group of people were gathered around a man serving tea. A young man looked at their old and tired donkey and asked them how they could treat their animal in such an unkind way. Touched by his words, they decided that the father will continue riding while the son would walk along. Along the way an older man chastised the father for being so selfish and let his son walk in that heat while he sat comfortably on the donkey. The embarrassed father switched place with his son, but less than 20 palms away, the son was soon reprimanded by a small crowd for letting his old father walk while he enjoyed the ride. Father and son decided that they will both walk again. As they approached the bridge leading to the town gate, two revellers rebuked them for making their tired donkey walk on such a day. Filled with remorse, the father and son felt that the only option left was for them to carry the donkey. They tied the donkey's legs to a strong tree branch which they carried on their shoulders. As they approached the bridge there was much jeering and laughter, the donkey got nervous, the branch broke and the donkey fell and drowned in the river.

As the crowd discussed and argued what the father and son should have done with their donkey, Nasredin, mounted his donkey and started making his way to the bazaar: "My brothers, those who really want to know the answer to what the father and son should have done, may follow me now and do as I do until we arrive at the bazaar". The crowd followed. Every few steps Nasredin would stop, shake his hands in the air, touch his feet and jump up yelling 'Ha!Ha!Hi!' The followers stopped and did the same. After some time however, some decided they had had enough, and made their way back to the caravanserai. At the bazaar, the remaining men wanted to know the meaning of all this. "Brothers, the ones who left along the way have understood the meaning of the story. I am going to spend some time at the bazaar, those who still do not have the answer, can follow me again on the way back to the caravanserai and do as I do" On his way back, only the old oasis dogs were following Nasredin and his donkey.

Chapter 10
Conclusion

We have now come to the end of our journey and the start of a new one. We have seen how social and emotional education (SEE) can be both taught and caught in the classroom and at the whole school, with the participation of the whole school community, the parents/caregivers and the local community. We have also discussed how schools may mobilise their resources and recruit additional support for pupils experiencing difficulties in accessing the SEE curriculum. We have also underlined that besides pupils' own SEE, the school needs to address the social and emotional needs of its staff and to support the parents'/caregivers' education and well-being. We have presented an overarching whole-school framework on how schools may embark on a comprehensive, integrated, multilevel and reflexive process to bring the heart into the classroom and into the whole school community.

The SEE framework presented in this book is not a romantic, 'alternative' vision of education. It is based on evidence, good practice and theory as well as the realities faced by our school children in the twenty-first century. It is also based on children's right for an adequate, meaningful and relevant education. It is also economically sound and cost effective, reducing the burden on health services, with less psychologists and mental health workers needed to 'fix' children in difficulty. Moreover, happy and socially competent individuals are in the end more productive in both schools and society. As Seligman et al. (2009, pp. 307–308) put it, 'well-being is now quantifiable and it complements and makes sense of GDP… The time has come for a new prosperity, a prosperity that combines well-being with wealth. The aim of wealth should be not to blindly produce more wealth, but to produce more well-being… Learning to value and to attain this new prosperity must start early—in the formative years of schooling'.

We now have the science to foster children's social and emotional education (Greenberg et al. 2003) and enough evidence about how educational systems without a heart can lead to pupils becoming alienated, disaffected and unprepared for life outside school. On the other hand, we have evidence that educational systems which made SEE a core aspect of their ethos and culture, lead to healthier, happier and more successful children, young people and families. Schools now have a very clear choice. Rather than 'educating for the past' (Gidley 2007), they need to be

C. Cefai, V. Cavioni, *Social and Emotional Education in Primary School*,   159
DOI 10.1007/978-1-4614-8752-4_10, © Springer Science+Business Media New York 2014

grounded in the current realities and challenges if they are to remain valid and relevant in the lives of children in the twenty-first century. We need both head and heart in education.

> The magic combination of inspiration, belief and perspiration is essential for those committed to improving students' achievement and their well-being. We know the way; what we need now is the will. (Elias and Weissberg 2000, p. 192)

Schools do not operate in isolation. They are a part of a number of social systems impacting the developmental trajectory in childhood and adolescence. The family, the community and socioeconomic, cultural and political factors, are key determinants in the growth and healthy development of children. A multidimensional approach to health and well-being with the various systems in the child's world complementing and supporting one another, would be an ideal context for our children to grow up in. Whilst striving to build such a context in partnership with other systems and institutions, schools have also a key role to play within their own sphere of influence. They are ideally placed to reach all children and have strong influence on children's social and emotional learning. This provides a great and unique opportunity for schools (Elias and Moceri 2012). This book carries a message of hope and optimism for educators. We can help to bring about a change in consciousness (Noddings 2012) and lay the foundations for a twenty-first century society where citizens thrive and maximise their growth in a context fuelled by collaboration, solidarity, equity, social justice and peace. As Albert Bandura (1997) put it, we can produce our own future, rather than simply foretell it. Whilst not ignoring the constraints and barriers we are set to meet in our path, we need to remain confident in our ability to bring change. We must not give up on children or let circumstances detract us from our commitment that we can make a positive difference in the lives of our children. 'We must accept finite disappointment, but never lose infinite hope' (Martin Luther King).

Spiderman

Rathlin Island off the north coast of Ireland

1307

The biting cold, low dark clouds and heavy fog added to the desolation of the harsh rugged terrain. An air of abandonment and despair hovered in the dark cave where the hunted, exhausted and bearded man was lying, defeated and humiliated. A sense of hopelessness pervaded his tired spirit, he just wanted to curl up and hibernate like the sleeping foxes in the caves nearby. He had lost his kingdom, his army crushed, his crown desecrated, his brothers executed, his sister captured, his neck hanging by a thread. The hunters were not far, the dark days and nights seemed endless as the harsh winter dragged on, gnawing at his wounded spirit. He eyed listlessly a small spider trying hard to swing across the ceiling in its attempts to spin its web. It fell back again and again, but continued swinging and falling back. He expected it to give up, to have at least one companion in his desolate predicament. The spider was not discouraged however, and continued swinging across the ceiling again and again until it finally reached the other side and put a hold there. Then it continued to spin its new web.

As a streak of weak sunshine entered the cave and lit the silvery web, a flush of warmth and hope filled the man's heart. If a spider can do it, so could he. He will try, try and try again. He will have his kingdom back! He recalled distant rumours of a mighty Mongol king in ancient Persia, Timur the Lame, who licking his wounds in defeat, also regained his strength and courage through an ant who kept trying to move a corn kernel up a wall time and again until at last she did it. Fired by the spider's determination and persistence, the transformed king regained his strength, courage and determination, and started gathering his dispersed men again. After 8 years, King Robert the Bruce was back on his throne. It is rumoured that his crown featured a golden spider spinning a web, while the words 'Try, Try and Try again' were carved in gold on his throne.

References

Adelman, H. S., & Taylor, L. (2010). *Mental health in schools: Engaging learners, preventing problems and improving schools.* Thousand Oaks: Corwin.

Adi, Y., Killoran, A., Janmohamed, K., & Stewart-Brown, S. (2007). *Systematic review of the effectiveness of interventions to promote mental well-being in primary schools: Universal approaches which do not focus on violence or bullying.* London: National Institute for Clinical Excellence.

Albers, C. A., Kratochwill, T. R., & Glover, T. A. (2007). Where are we and where do we go now? Universal screening for enhanced educational and mental health outcomes. *Journal of School Psychology, 45,* 257–263.

Alliance for Excellent Education. (2005). *Teacher attrition: A costly loss to the nation and to the states.* Washington: Author.

Anchorage School District (ASD). (2012). *Social and Emotional Learning (SEL).* www.asdk12.org/depts/SEL. Accessed 30 Dec 2012.

Arthur, J. (2005). The re-emergence of character education in British educational policy. *British Journal of Educational Studies, 53*(3), 239–254.

Askell-Williams, H., Dix, K. L., Lawson, M. J., & Slee, P. T. (2012). Quality of implementation of a school mental health initiative and changes over time in students' social and emotional competencies. *School Effectiveness and School Improvement: An International Journal of Research, Policy and Practice.*

Askell-Williams, H., Lawson, M. J., & Slee, P. T. (2010). Venturing into schools: Locating mental health initiatives in complex environments. *International Journal of Emotional Education, 1*(2), 14–33.

Askell-Williams, H., Lawson, M. J., & Murray-Harvey, R. (2005). Teaching and learning about mental illnesses: An Australian perspective. *International Journal of Mental Health Promotion, 9,* 26–36.

Bagner, D. M., Rodriguez, G. M., Blake, C. A., Linares, D., & Carter, A. S. (2012). Assessment of behavioral and emotional problems in infancy: A systematic review. *Clinical Child and Family Psychology Review, 15* (2), 113–128.

Bandura, A. (1997). *Self-efficacy: The exercise of control.* New York: Freeman.

Barmby, P. W. (2006). Improving teacher recruitment and retention: The importance of workload and pupil behaviour. *Educational Research, 48*(3), 247–265.

Bartolo, P., & Symth, G. (2009). Teacher education for diversity. In A. Swennen & M. Van der Klink (Eds.), *Becoming a teacher educator* (pp. 117–132). Netherlands: Springer.

Bartolo, P., Janik, I., Janikova, V., Hofsass, T., Koinzer, P., Vilkiene, V., Calleja, C., Cefai, C., Chetcuti, D., Ale, P., Mol Lous, A., Wetso, G. M., & Humphrey, N. (2007). *Responding to student diversity tutor's aanual.* Malta: Faculty of Education, University of Malta.

Battistich, V., Solomon, D., Watson, M. S., & Schaps, E. (1997). Caring school communities. *Educational Psychologist, 32,* 137–151.

Battistich, V., Schaps, E., & Wilson, N. (2004). Effects of an elementary school intervention on students' "connectedness" to school and social adjustment during middle school. *Journal of Primary Prevention, 24,* 243–262.

Benard, B. (2004). *Resiliency: What we have learned.* San Francisco: WestEd.

Benninga, J. S., Berkowitz, M. W., Kuehn, P., & Smith, K (2006). Character and academics: What good schools do. *Phi Delta Kappan, 87*(6), 448–452.

Bernard, M. E. (2012a). *The importance of social and emotional learning dispositions to the achievement and well-being of young children.* Melbourne: A Bernard Group Publication.

Bernard, M. E. (2012b). *You can do it! Education: A social-emotional learning program for increasing the achievement and well-being of children and adolescent.* Melbourne: A Bernard Group Publication.

Bernard, M. E. (2011). *The mindset of highly effective classroom teachers. Resilience.* Melbourne: A Bernard Group Publication.

Bernard, M. E. (2006). It's time we teach social-emotional competence as well as we teach academic competence. *Reading & Writing Quarterly, 22,* 103–119.

Bernard, M. E., Stephanou, A., & Urbach, D. (2007). *ASG Student Social and Emotional Health Report.* Australia: Australian Scholarships Group.

Bricheno, P., Brown, S., & Lubansky, R. (2009). *Teacher well-being: A review of the evidence.* London: Teacher Support Network.

Bierman, K. L., & Erath, S. A. (2006). Promoting social competence in early childhood: Classroom curricula and social skills coaching programs. In K. McCartney & D. Phillips (Eds.), *Blackwell handbook on early childhood development* (pp. 595–615). Malden: Blackwell.

Blank, L., Baxter, S., Goyder, L., Guillaume, L., Wilkinson, A., Hummel, S., & Chilcott, J. (2009). Systematic review of the effectiveness of universal interventions which aim to promote emotional and social well-being in secondary schools. London: National Institute for Clinical Excellence.

Blasé, J. (2009). The role of mentors of preservice and inservice teachers. In L. J. Saha & A. G. Dworkin (Eds.), *International handbook of research on teachers and teaching* (Vol. 1, pp. 171–182). New York: Springer.

Bond, L., Butler, H., Thomas, L., Carlin, J., Glover, S., Bowes, G., et al. (2007). Social and school connectedness in early secondary school as predictors of late teenage substance use, mental health, and academic outcomes. *Journal of Adolescent Health, 40*(4), e9–e18.

Booth, T., & Ainscow, M. (1998). From them to us: An international study of inclusion in education. London: Routledge.

Borg, M. G., & Riding, R. J. (1991). Occupational stress and satisfaction in teaching. *British Educational Research Journal, 17,* 263–281.

Borman, G., Slavin, R. E., Cheung, A., Chamberlain, A., Madden, N. A., & Chambers, B. (2007). Final reading outcomes of the national randomized field trial of Success for All. *American Educational Research Journal, 44*(3), 701–731.

Bowers, H., Manion, I., Papadopoulos, D., & Gauvreau, E. (2012). Stigma in school-based mental health: Perceptions of young people and service providers. *Journal of Child and Adolescent Health,* June, 165–170.

Bowlby, J. (1980). *Attachment and loss.* London: Hogarth.

Bradley, R., Doolittle, J., & Bartolotta, R. (2008). Building on the data and adding to the discussion: The experiences and outcomes of students with emotional disturbance. *Journal of Behavioral Education, 17,* 3–23.

Broderick, P. C., & Metz, S. (2009). Learning to BREATHE: A pilot trial of a mindfulness curriculum for adolescents. *Advances in School Mental Health Promotion, 2,* 35–46.

Bronfenbrenner, U. (1989). Ecological systems theory. *Annals of Child Development, 6,* 187–249.

Brown, C. G. (2012). A systematic review of the relationship between self-efficacy and burnout in teachers. *Educational and Child Psychology, 29*(4), 47–63.

Brown, M. B., & Bowen, L. M. (2008). The school-based health center as a resource for prevention and health promotion. *Psychology in the Schools, 45,* 28–38.

Brown, K. W., & Ryan, R. M. (2003). The benefits of being present: Mindfulness and its role in psychological well-being. *Journal of Personality and Social Psychology, 84,* 822–848.

Bryk, A. S., & Driscoll, M. E. (1988). *The school as community: Theoretical foundations, contextual influences, and consequences for students and teachers.* Madison: National Center on Effective Secondary Schools.

Bryk, A., Camburn, E., & Louis, K. L. (1999). Professional community in Chicago elementary school: Facilitating factors and organizational consequences. *Educational Administration Quarterly, 35*(Supplement), 751–781.

Bullough, R. V. (2009). Seeking eudaimonia: The emotions in learning to teach and to mentor. In P. A. Schutz & M. Zembylas (Eds.), *Advances in Teacher Emotion Research. The Impact on Teachers' Lives* (pp. 33–53). New York: Springer.

Bullough, R. V. (2011). Hope, happiness, teaching, and learning. In C. Day & J. C. Lee (Eds.), *New understandings of teacher's work. Emotions and educational change* (pp. 15–30). New York: Springer.

Burke, C. A. (2009). Mindfulness-based approaches with children and adolescents: A preliminary review of current research in an emergent field. *Journal of Child and Family Studies, 19*(2), 133–144.

Burrows, L. (2011a). Relational mindfulness in education. *Encounter: Education for Meaning and Social Justice, 24*(4), 24–29.

Burrows, L. (2011b). Opening our minds to new ideas and slowing us down to consider our options: Practising relational mindfulness in school communities. In R. Shute (Ed.), *Mental health and well-being: Educational perspectives.* Adelaide: Shannon Research Press.

Burrows, L. (2012). Mindfulness is everywhere. *Social and Emotional Learning Matters,* ENSEC Newsletter, Issue 3 November 2012, 11–13. http://www.enseceurope.org. Accessed 30 Dec 2012.

Bywater, T., & Sharples, J. (2012). Effective evidence-based interventions for emotional well-being: lessons for policy and practice. *Research Papers in Education, 27*(4), 398–408.

Cameron, E. (2011). *Development, climate change and human rights: From the margins to the mainstream?* Social Development Working Paper 123, World Bank, Washington DC.

Caprara, G. V., Pastorelli, C., Bandura, A., & Zimbardo, P. G. (2000). Prosocial foundations of children's academic achievement. *Psychological Science, 53*(2), 302–306.

Carlson, C., & Christenson, S. L. (2005). Evidence-based parent and family interventions in school psychology [Special issue]. *School Psychology Quarterly, 20*(4).

Catalano, R. F., Berglund, M. L., Ryan, J. A. M., Lonczak, H. S., & Hawkins, J. D. (2004). Positive youth development in the United States: Research findings on evaluations of positive youth development programs. *Annals of the American Psychological Society, 591,* 98–124.

Cavioni, V. (2013). Analisi degli effete a breve e a lungo termine di un programma universal di apprendimento socio-emotivo. Unpublished PhD, Department of Psychology, University of Pavia, Italy.

Cefai, C. (2007). Resilience for all: A study of classrooms as protective contexts. *Emotional and Behavioural Difficulties, 12*(2), 119–134.

Cefai, C. (2008). *Promoting resilience in the classroom. A guide to developing pupils' emotional and cognitive skills.* London: Jessica Kingsley Publishers.

Cefai, C., & Camilleri, L. (2011). *Building resilience in children. Risk and promotive factors amongst Maltese primary school children.* Malta: EuroCentre for Educational Resilience and Socio-Emotional Health, University of Malta.

Cefai, C., & Cooper, P. (2010). Students without voices: The unheard accounts of secondary school students with social, emotional and behaviour difficulties. *European Journal of Special Needs Education, 25*(2), 183–198.

Cefai, C., & Cooper, P. (2009). What is emotional education. *International Journal of Emotional Education, 1*(1), 1–7.

Centers for Disease Control and Prevention. (2012). *Parent engagement: Strategies for involving parents in school health.* Atlanta: U.S. Department of Health and Human Services.

Center for Disease Control and Prevention. (2013). Mental Health Surveillance Among Children—United States 2005–2011. *Morbidity and Mortality Weekly Report,* Supplement, *62* (2).

Chapman, S., Lister-Sharp, D., Sowden, A., & Stewart-Brown, S. (1999). *Systematic review of reviews of health promotion in schools.* New York: Centre for Reviews and Dissemination, University of York.

Cohen, J. (2006). Social, emotional, ethical, and academic education: Creating a climate for learning, participation in democracy, and well-Being. *Harvard Educational Review, 76*(2), 201–237.

Cole, T., Daniels, H., & Visser, J. (2005). The mental health needs of pupils with EBD. In R. Williams & M. Kerfoot (Eds.), *Child and adolescent mental health services.* Oxford: Oxford University Press.

Coleman, J., & Hagell, A. (2007). Adolescence, risk and resilience: A conclusion. In J. Coleman & A. Hagell (Eds.), *Adolescence, risk and resilience.* London: Wiley.

Collaborative for Academic, Social, and Emotional Learning. (2005a). *Safe and sound: An educational leader's guide to evidence-based social and emotional SEL programs.* http://www.casel.org/projects_products/safeandsound.php. Accessed 30 Dec 2012.

Collaborative for Academic, Social, and Emotional Learning & Mid-Atlantic Regional Laboratory for Student Success (2005b). *SEL parent packet- Ideas and tools for working with parents and families.* http://casel.org/in-schools/tools-for-families. Accessed 30 Dec 2012.

Collaborative for Academic, Social and Emotional Learning. (2006). *CASEL Practice Rubric For Schoolwide SEL Implementation.* http://casel.org/wpcontent/uploads/2011/04/Rubric.pdf. Accessed 30 Dec 2012.

Collaborative for Academic, Social, and Emotional Learning. (2008). *Social and Emotional Learning (SEL) Programs, Illinois Edition.* Chicago: CASEL.

Collaborative for Academic, Social, and Emotional Learning. (2012). 2013 CASEL Guide. Effective social and emotional learning programs preschool and elementary school edition. http://casel.org/guide. Accessed 30 Dec 2012.

Collishaw, S., Maughan, B., Goodman, R., & Pickles, A. (2004). Time trends in adolescent mental health. *Journal of Child Psychology and Psychiatry, and Allied Disciplines, 45*(8), 1350–1362.

Colman, I., Murray, J., Abbott, R. A., Maughan, B., Kuh, D., Croudace, T. J., & Jones, P. B. (2009). Outcomes of conduct problems in adolescence: 40 year follow-up of national cohort. *British Medical Journal, 338,* 208–211.

Conduct Problems Prevention Research Group. (1999). Initial impact of the fast track prevention trial for conduct problems: II. Classroom effects. *Journal of Consulting and Clinical Psychology, 67,* 648–657.

Conduct Problems Prevention Research Group. (2011). The effects of the fast track preventive intervention on the development of conduct disorder across childhood. *Child Development, 82*(1), 331–345.

Cooper, P., & Cefai, C. (2009). Contemporary values and social context: Implications for the emotional well-being of children. *Journal of Emotional and Behaviour Difficulties, 14*(2), 91–100.

Cooper, P., Bilton, C., & Kakos, M. (2011). The importance of a biopsychosocial approach to interventions for SEBD. In T. Cole, H. Daniels, & J. Visser (Eds.), *The routledge international companion to emotional and behavioural difficulties.* London: Routledge.

Cooper, P., & Jacobs, B. (2011). From inclusion to engagement: Helping students engage with schooling through policy and practice. Chichester: Wiley-Blackwell.

Craig, C. (2009). *Well-being in schools: The curious case of the tail wagging the dog.* Glasgow: Centre for Confidence and Well-being.

Crocker, J., & Park, L. E. (2004). The costly pursuit of self-esteem. *Psychological Bulletin, 130*(3), 392–414.

Dator, J. (2000). The futures for higher education: From bricks to bytes to fare thee well! In S. Inayatullah & J. Gidley (Eds.), *The university in transformation: Global perspectives on the futures of the university.* Westport: Bergin & Garvey.

Davidson, R. J, Dunne, J., & Eccles, J. S., et al. (2012). Contemplative practices and mental training: Prospects for American education. *Child Development Perspectives, 6*(2), 146–153.

Day, C. (2011). Uncertain professional identities: Managing the emotional contexts of teaching. In C. Day & J. C. Lee (Eds.), *New understandings of teacher's work. Emotions and educational change* (pp. 45–64). New York: Springer.

Day C., & Gu, Q. (2007). Variations in the conditions for teachers' professional learning and development: Sustaining commitment and effectiveness over a career. *Oxford Review of Education, 33*(4), 423–443.

Day, C., & Qing, G. (2009). Teacher emotions: Well being and effectiveness. In P. A. Schutz & M. Zembylas (Eds.), *Advances in teacher emotion research. The impact on teachers' lives.* New York: Springer.

Deci, E. L., & Ryan, R. M. (2000). The "what" and "why" of goal pursuits: Human needs and the self determination of behavior. *Psychological Inquiry, 11,* 227–268.

De Bono, E. (1992). Serious creativity: Using the power of lateral thinking to create new ideas. New York: Harper Business.

Denham, S. A., Bassett, H. H., & Zinsser, K. (2012). Early childhood teachers as socializers of young children's emotional competence. *Early Childhood Education Journal, 40,* 137–143.

Denham, S., Li, P., & Hamre, B. (2010). *Compendium of preschool through elementary school social-emotional learning and associated assessment measures.* Chicago CASEL. http://casel. org/wp-content/uploads/Compendium_SELTools.pdf. Accessed 30 Dec 2012.

Dent, R., & Cameron, R. J. (2003). Developing resilience in children who are in public care: the educational psychology perspective. *Educational Psychology in Practice, 19*(1), 3–19.

Department for Education and Skills. (2007). *Social and emotional aspects of learning for secondary schools (SEAL): Guidance booklet.* Nottingham: Department for Education and Skills.

Dever, B. V., Raines, T. C., & Barclay, C. M. (2012). Chasing the unicorn: Practical implementation of universal screening for behavioral and emotional risk. *Research in Practice, 6*(4), 108–118.

DfE. (2010). *The importance of teaching—the schools.* London: The Stationery Office.

DfES. (2005a). Learning behaviour. The report of the practitioners' group on school behaviour and discipline. www.teachernet.gov.uk/publications. Accessed 30 Dec 2012.

DFES. (2005b). Primary national strategy. Excellence and enjoyment: Social and emotional aspects of learning Guidance. London: DfES.

DfES. (2001a). Promoting children's mental health within early years and school settings. London: DfES.

DfES. (2001b). Special educational needs code of practice. London: DfES.

Diekstra, R. (2008a). Effectiveness of school-based social and emotional education programmes worldwide—part one, a review of meta-analytic literature. In *Social and motional education: an international analysis* (pp. 255–284). Santander: Fundacion Marcelino Botin, Santander.

Diekstra, R. (2008b). Effectiveness of school-based social and emotional education programmes worldwide—part two, teaching social and emotional skills worldwide. A meta-analytic review of effectiveness. In *Social and emotional education: an international analysis* (pp. 285–312). Santander: Fundacion Marcelino Botin, Santander.

Dix, K. L., Slee, P. T., Lawson, M. J., & Keeves, J. P. (2012). Implementation quality of whole-school mental health promotion and students' academic performance. *Child and Adolescent Mental Health, 17*(1), 45–51.

Dixon, T. (2012). Educating the emotions from Gradgrind to Goleman. *Research Papers in Education, 27*(4), 481–495.

Dodge, K. (2010). Introduction: Why focus on social and emotional learning? In society for research in child development. New findings on approaches to improving children's social and emotional learning implications for academic performance and behavior. http://casel.org/wp-content/uploads/SRCD-March-21-2011Presentation-Slides.pdf. Accessed 30 Dec 2012.

Domitrovich, C. E., Cortes, R., & Greenberg, M. T. (2007). Improving young children's social and emotional competence: A randomized trial of the Preschool PATHS program. *Journal of Primary Prevention, 28*(2), 67–91.

Dowdy, E., & Kim, E. (2012). Choosing informants when conducting a universal screening for behavioral and emotional risk. *Research In Practice, 6*(4), 1–10.

Downey, C., & Williams, C. (2010). Family SEAL—a home-school collaborative programme focusing on the development of children's social and emotional skills. *Advances in School Mental Health Promotion, 3,* 30–41.

Durlak, J. A., & Dupre, E. P. (2008). Implementation matters: A review of research on the influence of implementation on program outcomes and the factors affecting implementation. *American Journal of Community Psychology, 41,* 327–350.

Durlak, J. A., Weissberg, R. P., & Pachan, M. (2010). A meta-analysis of afterschool programs that seek to promote personal and social skills in children and adolescents. *American Journal of Community Psychology, 45,* 294–309.

Durlak, J. A., Weissberg, R. P., Dymnicki, A. B., Taylor, R. D., & Schellinger, K. (2011). The impact of enhancing students' social and emotional learning: A meta-analysis of school-based universal interventions. *Child Development, 82,* 474–501.

Dweck, C. (1999). Self-theories: Their role in motivation, personality, and development. Essays in social psychology. Philadelphia: Psychology Press.

Dworkin, G.A. (2009). Teacher Burnout and Teacher Resilience: Assessing the Impacts of the School Accountability Movement. In L. J. Saha & A. G. Dworkin (Eds.), *International handbook of research on teachers and teaching* (vol. 1). New York: Springer.

Ecclestone, K. (2012). From emotional and psychological well-being to character education: challenging policy discourses of behavioural science and 'vulnerability'. *Research Papers in Education, 27*(4), 463–480.

Ecclestone, K., & Hayes, D. (2009). Changing the subject: the educational implications of emotional well-being. *Oxford Review of Education, 35*(3), 371–389.

El Nokali, N. E., Bachman, H. J., & Votruba-Drzal, E. (2010). Parent involvement and children's academic and social development in elementary school. *Child Development, 81*(3), 988–1005.

Elias, M. J. (2003). *Academic and social-emotional learning.* Brussels: International Bureau of Education.

Elias, M. J. (2009). Teaching participatory competencies for success in school and life: How to bring social-emotional and character development into every classroom and subject area. Keynote address, Second ENSEC Conference, 9th–12th September, Izmir, Turkey.

Elias, M. J. (2010). Sustainability of social-emotional learning and related programs: lessons from a field study. *International Journal of Emotional Education, 2*(1), 17–33.

Elias, M. J., & Arnold, H. (2006). The educator's guide to emotional intelligence and academic achievement: Social-emotional learning in the classroom. Thousand Oaks, CA: Corwin Press.

Elias, M. J., & Moceri, D. C. (2012). Developing social and emotional aspects of learning: the American experience. *Research Papers in Education, 27*(4), 423–434.

Elias, M., & Synder, D. (2008). *Developing safe and civil schools: A coordinated approach to social-emotional and character development.* www.njasp.org/notes/confarc/DSACS_handouts_12_09.doc. Accessed 15 Apr 2011.

Elias, M. J., & Weissberg, R. P. (2000). Primary prevention: Educational approaches to enhance social and emotional learning. *Journal of School Health, 70*(5), 186–190.

Elias, M., Zins, J., Weissberg, R., Frey, K., Greenberg, M., Haynes, N., Kessler, R., Schwab- Stone, M., & Shriver, T. (1997). *Promoting Social and Emotional Learning.* Alexandria: ASCD.

Epstein, M. H., Ryser, G., & Pearson, N. (2002). Standardization of the behavioral and emotional rating scale: Factor structure, reliability, and criterion validity. *Journal of Behavioral Health Services & Research, 29,* 208–216.

Epstein, J. L., Sanders, M. G., Simon, B. S., Salinas, K. C., Jansorn, N. R., & Van Voorhis, F. L. (2002). *School, community, and community partnerships: Your handbook for action* (2nd ed.). Thousand Oaks: Corwin Press.

Essex, M. J., Kraemer H. C., Armstrong, J. M., Boyce, T. M., Goldsmith, H. H., Klein, M. H., Woodward, H., & Kupfer, D. J. (2006). Exploring risk factors for the emergence of children's mental health problems. *Archives of General Psychiatry, 63,* 1246–1256.

European Trade Union Committee for Education (ETUCE) (2007). Report on the ETUCE Survey on teachers' work-related stress. http://etuce.homestead.com/News/2008/March2008/DraftReport_WRS_EN.pdf. Accessed 30 Dec 2012.

Facer, K. (2012). Personal, relational and beautiful: education, technologies and John Macmurray's philosophy. *Oxford Review of Education, 38*(6), 709–725.

Farington, D. P., & Ttofi, M. M. (2009). School-based programs to reduce bullying and victimization. Campbell Systematic Reviews. Oslo: Campbell Collaboration. http://campbellcollaboration.org/lib/download/718/. Accessed 30th Dec 2012.

Farrell, P., & Humphrey, N. (2009). Improving services for pupils with social, emotional and behaviour difficulties: responding to the challenge. *International Journal of Emotional Education, 1*(1), 64–82.

Fan X., & Chen, M. (2001). Parental involvement and students' academic achievement: A meta-analysis. *Educational Psychology Review, 13*(1), 1–22.

Fielding, M. (2012). Education as if people matter: John Macmurray, community and the struggle for democracy, *Oxford Review of Education, 38*(6), 675–692.

Fergusson D. M., Horwood, L. J., & Ridder, E. M. (2005). Show me the child at seven: the consequences of conduct problems in childhood for psychosocial functioning in adulthood. *Journal of Child Psychology and Psychiatry, 46*, 837–49.

Flook, L., Smalley, S. L., Kitil, M. J., Galla, B. M., Kaiser-Greenland, S., Locke, J., Ishijima, E., & Kasari, C. (2010). Effects of mindful awareness practices on executive functions in elementary school children. *Journal of Applied School Psychology, 26*, 70–95.

Ford, T., Goodman, R., & Meltzer, H. (2003). The British Child and Adolescent Mental Health Survey 1999: The prevalence of DSM-IV disorders. *Journal of the American Academy of Child and Adolescent Psychiatry, 42*, 1203–1211.

Franklin, C., Kim, J. S., Ryan, T., Kelly, M., & Montgomery, K. L. (2012). Teacher involvement in school mental health interventions: A systematic review. *Children and Youth Services Review, 34*, 973–982.

Fredrickson, B. L. (2004). The broaden-and-build theory of positive emotions. *R Soc 359*, 1367–1377.

Fredrickson, B. L., & Branigan, C. (2005). Positive emotions broaden the scope of attention and thought-action repertoires. *Cognition and Emotion, 19*, 313–332.

Frenzel, A. C., Goetz, T., Stephens, E. J., & Jacob, B. (2009). Antecedents and effects of teachers' emotional experiences: An integrated perspective and empirical test. In P. A. Schutz and M. Zembylas (Eds.), *Advances in teacher emotion research the impact on teachers' lives* (pp. 129–151). New York: Springer.

Fundacion Marcellino Botin. (2008). *Social and emotional education: An international analysis.* Santander, Spain: Fundacion Botin.

Gaziel, H. H. (2004). Predictors of absenteeism among primary school teachers. *Social Psychology of Education, 7*, 421–434.

Geake, J. G., & Cooper, P. W. (2003). Implications of cognitive neuroscience for education. *Westminster Studies in Education, 26*, 10, 7–20.

Gergen, K. J. (2001). Psychological science in a postmodern world. *American Psychologist, 56*, 803–13.

Gibbs, S., & Powell, B. (2012). Teacher efficacy and pupil behaviour: The structure of teachers' individual and collective beliefs and their relationship with numbers of pupils excluded from school. *British Journal of Educational Psychology, 82*(4), 564–584.

Gidley, J. (2007). The evolution of consciousness as a planetary imperative: An integration of integral views. *Integral Review: A Transdisciplinary and Transcultural Journal for New Thought, Research and Praxis, 5*, 4–226.

Gilliam, W. S. (2005). Prekindergarteners left behind: Expulsion rates in state prekindergarten programs. New York: Foundation for Child Development.

Gilman, R. Scott Huebner, E., & Furlong, M. J. (Eds.) (2009). *Handbook of positive psychology in schools*. London: Routeledge.

Goddard, R. D., Hoy, W. K., Woolfolk Hoy, A. (2004). Collective efficacy beliefs: Theoretical developments, empirical evidence, and future directions. *Educational Researcher, 33*, 3–13.

Goleman, D. (1996). *Emotional intelligence*. London: Bloomsbury.

Goleman, D., Bennett, L., & Barlow, Z. (2012). *Ecoliterate: How educators are cultivating emotional, social, and ecological intelligence*. Jossey-Bass.

Goodman, R (1997). The strengths and difficulties questionnaire: A research note. *Journal of Child Psychiatry and Psychology, 38*(8), 581–585.

Goodman, R., Renfrew, D., & Mullick, M. (2000). Predicting type of psychiatric disorder from Strengths and Difficulties Questionnaire (SDQ) scores in child mental health clinics in London and Dhaka. *European Child Adolescent Psychiatry, 9,* 129–134.

Government of Australia. (1912). *Minutes of evidence of royal commission on education.* Australian Royal Commission on Education, pp. 64–65.

Graetz, B., Littlefield, L., Trinder, M., Dobia, B., Souter, M., Champion, C., Boucher, S., Killic-Moran, C., & Cummins, R. (2008). KidsMatter: A Population health model to support student mental health and well-being in primary schools. *International Journal of Mental Health Promotion, 10,* 13–20.

Graziano, P., Reavis, R., Keane, S., & Calkins, S. (2007). The role of emotion regulation and the student-teacher relationship in children's academic success. *Journal of School Psychology, 45,* 3–19.

Green, C. L., Walker, J. M. T., Hoover-Dempsey, K. V., & Sandler, H. M. (2007). Parents' motivations for involvement in children's education: an empirical test of a theoretical model of parental involvement. *Journal of Educational Psychology, 99*(3), 532–544.

Greenberg, M. T. (2010). School-based prevention: Current status and future challenges. *Effective Education, 2,* 27–52.

Greenberg, M. (2011). *Promoting well-being in schools: Current status and future challenges.* Keynote address at the Third ENSEC Conference, Manchester, UK, 29th June—3rd July 2011.

Greenberg, M. T., & Rhoades, B. L. (2008). *State-of-science review: Self regulation and executive function—What can teachers and schools do?* London: Office of Science and Innovation Foresight Project: Mental Capital and Mental Well-being.

Greenberg, M. T., Riggs, N. R., & Blair, C. (2007). The role of preventive interventions in enhancing neurocognitive functioning and promoting competence in adolescence. In E. F. Walker & D. Romer (Eds.), *Adolescent psychopathology and the developing brain: Integrating brain and prevention science* (pp. 441–462). New York: Oxford University Press.

Greenberg, M., Domotrovich, C. E., Graczyk, P. A., & Zins, J. E. (2005). *The study of implementation in school-based preventive interventions: theory, research and practice.* Rockville: SAMHSA.

Greenberg, M. T., Weissberg, R. P., O'Brien, M. U., Zins, J. E., Fredericks, L., Resnik, H., & Elias, M. J. (2003). Enhancing school-based prevention and youth development through coordinated social, emotional, and academic learning. *American Psychologist, 58,* 466–474.

Greer, F. W., Wilson, B. S., DiStefano, C., & Liu, J. (2012). Considering social validity in the context of emotional and behavioral screening. *Research In Practice, 6*(4), 148–159.

Hallam, S., Rhamie, J., & Shaw, J. (2006). *Evaluation of the primary behaviour and attendance pilot.* Nottingham: Department for Education and Skills.

Hamre, B. K., & Pianta, R. C. (2001). Early teacher-child relationships and the trajectory of children's school outcomes through eighth grade. *Child Development, 72*(2), 625–638.

Hattie, J. (2009). *Visible Learning: A synthesis of over 800 meta-analyses relating to achievement.* London: Routledge.

Hargreaves, A. (1998). The emotional practice of teaching. *Teacher Education, 14*(8), 835–854.

Hargreaves, A. (2000). Mixed emotions: Teachers' perceptions of their interactions with students. *Teaching and Teacher Education, 16,* 811–826.

Henderson, A. T., & Mapp, K. L. (2002). *A new wave of evidence: The impact of school, family, and community connections on student achievement.* Austin: Southwest Educational Development Laboratory.

Hoagwood, K. E., Olin, S. S., Kerker, B. D., Kratochwill, T. R., Crowe, M., & Saka, N. (2007). Empirically based school interventions target at academic and mental health functioning. *Journal of Emotional and Behavioral Disorders, 15,* 66–94.

Howard, S., & Johnson, B. (2004). Resilient Teachers: Resisting Stress and Burnout. *Social Psychology of Education, 7*(3), 399–420.

Howse, R., Calkins, S. D., Anastopoulos, A., Keane, S., & Shelton, T. (2003). Regulatory contributors to children's kindergarten achievement. *Early Education and Development, 14,* 101–119.

Humphrey, N., Lendrum, N., & Wigelsworth, M. (2010). *Social and emotional aspects of learning (SEAL) programme in secondary schools: national evaluation.* London: Department for Education.

Humphrey, N., Kalambouka, A., Bolton, J., Lendrum, A., Wigelsworth, M., Lennie, C., & Farrell, P. (2008). *Primary Social and Emotional Aspects of Learning (SEAL) Evaluation of Small Group Work.* Nottingham: Department for Children, Schools and Families.

Huppert, F. A., & Johnson, D. M. (2010). A controlled trial of mindfulness training in schools: The importance of practice for an impact on well-being. *The Journal of Positive Psychology, 5*(4), 264.

Ingersoll, R. M. (2001). *Teacher turnover, teacher shortages, and the organization of schools.* Seattle: Center for the Study of Teaching and Policy.

Ingersoll, R. M. (2003). *Who controls teachers' work?* Cambridge: Harvard University Press.

Ingersoll, R., & Strong, M. (2011, June). The impact of induction and mentoring programs for beginning teachers: A critical review of the research. *Review of Educational Research, 81*(2), 201–233.

James, O. (2007). *Affluenza: How to be successful and stay sane.* London: Vermillion.

Jamieson, B. (2006). State of the Teaching Profession *Professionally Speaking,* September. www.oct.ca/publications/professionally_speaking/september_2006/survey.asp. Accessed 30th Dec 2012.

Jennings, P. A., & Greenberg, M. T. (2009). The Prosocial Classroom: Teacher social and emotional competence in relation to child and classroom outcomes. *Review of Educational Research, 79,* 491–525.

Jennings, P., Lantieri, L. & Roeser, R. W. (2012). Supporting Educational Goals through Cultivating Mindfulness. Approaches for Teachers and Students. In P. M. Brown, M. W. Corrigan & A. Higgins-d' Alessandro (Eds.), *Handbook of Prosocial Education Volume 1* (p. 371–396). Blue Ridge Summit: Rowman & Littlefield.

Jeynes, W. H. (2007). The relationship between parental involvement and urban secondary school student academic achievement: a meta-analysis. *Urban Education, 42,* 82–110.

Johnson, S. M., Berg, J. H., & Donaldson, M. L. (2005). *Who stays in teaching and why: A review of the literature on teacher retention.* Cambridge: Harvard Graduate School of Education.

Johnson, B., Down, B., Le Cornu, R., Sullivan, A. M., Peters, J., Pearce, J., & Hunter, J. (2010). *Early Career Teacher Resilience.* http://www.ectr.edu.au/. Accessed 30th Dec 2012.

Johnson, D. W. & Johnson, F. P. (2008). *Joining Together. Group Theory and Group Skills.* (10th ed.) Allyn & Bacon.

Johnson, S., Cooper, C., Cartwright, S., Donald, I., Taylor, P., & Millet, C (2005). The experience of work-related stress across occupations. *Journal of Managerial Psychology, 20*(2), 178–187.

Johnson Moore, S. (2004). *Finders and Keepers: Helping New Teachers Survive and Thrive in Our Schools.* San Francisco: Jossey Bass.

Kabat-Zinn, J. (2004). *Coming to Our Senses: Healing Ourselves and the World Through Mindfulness.* New York: Hyperion Books.

Kalambouka, A., Farrell, P., Dyson, A. & Kaplan, I. (2007). The impact of placing pupils with special educational needs in mainstream schools on the achievements of their peers. *Educational Research, 39,* 365–382.

Kaminski, J. W., Valle, L. A., Filene, J. H., & Boyle, C. L. (2008). A meta-analytic review of components associated with parent training program effectiveness. *Journal of Abnormal Child Psychology, 36*(4), 567–589.

Kamphaus, R. W. (2012). Screening for behavioral and emotional risk: Constructs and practicalities. *Research In Practice, 6*(4), 89–97.

Kamphaus, R. W., & Reynolds, C. R. (2007). *BASC-2 Behavioral and Emotional Screening System.* Minneapolis: Pearson Assessments.

Kauffman, J. (2012). *Characteristics of Emotional and Behavioural Disorders of Children and Youth.* (10th ed.). New Jersey: Merrill Prentice Hall.

Kelchtermans, G. (2011). Vulnerability in teaching: The moral and political roots of a structural condition. In C. Day & J. C. Lee (Eds.), *New Understandings of Teacher's Work. Emotions and Educational Change* (p. 65–83). New York: Springer.

Kelchtermans, G. Ballet, K., & Piot, P. (2009). Surviving diversity in times of performativity: Understanding teachers' emotional experience of change. In P.A. Schutz & M. Zembylas (Eds.), *Advances in Teacher Emotion Research The Impact on Teachers' Lives* (p. 215–232). New York: Springer.

Kelley, L. M. (2004). Why induction matters. *Journal of Teacher Education, 55*(5):438–448.

Kemeny, M. E., Foltz, C., Cavanagh, J. F., Cullen, M., Giese-Davis, J., Jennings, P., Rosenberg, E. L., Gillath, O., Shaver, P. R., Wallace, B. A., Ekman, P. (2012). Contemplative/emotion training reduces negative emotional behavior and promotes prosocial responses. *Emotion, 12*(2), 338–350.

Kidger, J. L., Gunnell, D., Biddle, J., Campbell, L. R., & Donovan, J. L. (2010). Part and parcel of teaching? Secondary school staff's views on supporting student emotional health and well-being'. *British Educational Research Journal, 36,* 919–935.

KidsMatter (2012a) *Australian Primary School Mental Health Initiative.* www.kidsmatter.edu.au/primary/. Accessed 30th Dec 2012.

KidsMatter (2012b) *Family Matters.* http://www.kidsmatter.edu.au/families. Accessed 30th Dec 2012.

Kimber, B. (2011). *Primary Prevention of Mental Health Problems among Children and Adolescents through Social and Emotional Training in School.* Stockholm: Department of Public Health Sciences, Division of Social Medicine, Karolinska Institutet.

Kroeger, S., C. Burton, A. Comarata, C. Combs, C. Hamm, R. Hopkins, & B. Kouche. (2004). Student voice and critical reflection: Helping students at risk. *Teaching Exceptional Children, 36*(3), 50–57.

Kusche, C. A., & Greenberg, M. T. (1994). *The PATHS curriculum.* Seattle: Developmental Research and Programs, Inc.

Kuyken, W., Weare, K., Ukoumunne, O. C., Vicary, R., Motton, N., Burnett, R., Cullen, C., Hennelly, S., & Huppert, F. (2013). Effectiveness of the Mindfulness in Schools Programme: Non-randomised controlled feasibility study. *British Journal of Psychiatry, 203* (2), 126–131.

Lane, K. L., & Menzies, H. M. (2003). A school-wide intervention with primary and secondary levels of support for elementary students: Outcomes and considerations. *Education and Treatment of Children, 26,* 431–451.

Lane, K. L., Weisenbach, J. L., Little, M. A., Phillips, A., & Wehby, J. (2006). Illustrations of function-based interventions implemented by general education teachers: Building capacity at the school site. *Education and Treatment of Children, 29,* 549–671.

Lantieri, L. (2009a). Putting the oxygen masks on ourselves first. *Reclaiming Youth International e-Newsletter: May.* http://www.reclaiming.com/content/node/65. Accessed 30 Dec 2012.

Lantieri, L. (2009b). Social emotional intelligence cultivating children's hearts and spirits. *LILIPOH* Spring, 11–12, 15. http://www.lindalantieri.org/documents/Lilipoh55_SocialEmotional_000.pdf. Accessed 30 Dec 2012.

Lantieri, L. (2009c). Building inner resilience. *Mind and Life Institute 2009 Autumn Newsletter,* 9–10. http://www.lindalantieri.org/documents/ml.autumn.09.newsletter.pdf. Accessed 30 Dec 2012.

Lantieri, L. (2010). *Social and emotional learning—An idea whose time has come.* http://www.reclaimingbooks.com/content/node/124. Accessed 30 Dec 2012.

Lantieri, L., Nagler Kyse, L. Harnett, S., & Malkmus, C. (2011). Building inner resilience in teachers and students. In G. M. Reevy & E. Frydenberg (Eds.), *Personality, stress, and coping: Implications for education* (pp. 267–292). Charlotte, NC: Information Age Publishing, Inc.

Lavellee, K. L., Bierman, K. L., Nix, R. L., & the Conduct Problems Prevention Research Group (2005). The impact of first-grade "friendship group" experiences on child social outcomes in the Fast Track Program. *Journal of Abnormal Child Psychology, 33,* 307–324.

Layard, R., & Dunn, J. (2009). *A good childhood*. London: Penguin.

Leadbetter, J., & Leadbetter, P. (1993). *Special children. Meeting the challenge in primary schools*. London: Cassell.

Leitch, R., & Mitchell, S. (2007). Caged birds and cloning machines: How student imagery 'speaks' to us about cultures of schooling and student participation. *Improving Schools, 10*, 53–71.

Leithwood, K., & Beatty, B. (2008). *Leading with teacher emotions in mind*. Thousand Oaks, CA: Corwin Press.

Lendrum, A., Humphrey, N., & Wigeslworth, M. (2013). Social and emotional aspects of learning (SEAL) for secondary schools: Implementation difficulties and their implications for school-based mental health promotion. *Journal of Child and Adolescent Health, 18* (3), 158–164.

Libbey, H. P. (2004). Measuring student relationships to school: Attachment, bonding, connectedness, and engagement. *Journal of School Health, 74*, 274–283.

Lutz, A., Brefczynski-Lewis, J., Johnstone, T., & Davidson, R. J. (2008). Regulation of the neuralcircuitry of emotion by compassion meditation: Effects of meditative expertise. *PLoS ONE, 3*(3), e1897.

Maes, L., & Lievens, J. (2003). Can school make a difference? A multilevel analysis of adolescent risk and health behaviour. *Social Science and Medicine, 56*, 517–529.

Marable, M. A., & Raimondi, S. L. (2007). Teachers perception of what was most (and least) supportive during their first year of teaching. *Mentoring Tutoring, 15*(1), 25–37.

McGrath, H., & Noble, T. (2011). *Bounce back. A well-being & resilience program*. Melbourne: Pearson Education.

McLaughlin, M. W., & Talbert, J. (2006). *Building school-based teacher learning communities*. New York: Teachers College Press.

Martinez, C. R., DeGarmo, D. S., & Eddy, M. J. (2004). Promoting academic success among Latino youth. *Hispanic Journal of Behavioral Sciences, 26*, 128–151.

Marzano, R. J., Marzano, J. S., & Pickering, D. J. (2003). *Classroom management that works*. Alexandra, VA: ASCD.

Maslow, A. (1971). *The further reaches of human nature*. London: Penguin.

Masten, A. S. (2007). Resilience in developing systems: Progress and promise as the fourth wave rises. *Development and Psychopathology, 19*(3), 921–930.

Masten, A. S. (2001). Ordinary magic: Resilience processes in development. *American Psychologist, 56*, 227–238.

Masten, A. S., Best, K. M., & Garmezy, N. (1990). Resilience and development: Contributions from the study of children who overcome adversity. *Development and Psychopathology, 2*(4), 425–444.

Mayer, J., & Salovey, P. (1997). What is emotional intelligence. In P. Salovey & D. Sluyter (Eds.), *Emotional development and emotional intelligence: Educational implications* (pp. 10–11). New York: Basic Books.

McLaughlin, C. (2008). Emotional well-being and its relationship to schools and classrooms: A critical reflection. *British Journal of Guidance and Counselling, 36*, 4.

Merrell, K. W. & Gueldner, B. A. (2010). Social and Emotional Learning. *Promoting Mental Health and Academic Success*. New York: The Guilford Press.

Miles, S., & Stipek, D. (2006). Contemporaneous and longitudinal associations between social behavior and literacy achievement in a sample of low-income elementary school children. *Child Development, 77*, 103–117.

MindMatters. (2012). *Whole School Matters*. Commonwealth of Australia. http://www.mindmatters.edu.au/verve/_resources/Whole_School_Matters_2012_draft_2.pdf. Accessed 30 Dec 2012.

Mind Matters. (2005). *The Mentoring Journal*. Commonwealth of Australia. http://www.mindmatters.edu.au/verve/_resources/interpersonal_journal_mentoring.pdf. Accessed 30 Dec 2012.

Montgomery, C. And Rupp, A.A. (2005). A meta-analysis for exploring the diverse causes and effects of stress in teachers. *Canadian Journal of Education 28*(3), 458–486.

Mooij, T., & Smeets, E. (2009). Towards systemic support of pupils with emotional and behavioural disorders. *International Journal of Inclusive Education,* (13)6, 597–616.

Moon, B. (2007). *Research analysis: Attracting, developing and retaining effective teachers – a global overview of current policies and practices.* Paris, France: UNESCO.

Morrison Gutman, L., Brown, J., Akerman, R. and Obolenskaya, P. (2010). *Change in well-being from childhood to adolescence: risk and resilience.* London: Institute of Education, University of London.

Mosley, J. (1993). *Turn Your School Round.* Wisbech, Cambridgeshire: LDA.

Mosley, J. (2009). Circle Time and Socio-Emotional Competence. In C. Cefai & P. Cooper (Eds.), *Promoting Emotional Education.* London: Jessica Kinsgley Publishers.

Murray, J., (2005). *Social-emotional climate and the success of new teachers.* Wellesley, MA: Wellesley Centers for Women.

Myers, K. (2012). Marking time: some methodological and historical perspectives on the 'crisis of childhood'. *Research Papers in Education,* 27, 4: 409–422.

National Curriculum Council Focus Group for Inclusive Education (2002). *Creating Inclusive Schools. Guidelines for the Implementation of the National Curriculum Policy on Inclusive Education.* Malta: Ministry of Education.

New Economics Foundation. (2009). *National accounts of well-being: bringing real wealth onto the balance sheet.* London: New Economics Foundation.

National Institute for Health and Clinical Excellence (2008). *Promoting children's social and emotional well-being in primary education.* London:National Health Service.

Nias, J. (1999). 'Primary Teaching as a Culture of Care.' In J. Prosser (ed.), *School Culture.* London: Paul Chapman.

Nieto, S. (2003). *What keeps teachers going?* New York: Teachers College Press.

Noble, T. & McGrath, H. (2008). The positive educational practices framework: A tool for facilitating the work of educational psychologists in promoting pupil well-being. *Educational & Child Psychology, 25,* 2:119–134.

Noddings, N. (1992). *The Challenge of Care in Schools* New York: Teachers College Press.

Noddings, N. (1995). Teaching themes of care. *Phi Delta Kappa 96,* 675–679.

Noddings, N. (2012). The Caring Relation in Teaching. *Oxford Review of Education,* 38, 6:771–781.

OECD. (2005). *Teachers Matter. Attracting, developing and retaining effective teachers.* http://www.oecd.org/education/preschoolandschool/34990905.pdf. Accessed 30th Dec 2012.

OECD. (2009). *Teaching and Learning International Survey (TALIS).* www.oecd.org/edu/talis/firstresults. Accessed 30th Dec 2012.

Ofsted. (2007). *Developing social, emotional and behavioural skills in secondary schools.* www.ofsted.gov.uk. Accessed 30th Dec 2012.

Ogden, T. & Sorlie, M. A. (2009). 'Implementing and evaluating empirically based family and school programmes for children with conduct problems in Norway', *International Journal of Emotional Education,* 1 (1), 96–107.

Oliver, M. (2004). If I had a hammer: The social model. In J. Swain., S. French., C. Barnes., & C. Thomas (Eds.), *Disabling Barriers- Enabling Environments.* 2nd edition. London: Sage.

Oliver, M. (1996). *Understanding Disability: From theory to practice.* Basingstoke: MacMillan Press.

Olsen, J., & Cooper, P. (2001). *Dealing With Disruptive Students in the Classroom.* London: Kogan Page Ltd.

Oplatka, I. (2009). Emotion Management and Display in Teaching: Some Ethical and Moral Considerations in the Era of Marketization and Commercialization. In P.A. Schutz and M. Zembylas (editors), *Advances in Teacher Emotion Research The Impact on Teachers' Lives* (p. 55–71). New York: Springer.

Osher, D., Sprague, J., Weissberg, R. P., Axelrod, J., Keenan, S., Kendziora, K., et al. (2007). A comprehensive approach to promoting social, emotional, and academic growth in contemporary schools. In A. Thomas & J. Grimes (Eds.), *Best practices in school psychology* (Vol. 5, 5th ed., pp. 1263–1278). Bethesda, MD: National Association of School Psychologists.

Pace, S. (2011). *Primary School Teachers' Perception of Emotional Intelligence in Children's Education.* Unpublished Masters dissertation. Faculty of Education, University of Malta, Malta.

Palmer, S. (2006). *Toxic childhood: How the modern world is damaging our children and what we can do about it.* London: Orion.

Payton, J., Weissberg, R. P., Durlak, J. A., Dymnicki, A. B., Taylor, R. D., Schellinger, K. B., & Pachan, M. (2008). *The positive impact of social and emotional learning for Kindergarten to eighth-grade students. Findings from three scientific reviews.* Chicago: CASEL.

Pianta, R. C. (1999). *Enhancing relationships between children and teachers.* Washington: American Psychological Association.

Pianta, R C & Stuhlman, M. W. (2004). Teacher-child relationships and children's success in the first years of school. *School Psychology Review, 33(3),* 444–458.

Pianta, R. C., La Paro, K. M., Payne, C., Cox, M. J., & Bradley, R. (2002). The relation of kindergarten classroom environment to teacher, family, and school characteristics and child outcomes. *Elementary School Journal, 102,* 225–238.

Pianta, R. C., & Walsh, D. J. (1998). Applying the construct of resilience in schools: Cautions from a developmental systems perspective. *School Psychology Review, 27*(3), 407–417.

Pring, R. (2012). Putting persons back into education. *Oxford Review of Education, 38*(6), 747–760.

Ransford, C. R., Greenberg, M. T., Domitrovich, C. E., Small, M., & Jacobson, L. (2009). The role of teachers' psychological experiences and perceptions of supports on the implementation of a social and emotional learning curriculum. *School Psychology Review, 38*(4).

Ravitch, D. (2010). *The death and life of the great American school system.* New York: Basic Books.

Reinke, W. M., Stormont, M., Herman, K. C., Puri, R., & Goel, N. (2011). Supporting children's mental health in schools: Teacher perceptions of needs, roles, and barriers. *School Psychology Quarterly 26,* 1–13.

Response Ability. (2009). *Social and emotional well-being. A teachers' guide.* Newscastle: Hunter's Institute, Commonwealth of Australia.

Resnick, M. D., Bearman, P. S., Blum, R. W., Bauman, K. E., Harris, L. J., & Jones, J. (1997). Protecting adolescents from harm: Findings from the national longitudinal study on adolescent health. *Journal of the American Medical Association, 278,* 823–832.

ReSURV. (2012). *Pupil Well-being.* http://www.pupilwell-being.com/. Accessed 30th Dec. 2012.

Reynolds, H. L., Brondizio, E. S., & Robinson, J. M. (2010). *Teaching environmental literacy: Across campus and across the curriculum.* Bloomington: Indiana University Press.

Rones, M., & Hoagwood, K. (2000). School-based mental health services: A research review. *Clinical Child and Family Psychology Review, 3*(4), 223–241.

Roeser, R. W., & Peck, S. C. (2009). An education in awareness: Self, motivation and self-regulation in contemplative perspective. *Educational Psychologist, 44,* 119–136.

Roeser, R. W., Skinner, E., Beers, J., & Jennings, P. A. (2012). Mindfulness training and teachers' professional development: An emerging area of research and practice. *Child Development Perspectives, 6*(2), 167–173.

Roffey, S. (2010). Content and context for learning relationships: A cohesive framework for individual and whole school development. *Educational and Child Psychology, 27*(1), 156–167.

Roffey, S. (2011). *Changing behaviour in schools. Promoting positive relationships and well-being.* London: Sage.

Romano, E., Tremblay, R. E., Vitaro, F., Zoccolillo, M., & Pagani, L. (2001). Prevalence of psychiatric diagnosis and the role of perceived impairment: findings from an adolescent community sample. *Journal of Child Psychology and Psychiatry, 42,* 451–461.

Rowlings, L. (2012). Personal communication to author, May 2012.

Rutter, M., & Smith, D. (1995). *Psychosocial disorders in young people.* Chichester: Wiley.

Rutter, M., & English and Romanian Adoptees Study Team. (1998). Developmental catch-up, and deficit, following adoption after severe global early privation. *Journal of Child Psychology and Psychiatry, 39,* 465–76.

Schonert-Reichl, K. A., & Lawlor, M. S. (2010). The effects of a mindfulness-based educational program on pre- and early adolescents' well-being and social and emotional competence, *Mindfulness*. http://thehawnfoundation.org/wp-content/uploads/2012/12/KSR-MSL_Mindfulness_2010-copy.pdf. Accessed 30th Dec. 2012.

Schwarzer, R., & Hallum, S. (2008). Perceived teacher self-efficacy as a predictor of job stress and burnout: Mediation analyses. *Applied Psychology: An International Review, 57,* 152–171.

Seligman, M. (2011). Flourish: *A visionary new understanding of happiness and well-being.* New York: Free Press.

Seligman, M. E. P., & Csikszentmihalyi, M. (2000). Positive psychology: An introduction. *American Psychologist, 55,* 5–14.

Seligman, M. E. P., Gillham, J., Reivich, K., Linkins, M., & Ernst, R. (2009). Positive education. *Oxford Review of Education, 35*(3), 293–311.

Sergiovanni, T. J. (1994). *Building school communities.* San Francisco: Jossey-Bass.

Sergiovanni, T. J. (1996). Learning community, professional community and the school as a centre of inquiry. *Principal Matters, 4,* 1–4.

Shapiro, S. L., Schwartz, G. E., & Bonner, G. (1998). Effects of mindfulness-based stress reduction on medical and premedical students. *Journal of Behavioral Medicine, 21,* 581–599.

Shaw, D. S., Dishion, T. J., Supplee, L., Gardner, F., & Arnds, K. (2006). A family-centered approach to the prevention of early-onset antisocial behavior: Two-year effects of the family check-up in early childhood. *Journal of Consulting and Clinical Psychology, 74,* 1–9.

Shucksmith, J., Summerbell, C., Jones, S., & Whittaker, V. (2007). *Mental well-being of children in primary education (targeted/indicated activities).* London: National Institute of Clinical Excellence.

Siegel, D. J. (2007). *The mindful brain: Reflection and attunement in the cultivation of well-being.* New York: WW Norton.

Skaalvik, E. M., & Skaalvik, S. (2010). Teacher self-efficacy and teacher burnout: A study of relations. *Teaching and Teacher Education, 26,* 1059–1069.

Sklad, M., Diekstra, R., De Ritter, M., & Ben, J. (2012). Effectiveness of school-based universal social, emotional, and behavioral programs: Do they enhance students' development in the area of skill, behavior, and adjustment? *Psychology in the Schools, 49*(9), 892–909.

Slee, P. T., Lawson, M. J., Russell, A., Askell-Williams, H., Dix, K. L., Owens, L., & Spears, B. (2009). *Kids matter evaluation final report.* Adelaide: Flinders University.

Slee, P., Murray-Harvey, R., Dix, K. L., Skrzypiec, G., Askell-Williams, H., Lawson, M., & Krieg, S. (2012). *KidsMatter Early Childhood Evaluation Report.* Adelaide, Australia: Shannon Research Press.

Smith, A., Brice, C., Collins, A., Mathews, V., & McNamara, R. (2000). *The scale of occupational stress. A further analysis of the impact of demographic factors and type of job.* UK: HSE Books.

Smith, T. M., & Ingersoll, R. M. (2004). What are the effects of induction and mentoring on beginning teacher turnover? *American Educational Research Journal, 41*(3), 681–714.

Solomon, D., Battistisch, V., Watson, M., Schaps, E., & Lewis, C. (2000). A six district study of educational change: Direct and mediated effects of the child development project. *Social Psychology of Education, 4,* 3–51.

Spera, C., & Wentzel, K. R. (2003). Congruence between students' and teachers' goals: Implications for social and academic motivation. *International Journal of Educational Research, 39*(4–5), 395–413.

Spratt, J., Shucksmith, J., Philip, K., & Watson, C. (2010). 'Part of who we are as a school should include responsibility for well-being': links between the school environment, mental health and behaviour. In J. Rix, M. Nind, K. Sheehy, K. Simmons, J. Parry & R. Kumrai (Eds.), *Equality, participation and inclusion* (2nd ed., pp. 284–296). London: Routledge.

Stormshak, E. A., Dishion, T. J., Light, J., & Yasui, M. (2005). Implementing family-centered interventions within the public middle school: Linking service delivery to change in problem behavior. *Journal of Abnormal Child Psychology, 33,* 723–733.

Stormshak, E. A., Bierman, K. L., McMahon, R. J., Lengua, L., & Conduct Problems Prevention Research Group. (2000). Parenting practices and child disruptive behavior problems in early elementary school. *Journal of Clinical Child Psychology, 29,* 17–29.

Sultana, R. G. (2009). Competence and competence frameworks in career guidance: complex and contested concepts. *International Journal of Educational Vocational Guidance, 9,* 15–30.

Tanti Rigos, V. (2009). *Maltese teachers; causal attributions, cognitive and emotional responses to students with emotional and behavioral difficulties.* Unpublished M.Ed. dissertation. Faculty of Education, University of Malta.

Teacher Support Network. (2009). *The path to better health and well being in education.* London: Author.

Teddlie, C., & Reynolds, D. (2000). *The international handbook of school effectiveness research.* London: Falmer Press.

Thomas, W. (2010). *Mindfulness, well-being and performance.* www.sharphamtrust.org/uploads/userfiles/Mindfulness_in_SEL[1].pdf. Accessed 30 Dec 2012.

UNESCO. (2005). *Guidelines for inclusion: Ensuring access to education for all.* Paris: Author.

UNICEF. (2007). *A world fit for us: the children's statement from the United Nations.* New York: Author.

UK Department for Education (2011). *What impact does the wider economic situation has on teachers' career decisions. A literature review.* London Metropolitan University: Institute for Policy Studies in Education.

United Nations (2006). *Convention on the rights of persons with disabilities.* New York: United Nations.

Valli, L., & Buese, D. (2007). The changing roles of teachers in an era of high-stakes accountability. *American Educational Research Journal, 44*(3), 519–558.

Van Veen, K., & Sleegers, P. (2009). Teachers' emotions in a context of reforms: To a deeper understanding of teachers and reforms. In P. A. Schutz & M. Zembylas (Eds.), *Advances in teacher emotion research: The impact on teachers' lives* (pp. 233–251). New York: Springer.

Vostanis, P., Humphrey, N., Fitzgerald, N., Deighton, J., & Wolpert, M. (2013). How do schools promote emotional well-being among their pupils? Findings from a national scoping survey of mental health provision in English schools. *Journal of Child and Adolescent Health, 18*(3), 151–157.

Waddell, C, Peters, R. V., Hua, R. M., & McEwan, K. (2007). Preventing mental disorders in children: A systematic review to inform policy-making. *Canadian Review of Public Health, 98*(3), 166–173.

Walker, H. M., & Severson, H. H. (1990). *Systematic screening for Behavior disorders (SSBD).* Longmont: Sopris West.

Watkins, C (2010). Learning, performance and improvement. *Institute of Education International Network for School Improvement.* Research Matters Series, No. 34.

Watkins, C. (2005). *Classrooms as learning communities. What's in it for schools?* Oxford: Routledge.

Watkins, C., & Wagner, P. (2000). *Improving school behaviour.* London: Sage/Paul Chapman.

Watson, D., Emery, C., & Bayliss, P. (2012). *Children's social and emotional well-being in schools. A critical perspective.* Bristol: The Policy Press.

Weare, K. (2010a). Mental health and social and emotional learning: Evidence, principles, tensions, balances. *Advances in school mental health promotion, 3*(1), 5–17.

Weare, K. (2010b). *Mindfulness, the missing piece for SEL?* www.sharphamtrust.org/uploads/userfiles/Mindfulness_in_SEL[1].pdf. Accessed 30 Dec 2012.

Weare, K. (2004). *Developing the emotionally literate school.* London: Sage.

Weare, K., & Gray, G. (2003). *What works in developing children's emotional and social competence and well-being?* Nottingham: DfES Publications.

Weare, K., & Nind, M. (2011). Mental health promotion and problem prevention in schools: What does the evidence say? *Health Promotion International, 26*(S1), i29-i69.

Weissberg, R. (2008). *The positive impact of SEL for kindergarten to eighth-grade students: Findings from three scientific reviews.* www.casel.org/publications. Accessed 30 Dec 2013.

Weissberg, R. P., & Greenberg, M. T. (1998). School and community competence enhancement and prevention programs. In W. Damon (Ed.), *Handbook of child psychology: Child psychology in practice* (Vol. 4, pp. 877–954). New York: Wiley.

Weissberg, R. P., Walberg, H. J., O'Brien, M. U., & Kuster, C. B. (Eds.). (2003). *Long-term trends in the well-being of children and youth.* Washington, DC: Child Welfare League of America Press.

Wells, J., Barlow, J., & Stewart-Brown, S. (2003). A systematic review of universal approaches to mental health promotion in schools. *Health Education, 103*(4), 197–220.

Werner, E., & Smith, R. (1992). *Overcoming the odds: High-risk children from birth to adulthood.* New York: Cornell University Press.

Westheimer, J. (1998). *Among school teachers.* New York: Teachers College Press.

Whaley, A., & Davis, K. (2007). Cultural competence and evidence-based practice in mental health services: A complementary perspective. *American Psychologist, 62*(6), 563–574.

Wilkinson, J., Ingvarson, L., Kleinhenz, E., & Beavis, A. (2005). *Primary teacher work study report.* Melbourne: Australian Council for Educational Research (ACER).

Williamson, J., & Myhill, M. (2008). Under "constant bombardment": Work intensification and the teachers' role. In D. Johnson & R. Maclean (Eds.). *Teaching: Professionalization, development and leadership* (pp. 25–43). Dordrecht, The Netherlands: Springer.

Wilson, S. J., & Lipsey, M. J. (2007). Effectiveness of school-based intervention programs on aggressive behavior: Update of a meta-analysis. *American Journal of Preventive Medicine, 33*(Suppl. 2), S130–S143.

Wilson, S. J., Lipsey, M. W., & Derzon, J. H. (2003). The effects of school-based intervention programs on aggressive behavior: A meta-analysis. *Journal of Consulting and Clinical Psychology, 71*(1), 136–149.

Winzelberg, A. J., & Luskin, F. M. (1999). The effect of a meditation training in stress levels in secondary school teachers. *Stress Medicine, 15,* 69–77.

World Health Organisation. (2007). *What is a health promoting school?* http://www.who.int/school_youth_health/gshi/hps/en/index.html. Accessed 30th Dec 2012.

World Health Organisation. (2011a). *Mental health: A state of well-being.* http://www.who.int/features/factfiles/mental_health/en/index.html. Accessed 30th Dec 2012.

World Health Organisation. (2011b). *Mental health: Strengthening mental health promotion.* http://www.who.int/mediacentre/factsheets/fs220/en/. Accessed 30th Dec 2012.

World Health Organization. (2012). *Public health action for the prevention of suicide.* Geneva: Author.

World Health Organisation. (2013). School health and youth health promotion. www.who.int/school_youth_health/en/. Accessed 30th July 2013.

Willms, J. D. (2003). *Student engagement at school: A sense of belonging and participation. Results from PISA 2000.* Paris: OECD.

Zembylas, M., & Schutz, P. A. (2009). Research on teachers' emotions in education: Findings, practical implications and future agenda. In P. A. Schutz & M. Zembylas (Eds.), *Advances in teacher emotion research. The impact on teachers' lives* (pp. 367–377). New York: Springer.

Zins, J. E. (2001). Examining opportunities and challenges for school-based prevention and promotion: Social and emotional learning as an exemplar. *Journal of Primary Prevention, 21*(4), 441–446.

Zins, J. E., Weissberg, R. P., Wang, M. C., & Walberg, H. J. (Eds.). (2004). *Building academic success through social and emotional learning: What does the research say?* New York: Teachers College Press.

Index

C. Cefai, V. Cavioni, *Social and Emotional Education in Primary School*,
DOI 10.1007/978-1-4614-8752-4, © Springer Science+Business Media New York 2014